W9-BSS-414

SHAGGY MUSES

SHAGGY MUSES

The Dogs Who Inspired Virginia Woolf,
Emily Dickinson, Elizabeth Barrett Browning,
Edith Wharton, and Emily Brönte

MAUREEN ADAMS

BALLANTINE BOOKS / NEW YORK

Published in the United States by Ballantine Books,
an imprint of The Random House Publishing Group,
a division of Random House, Inc., New York.

BALLANTINE and colophon are registered trademarks
of Random House, Inc.

Due to space limitations, pages 283–286 constitute
an extension of this copyright page.

Library of Congress Cataloging-in-Publication Data

Adams, Maureen.
Shaggy muses : the dogs who inspired Virginia Woolf, Emily Dickinson,
Elizabeth Barrett Browning, Edith Wharton, and Emily Brontë /
by Maureen Adams.
p.   cm.
Includes bibliographical references.
ISBN-13: 978-0-345-48406-2 (acid-free paper)
ISBN-10: 0-345-48406-1 (acid-free paper)
1. Women authors, English—Biography.   2. Women authors, American—
Biography.   3. Women dog owners—Biography.
4. Dogs—Biography.   5. Human-animal relationships.   I. Title.

PR111.A33 2007
820.9'9287—dc22   2006101291

Printed in the United States of America on acid-free paper

www.ballantinebooks.com

2   4   6   8   9   7   5   3   1

First Edition

Book design by Susan Turner

For Marty

Preface

ELEVEN YEARS AGO, my curiosity about the human-dog bond was transformed into a compelling interest when Cody, my Golden Retriever, died. I am a psychologist, and I often reassure clients who are mourning the death of a dog that such emotion is normal and appropriate. However, this knowledge did not comfort me when I lost Cody. Even though he had lived a rich, full life, and I had done everything I could to make sure he had a "good death," I was bereft when he died.

Cody was part of my daughter and son's childhood in Kansas City, Missouri. He was a puppy when Andrew was a toddler, and the two of them used to tumble on the lawn like littermates. First-grader Kate dressed Cody in doll clothes and took him for rides in a stroller. The three of them grew up together. When Kate was old enough to babysit for Andrew, I knew that Cody would watch over them both. That proved to be true the night some boys, intent on stealing our new television, broke into the house. While Kate huddled upstairs calling our neighbor for help, Cody shed his usual sweet Golden Retriever temperament. Growling and snapping, he chased the boys through the house and out the back door. The neighbor arrived to find the television in the yard and Cody upstairs calming Kate and Andrew.

When my husband was offered a position at a California winery, he was eager to accept, but the children and I were reluctant to leave Kansas City. For nine years, I had been teaching English at the University of Missouri, and I was fond of my students and colleagues. Kate and Andrew were happy with their school and friends. After much deliberation, we decided to make the change, and Cody became part of our family's transition from Missouri to California. Throughout the trip, he seemed to express the whole family's anxiety about moving from the Midwest. When we picked him up in the baggage claim area at the San Francisco airport, he greeted us with ringing barks of protest, which continued throughout the two-hour car ride to our new home in Sonoma. On the way, he saw his first cow, which inspired even more frantic barking. Finally at the new house, Cody saw the swimming pool—another first for him—and ran around it in circles of joy, exhilarated to be free again. The children joined him, running and laughing in relief. Cody's exuberance made us all begin to feel at home.

In the next few months, Cody assumed another role. I had a difficult time adjusting to the move and became depressed. Cody would sit patiently when I cried and would stay up with me on the nights I could not sleep. Always calm, unperturbed by tears or anger, Cody would lean against me or lay his head on my lap. His solid presence demanded nothing of me: I did not have to pretend to be all right or feel guilty about being unable to overcome my unhappiness.

Eventually, thanks to a supportive family, a caring and skilled psychotherapist, and Cody, I emerged from depression. At the same time, I found a new direction for my life. I was inspired by the insights I had gained during psychotherapy, and a longtime interest in the field was rekindled. As a result, I began studying to become a psychologist.

During the next years, as I balanced family life with the demands of courses and internships, Cody moved to the background of my attention. Yet I could not ignore his growing stiffness on our morning walks or his whitening muzzle. Even though I saw these signs, his aging still seemed to happen overnight. One day, Cody was running circles around the pool; the next, he was too crippled to climb stairs.

A morning came when Cody did not get up, and he refused to eat or drink. I went for a long walk in the hills and remembered the way the white plume of his tail had shone through the tall grass as he ran ahead of me. I realized we had taken our last walk together weeks ago. I went home and called the veterinarian, who agreed to come to the house and euthanize Cody. Throughout that long day, the family took turns sitting by Cody, petting and talking to him. He appeared detached, but it comforted us to spend time with him. When the veterinarian arrived, Cody did not even look at him but continued to gaze steadily at me. I stroked his paw and kept telling him goodbye. The light in his eyes dimmed, and Cody was gone. We wrapped him in an afghan and buried him in the backyard under the redwoods.

Months later, I was still heartbroken. Cody had been so much a part of everyday life that we all experienced continual small shocks that reminded us he was gone. When we opened the back door, no high-pitched, dolphinlike cries of welcome greeted us. At dinner, there was no hovering presence under the table. In the evenings, we all walked around the place by the fire where he once slept.

Grief for Cody pushed me to examine this question: What explains our intense emotional attachment to our dogs? Determined to understand more about this powerful alliance, I undertook a serious study of the human-dog bond. All the research skills and energy I had applied to my graduate studies I now put to use learning about dogs and their connection to humans. I examined this tie from many points of view: historical, anthropological, psychological, and mythological. However, none fully explained the intense emotions I and others have felt for our dogs. For that, I turned once more to my knowledge of poetry and literature. I began with Emily Dickinson, whose poems I have loved since childhood.

One day, I discovered a note she had written to her literary mentor announcing the death of her dog: "Carlo died: Would you instruct me now?" I was stunned by the strong reaction I had to these few words. The spare language evoked the bleakness I had experienced after losing Cody. I kept wondering about the question "Would *you* instruct me now?" (emphasis added). Had Emily Dickinson relied on Carlo to somehow guide her poetry, to act as a muse? Rereading a collection of her letters, I made a second discovery: Emily Dickinson referred to Carlo as "my mute confederate" and "my Shaggy Ally."

These casual terms of endearment, used by a writer so careful and deliberate with words, struck an immediate chord in me. I knew for certain that Emily Dickinson had cared about Carlo in the same way I cared about Cody.

Intrigued, I looked for other writers who wrote about their relationships with their dogs. Some were men, notably Lord Byron, Thomas Mann, and John Steinbeck. Still, I was drawn to women, especially to those who had depended on dogs for emotional support during childhood and in times of transition, because their experiences were closer to my own. Gradually, a small group seemed to fall naturally into place around Emily Dickinson and Carlo: Elizabeth Barrett Browning, Emily Brontë, Edith Wharton, and Virginia Woolf. Had their dogs also acted as mute confederates and Shaggy Allies?

At first, I found it difficult to determine just how significant their dogs had been to them. With the exception of Elizabeth Barrett Browning's Flush, most were either overlooked by biographers or given only slight attention. And yet, photographs and paintings in the biographies often depicted the women with their dogs. For example, almost every book about Emily Brontë included at least one of her drawings of the Brontë dogs. To me, these images suggested that the dogs had indeed been an integral part of each woman's daily life.

Other sources confirmed this impression. Letters, memoirs, and recollections written by the writers' friends, family members, servants, and neighbors often mention the dogs. In research libraries and archives of the women's unpublished writing, I found drawings they themselves had made of their dogs—sketches tucked away in notebooks and scrawled in the margins of letters. I delved into contemporary newspaper articles, Victorian pet-keeping practices, village dog-tax records, and inscriptions on tombstones—all of which helped me place these stories in the context of the times in which the writers lived. Ultimately, though, the writers' own words—their diaries, letters, poems, or novels—truly revealed the powerful bond each woman had with her dog.

Ranging from lapdog to mastiff, their dogs acted as loyal companions, staunch protectors, and patient comforters. Elizabeth Barrett Browning was coaxed out of a life-threatening depression by Flush, a cheerful, lively Cocker Spaniel puppy. Emily Brontë's strong attachment to Keeper, a formidable Mastiff, began with a violent power struggle. Emily Dickinson, anxious and reclusive, ventured outside her father's house only when accompanied by Carlo, her immense Newfoundland. Edith Wharton, regal and formal in her circle of male admirers, played silly games when she was alone with Linky, one of her many adored Pekingese. And Virginia Woolf relied on a succession of dogs—the vigilant sheepdog Gurth, the scruffy mongrel Grizzle, and finally the playful spaniel Pinka—to help her connect with the people she loved most.

The attachments of these five women to their dogs mirrored the attachments I have had with my own. Like Emily Brontë, I have had a relationship with a difficult dog who responded to me with devoted loyalty. Like Emily Dickinson, I have felt alone and powerless in the world, and a dog has made me feel safe. Recently, a joyful little dog like Flush has filled my days with play and happiness. And I count on long walks with dogs to lift the solitude that comes when writing, as did Virginia Woolf and Emily Brontë. Dogs help me to feel more at home in the world, as generations of lapdogs did for Edith Wharton in her years of restless travel between the United States and Europe.

In every one of my life's passages, there has been a dog, or the memory of one, to act as a protector, a companion, and a comforter. Like Flush, Keeper, Carlo, Linky, and Pinka, my dogs have been a constant support for my own creative life. Cody's successors are sleeping at my feet—a Clumber Spaniel named Kipper and a Pug named Higgins. The sound of their snores provides a soothing and familiar background as I write.

Contents

Author's Note

THE FIVE WOMEN IN THIS BOOK WERE ALL WRITERS WHO LOVED language. They sprinkled ampersands and dashes throughout their private writing, they invented words, and they experimented with spelling. To maintain the lively informality of the women's letters and diaries and to reduce the use of *sic*, I retained their idiosyncratic spelling, punctuation, and capitalization. I quoted them verbatim, with only the rare change of an apostrophe here or there to fit contemporary usage. I also corrected the spelling of a few words to ensure they could be understood. Unless indicated otherwise, all ellipses are mine.

Deciding what names to use when referring to the people in this book has been tricky because of the age-old custom of married women changing their surnames. So I have skirted the problem by referring to the authors by their first names ("Edith"), interspersed with the names by which they are most known ("Edith Wharton"). So that the women's parents could be easily recognized, I tend to refer to them with a title—for example, Mrs. Dickinson, Mr. Barrett, Mr. Brontë.

An even thornier problem has been how to refer to the dogs. Although many animal lovers today choose the word *companion* to describe a beloved dog, the women in this book referred to their dogs as "pets" and themselves as "owners," even "mistresses." Because most of the references to the dogs are in the women's own words, I decided to use their terminology. And when the sex of the dog is unknown, I have used the masculine pronoun because I prefer not to refer to a dog as "it," and I dislike the awkward she/he construction.

A final remark is about Emily Dickinson. She rarely titled her poems, so they are therefore known and referred to by their first lines, not by a title.

SHAGGY MUSES

ELIZABETH BARRETT
BROWNING and FLUSH

"He & I are inseparable companions,
and I have vowed him my perpetual society
in exchange for his devotion."

ELIZABETH BARRETT BROWNING

O̶N A BITTER AFTERNOON in January 1841, a coach stopped outside a small house in the British seaside town of Torquay, bleak and deserted in the off-season. The coachman lifted out a wicker basket, and a young Cocker Spaniel peeked through the thick blankets. The six-month-old puppy sniffed the sea for the first time and wagged his tail excitedly. His dark eyes shone as he pushed his way through the layers of covering, eager to track the enticing scents in the air. The puppy's determined efforts to free himself from the basket made the man laugh, whereupon the little dog leaped into his arms and began licking his face. The coachman ruffled the dog's sleek head, muttering, "Miss Mitford is going to miss you, but here we are, and mind your manners." With the puppy tucked under his arm, the coachman rang the bell. Waiting for the door to open, he shivered in the wind and thought of the green lanes and meadows of home. He wondered how this little spaniel, bred to hunt rabbits and quail, would fare as a companion to a sickly recluse. The puppy's name was Flush, and he was being delivered to the poet Elizabeth Barrett. That afternoon marked the beginning of one of the most celebrated human-dog relationships in literature.

Elizabeth Barrett, 1859. *Chalk by Field Talfourd.*

When Flush arrived in Elizabeth's life, she was thirty-five and bedridden. As a girl, however, she had been healthy and active. Born in 1806, she was the eldest of twelve children who grew up on an estate called Hope End, consisting of 475 isolated acres on the border between England and Wales. There Mr. Barrett built a Turkish-style house, fondly remembered by Elizabeth as "crowded with minarets & domes, & crowned with metal spires & crescents." Mrs. Barrett, who was from a large, closely knit family, filled their home with visiting relatives. The Barrett children and their cousins rode horses, climbed haystacks, and played hide-and-seek in the underground passage between the house and the gardens. Elizabeth was usually the leader and often a risk-taker. Neighbors remembered her, with a "pale spiritual face and a profusion of dark curls," driving her pony carriage at breakneck speed through the steep Herefordshire lanes.

In adolescence, Elizabeth began to suffer symptoms of ill health, primarily backaches, shortness of breath, and lack of appetite. Because the Barretts' first daughter, Mary, had died when she was only three and a half, Mr. and Mrs. Barrett took Elizabeth's complaints seriously and consulted numerous doctors, to no avail. Finally, they brought her to the Spa Hotel in Gloucester, where a specialist examined her and decided to treat her as if she had a spinal disease, even though he was unsure of the diagnosis. He recommended that she remain there for months of rest in a spine crib, a hammock strung four feet above the ground. He also prescribed daily doses of laudanum (a mixture of opium and alcohol) for the fifteen-year-old, a common medication at that time.

Looking at Elizabeth's illness from a contemporary perspective, it seems to have had several causes: a form of scoliosis, a condition in which the spine curves abnormally; tuberculosis; and perhaps an eating disorder. No clear diagnosis emerges from the surviving medical records. In nineteenth-century England, middle-class girls were considered fragile once they started to menstruate, but Elizabeth's younger sisters Arabel and Henrietta, who had also complained of illnesses when they entered their teens, soon regained good health.

Elizabeth's infirmities certainly included an emotional component. One of the first times she was seriously ill occurred when her favorite brother, Edward, whom she always called "Bro," departed for boarding school. She was unhappy about losing her playmate and was also angry and frustrated because she yearned to go to school herself. Because Elizabeth was a girl, this would never be allowed, even though she was scholarly and precocious. Before she was ten, she had read *Paradise Lost* and the major works of Shakespeare; although she was primarily self-taught, she outdistanced her brothers in Latin and Greek, and she could read French, Italian, and Portuguese.

At the Spa Hotel, lying in her spine crib, Elizabeth read constantly, kept a notebook documenting her symptoms, and wrote poetry. Before her illness, her father had arranged to have fifty copies of her epic poem *The Battle of Marathon* published. As soon as Elizabeth saw her words in print, she knew she would be a poet: "Literature was the star which in prospect illuminated my future days. . . . It was the spur . . . the aim . . . the very soul of my being." When the sixteen-year-old returned to Hope End after her time at the spa, she was still suffering from bouts of weakness. Still, she spent the next few years determinedly finishing a poetic essay modeled after Poe and Milton, called *An Essay on Mind*. One of Elizabeth's aunts paid to have the essay and other poems published in a two-volume work, which the relatives distributed to all their friends. A classics scholar, Sir Uvedale Price, wrote to congratulate Elizabeth on the book, beginning what would become Elizabeth's extensive literary correspondence.

Soon Elizabeth's poems, all with the long descriptive titles so popular at the time, began to appear in literary magazines: *The New Monthly Magazine* printed "Stanzas, Excited by Some Reflections on the Present State of Greece," and *The Globe and Traveller* published "Lines on the Death of Lord Byron." Even though her poems were unsigned, which was considered proper for a young lady, especially one with a father as conservative as Mr. Barrett, Elizabeth felt she was beginning her vocation as a poet.

Then, in 1828, when Elizabeth was twenty-two, her mother died suddenly. Mary Barrett had been weakened by the birth of her last child but seemed to be regaining strength. In an effort to hasten her recovery, she had gone with her sister to a seaside resort. Within days, the news of her death reached Hope End. Elizabeth was overwhelmed, unable to cry or even to talk about her mother. As the oldest daughter, she would have been expected to take over the care of the younger children and to run the household of the large country estate, but her poor health prevented this. Instead, an aunt assumed Mrs. Barrett's duties, and Elizabeth was spared the domestic and social obligations that fell to Arabel and Henrietta. As mourning relatives filled the house, Elizabeth remained alone in her room, reading and writing letters and poems. Her role as an invalid was now firmly established.

Four years later, in 1832, Elizabeth experienced another loss when her father sold the family home at Hope End. Mr. Barrett depended for his income on a sugar plantation in Jamaica in the hills overlooking Montego Bay, where he had grown up. His brother Samuel now managed the property, called Cinnamon Hill, and Mr. Barrett regularly sent his sons to help their uncle. However, poor sugar harvests, slave rebellions, and a drawn-out lawsuit had led to such serious financial problems that in order to keep Cinnamon Hill, Mr. Barrett was forced to sell Hope End. Elizabeth was upset at the thought of moving, although, after her mother's death, Hope End was no longer the happy home it had once been.

The Barretts moved first to the coast at Sidmouth, in the southwest of England. Long walks on the beach improved Elizabeth's health, but she was bored by the town's social life, which consisted of dances and cricket matches. She was happier staying in her room: "I live with my books and my writings and my dear family." Three years later, the family moved from Sidmouth to London. At first, Elizabeth hated the congestion and noise of the city; before long, however, she enjoyed its stimulation, even though she experienced it only vicariously, through books, newspapers, and her family.

When it was Bro's turn to go to Jamaica to help Uncle Samuel, Elizabeth was filled with anxiety for him. As a distraction, she immersed herself in translating Aeschylus's *Prometheus Bound* from the Greek. Elizabeth was delighted that a commercial publisher had accepted her translation, along with nineteen poems, but she was not pleased with the ensuing reviews. *The Athenaeum*, a respected literary weekly, announced, "We advise those who adventure in the hazardous lists of poetic translation to touch anyone rather than Aeschylus; and they may take warning by the author before us." Yet the audacity of a woman, especially a young one (she was twenty-seven), taking on such a task endeared Elizabeth to many readers. She developed a circle of admirers, mostly older, intellectual men whom she never met in person but to whom she wrote long letters in which she discussed literature, politics, and philosophy.

Although Elizabeth was constructing a rich intellectual life through her poetry and her letters, she remained an adolescent in many ways. Awkward and nervous when facing anything new, she dreaded social encounters. Her cousin John Kenyon, part of London's literary world, persuaded Elizabeth to meet the popular author Mary Russell Mitford, known to everyone as Miss Mitford. He overcame his cousin's shyness by introducing the two women at the London Zoo. Elizabeth immediately warmed to Miss Mitford's friendliness, while the older woman was struck by Elizabeth's quiet demeanor: "Very pretty, very gentle, very graceful with a look of extreme youth which is in itself a charm." The two began writing each other several times a week—letters filled with speculation about authors, publishers, and reviewers—and they became dear friends.

In 1838, *The Seraphim and Other Poems* was published, with "Elizabeth B. Barrett" printed on the title page. Her father was so proud of these religious poems that he had finally allowed her name to appear in print. All the major literary publications reviewed the book, including *The Examiner*, which proclaimed Elizabeth "a genuine poetess, of no common order."

The same year, when Elizabeth was thirty-two, the Barretts moved for the last time, settling into 50 Wimpole Street, where, with Bro safely returned from Jamaica, they were once more together under one roof. Shortly thereafter came the news that Uncle Samuel had died in Jamaica, leaving Elizabeth a share in his trading ship. Years earlier, her Grandmother Moulton had also left her a legacy. Thus, Elizabeth was the only one of her siblings with some financial independence. And yet she remained emotionally reliant on her family. They considered their "Ba" amusing and endearing but did not treat her as an adult. By the time she was in her mid-thirties, Elizabeth's future seemed certain: She would stay in her room in her father's house and write for the rest of her life. Then another illness intervened.

In the winter of 1838, Elizabeth had developed a cough so worrisome that, by August, Dr. Chambers, who was also Queen Victoria's physician, declared Elizabeth would not survive another damp London winter. Although Mr. Barrett was reluctant to split up the family again, he finally agreed to send Elizabeth to the seaside town of Torquay, where he leased a small house on a cliff. Her brothers Bro and George, her sister Henrietta, and her personal maid Crow (ladies' maids were customarily called by their last names) accompanied Elizabeth to Torquay, where an aunt supervised the household and everyone waited for Elizabeth to regain her strength. Yet she did not improve.

Month after month passed. Although Elizabeth tried to keep up a brave front for her family, she wrote the truth of her lingering illness to Miss Mitford, who was assuming an increasingly maternal role in her life. She wrote her friend almost daily, occasionally complaining of her symptoms, but more often focusing on Bro's efforts to cheer her up. He gave his sister little gifts, "such pretty blue *two* vases," and spent hours with her discussing politics and philosophy.

A second winter passed in Torquay; then, in February 1840, came word from Jamaica that Elizabeth's younger brother Sam had died of fever at Cinnamon Hill. Elizabeth fainted when she heard the news and was intermittently delirious for a month. Mr. Barrett attempted to console her, but it was Bro's words that meant the most to her. The two were only a year apart and had always been each other's favorite, giving each other the family nicknames "Bro" and "Ba." To keep his sister company, thirty-three-year-old Bro had left his busy London life and moved to Torquay. As they comforted each other after Sam's death, the affection between them deepened.

Gradually, Elizabeth recovered, and her father returned to London. The weather grew warm; the seaside town filled with tourists. Seeing the improvement in Elizabeth's health, Bro resumed his social life. On July 11, a calm, sunny morning, he stopped in his sister's room before setting off to sail with two friends. Elizabeth, perhaps hurt that he was leaving her for an entire day, said goodbye with a "pettish word."

Neither Bro nor his companions returned. Elizabeth later described waiting for word of their fate: "For three days we waited—& I hoped while I could—oh—that awful agony of three days! And the sun shone as it shines today, & there was no more wind than now; and the sea under the windows was like this paper for smoothness—& my sisters drew the curtains back that I might see for myself how smooth the sea was, & how it could hurt nobody—& other boats came back one by one." Then one body was recovered, and all hope died. Bro's body did not wash ashore for another week; as she waited, Elizabeth regressed into frozen numbness, unresponsive to anyone.

Elizabeth lay in the room where she had last seen Bro and where she had said the words she now bitterly regretted. She ate little, rarely slept, and appeared to be close to death. When her mother and then Sam had died, Elizabeth had been unable to ease her suffering with tears. Nor could she weep for Bro. Her unexpressed grief for those earlier losses, combined with her anguish over Bro, left Elizabeth bereft and hopeless. She could not bear the sight or even the sound of the sea, which she said reminded her of the groans of the dying. She abandoned her writing. The curtains were drawn, and the room was kept in darkness. Her father sat by her side; her sisters and brothers visited. No one could assuage Elizabeth's despair. Mr. Barrett, alarmed by his daughter's condition, reported on her deterioration: "It is a wonder to me that she lives."

Miss Mitford offered the first glimmer of hope to the stricken poet. After Bro's death, Elizabeth had ceased all correspondence. When she finally felt able to write to Miss Mitford, Elizabeth said she felt "bound, more than I ever remember having felt, in chains, heavy and cold enough to be iron—and which have indeed entered into the soul." Miss Mitford understood immediately that her young friend was desperate. Although the older woman could not, as she wished, rush to Torquay because her father was ill, she knew what to do. She would send a puppy in her place, and not just any puppy: She offered Elizabeth the son of her own dog. As if to emphasize the connection, Miss Mitford gave the puppy the same name—Flush.

Elizabeth had not responded to anyone's overtures for five months, but she immediately answered her friend's letter. For the first time since Bro's death, Elizabeth showed stirrings of excitement: "Why there is nothing to be done but to be ready to receive him at the earliest moment." A flurry of letters followed as Elizabeth first accepted Flush, then rejected him, and then accepted him again. She worried that a purebred Cocker Spaniel was too valuable a gift; she also wondered if an active sporting dog could be happy sharing her confined life. The letters back and forth meant that Elizabeth was finally showing some interest in the outside world. The time she spent coming to a decision about Flush was time not spent thinking about Bro. As she fretted over what she should do, she was no longer absorbed in the self-preoccupation and endless rumination that so often characterize grief. Thus, before Flush and Elizabeth had even met, he had begun to turn her mind away from death and toward life.

Miss Mitford, not swayed by Elizabeth's scruples about accepting the puppy, said that every time Elizabeth looked into Flush's
eyes, she would see Miss Mitford's "affectionate feeling" shining in
them. Once Flush was explicitly linked with Miss Mitford's loving
concern for Elizabeth, there was no more arguing. Elizabeth accepted the puppy, even though she still worried he would be unhappy with her quiet life: "But I shall make it up to him, at least
something of it, in love and care. I must love him, coming from
you."

As soon as Flush arrived in Torquay, the somber atmosphere in
the Barrett household began to lift. Elizabeth was instantly captivated by the golden puppy and, within days of his arrival, wrote
Miss Mitford: "How I thank you for Flush!—Dear little Flush—
growing dearer every day!" Flush's calm temperament and his
beauty pleased his new mistress: "Such a quiet, loving intelligent
little dog—& so very very pretty! He shines as if he carried sunlight
about on his back!" Flush shone like a beacon in the darkness and
gloom of Elizabeth's life. For months, she had been indifferent to
the people around her, but she paid close attention to their reactions to her puppy. She proudly reported to Miss Mitford that
everyone was impressed with Flush: "He is much admired for
beauty—particularly for that white breastplate which marks him
even among dogs of his colour—Flush the silvershielded!"

As Flush grew more familiar with his surroundings, he began to
be less docile, revealing his high spirits and his pleasure at being the
center of attention. Elizabeth was as entranced by these aspects of
his personality as she had been with his earlier calm: "He dances
and dances, & throws back his ears almost to his tail in Bacchic rap-
ture. More than once he has lost his balance & fallen over." Perhaps
she recognized in Flush her own formerly exuberant love of life.

Flush and Elizabeth would spend eight months together in
Torquay, from January until late August of 1841, a period removed
from Elizabeth's usual life, a time out of time. From their very first
weeks together, the pair established a secure base for their lifelong
loyalty to each other. Flush easily and naturally carried out his man-

date from Miss Mitford to express her love to Elizabeth: "How he makes me think of you! How every pleasure he gives me is one drawn from you! How I love him *for your sake!*" Flush evoked Miss Mitford's loving concern for Elizabeth in moments such as this daily morning ritual: "The first person who comes to wake me in the morning is Flush—to wake me and remind me of you. There he comes, all in the dark . . . before the shutters are open . . . pushes through the bedcurtains and leaps into the nearest place by me and bites each of my hands very gently."

On those dark mornings, as Flush settled in next to Elizabeth and nibbled her hands, he was becoming more than a transitional object linking her to Miss Mitford; he was a living being that Elizabeth cared about for his own sake. There had always been dogs at Hope End, but they had belonged to Elizabeth's brothers. She had been fond of doves, keeping them in a cage in her room. Now she found that Flush's warm body, his soft bites, and the smell of his puppy breath all comforted her, as the soft cooing of her birds had once done. Through such wordless moments of connection, repeated every day, the two were developing a deep attachment to each other. In fact, the closeness between them was growing in the same way as the relationship does between a mother and her infant: through consistent proximity, eye contact, and touch.

Like a child, Flush distracted Elizabeth by coaxing her to play with him. He invented a favorite game that he insisted on repeating over and over. As Elizabeth reclined on her sofa, Flush would climb from the armrest to the top of her head and perch there "with his silky ears flapping about mine" for several minutes. Then, with no warning, he would tumble down over her shoulders "like an avalanche." Although Elizabeth considered the game "eccentric and perverse" and worried that Flush might break her bones, she tolerated it because he enjoyed it so.

The household once more heard the sound of Elizabeth laughing as she caught sight of Flush strutting about on his "little bantam rooster legs" and eating macaroon cookies snatched from the kitchen. Charmed by the new pet and grateful for his effect on Elizabeth, the servants all spoiled Flush. He responded to their attention, as any puppy would, by escalating his demands. If anyone refused to give him a treat or dared to speak harshly to him, Flush promptly ran to Elizabeth: "In every disappointment & fright he always comes to me, that I may do my best for him." She would pick him up and soothe him, at the same time soothing herself.

Elizabeth valued Flush for his attractiveness and his cheerful temperament, but most of all, because he was devoted entirely to her. This was a new experience for Elizabeth. Her mother had been warm and loving but so busy tending the younger children that Elizabeth often felt overlooked. She was her father's acknowledged favorite, although Mr. Barrett spent long days in the city and was absent for weeks at a time on business trips. Her brothers and sisters were getting on with their lives between visits to Torquay: George was establishing a law practice; the other brothers were attending school; and her sisters were involved in charity work and overseeing the housekeeping. Elizabeth felt drab and unappealing in comparison. When Flush chose to stay with her, she felt as if a healing balm were being applied to her battered spirits: "And when my sisters & brothers are with me, there he lies—quite downhearted—responding to no notice—waiting patiently, as it seems, until he can celebrate their departure by a round of leaps!"

Trying to describe Flush, Elizabeth turned to her books, which had been unopened since Bro's death. In a poem by Edmund Spenser, she found just the right word for Flush—*joyaunce*. Her return to the world of literature marked a tentative revival of Elizabeth's intellectual curiosity, and she at last resumed her extensive correspondence, which often featured her new puppy. She announced to Hugh Stuart Boyd, a blind scholar who had been her first mentor and who was one of her most faithful correspondents: "I have . . . a little spaniel dog, which was sent to me by Miss Mitford, for company." To Richard Horne, a fellow poet, Elizabeth emphasized Flush's connection to Miss Mitford: "I have a little spaniel called Flush, the descendant of Miss Mitford's spaniel,

Flush the Famous, which she sent me *for company* & besides to re-mind me of her."

Years later, when Elizabeth looked back at the year after Bro's death, she described feelings of utter despair: "After what broke my heart at Torquay, I lived on the outside of my own life, blindly and darkly from day to day, as completely dead to hope." Flush had al-leviated her misery; in gratitude, Elizabeth made a promise she would keep for the rest of Flush's life: "He & I are inseparable com-panions, and I have vowed him my perpetual society in exchange for his devotion."

One year after Bro's death, Elizabeth's doctor said she was finally well enough to return to London. Once August 25 was set as the date for departure, Elizabeth became agitated and unsettled. She complained of a racing heart, shortness of breath, and nausea—symptoms of anxiety that were all too familiar to her: "When I was a child I had fits of fearfulness sometimes. I used to be frightened of the dark, and could not go to sleep unless the nurse sat there with a candle; and I well remember how I used to think: 'I shall not like to be grown up because then I shall have nobody to take care of me,'—nobody to *trust to.*" In the past, Elizabeth had relied on her nurse or her parents during her "fits of fearfulness." Now she found that Flush could help her feel safe.

For the ten-day journey back to London, Elizabeth lay flat on a pallet especially constructed for her; even so, she was jounced and jarred by the carriage. She concentrated on Flush and found that the sight of the small spaniel standing on his hind legs with his paws on the coach window diverted her from her discomfort: "His glit-tering ears dancing up and down over his nose—the eyes dilating with the prospect. Through all my exhaustion, I couldn't help now and then smiling at Flush." When they finally arrived at the Barrett home at 50 Wimpole Street, Flush "oversaw" the servants who car-ried Elizabeth up to her room. He must have raced ahead of them up the stairs because he was there waiting when she reached her bed: "And when I was laid down safely, the first living thing I . . . [saw] was Flush standing on his hind legs to reach up and kiss me." He had never been in the house before, but it was he who welcomed Elizabeth home.

At first, Flush was overwhelmed by the hustle and bustle of Wimpole Street, so different from the funereal hush of Torquay. The London house was filled with servants and the large Barrett family: the imposing Mr. Barrett; the sisters, Henrietta and Arabel; and the surviving brothers, Charles, George, Henry, Alfred, Septimus, and Octavius. Wimpole Street was close to shops, so the hubbub of city life was right outside the door. Horse-drawn drays kept up a steady rumble, while shouting servants dodged in and out of the traffic. In the evenings, carriages carrying well-dressed ladies and gentlemen to concerts and the theater clattered over the cobblestones. Flush protested the tumult by barking at the Barrett brothers and their huge dogs, a Bloodhound named Catiline and a Mastiff named Resolute.

Elizabeth worried about her father's reaction to the commotion Flush caused: "I was in despair—not so much for myself as for Papa who is not perhaps very particularly fond of dogs and most particularly fond of silence." However, in a remarkably short time, Flush won over Mr. Barrett, the boys, their dogs, and the entire household: "Everybody likes Flush—everybody in the house. Even after he has done all the mischief possible, torn their letters, spoilt their books, bitten their shoes into holes—everybody likes Flush."

Elizabeth resumed her former London life as a brilliant poet cocooned within the warmth and safety of her family. Although her existence was limited and constricted, it was also familiar and comfortable. She took up her customary position on the sofa in her room as Henrietta and Arabel brought her mail, trinkets from the shops, and—always—gossip. The youngest boys, Sette and Occy, ran errands and entertained her with tales of their exploits at school and fencing class. In the evenings, Mr. Barrett returned with books and newspapers for Elizabeth and special cakes for Flush.

Elizabeth's personal maid, Crow, continued to care for her as if she were a child, brushing her hair, dressing and undressing her, and bringing her meals upstairs on a tray. Elizabeth's childlike dependence was evident when Crow announced she was leaving to get married. Instead of congratulating the woman who had been with her for five years, Elizabeth pouted: "Now, I may have the window open all day—I may take double morphine draughts if I like! I may go to bed as late as I please,—& talk as long. It is a liberty I am not grown strong enough for—& I feel the weight of it." Crow was the first servant Elizabeth had become close to, and she dreaded having to adjust to Crow's replacement, a maid named Wilson. Elizabeth used Flush to express her feelings of childish indignation about being abandoned. "Poor Flushie misses Crow dreadfully—& you would smile to see the utter disdain with which he looks at Wilson when she desires him to do anything—as if to say—'Obey *you*! Indeed!' "

Once Wilson was settled in, Elizabeth resumed her daily routines, which Flush shared. Every morning, they had coffee together, and Flush insisted on drinking from a china cup like Elizabeth's even though it made him sneeze. Then Wilson bathed and dried him with one of Elizabeth's paisley shawls. Most mornings, Arabel took him for walks in the park or to the shops with her. The rest of the day, Flush lay on Elizabeth's lap or at her feet while she read or wrote. They spent a great deal of time eating, or rather, Flush ate and Elizabeth watched him. "Here is Flush, rejoicing like Bacchus himself, among the grapes! Eating one grape after another, with exceeding complacency, shown by swingings of the tail."

Elizabeth read a newspaper account of a dog that could play dominoes, and she at once decided to teach Flush to play. She realized he would first need to count; accordingly, she entertained the family with Flush's arithmetic lessons, holding up pieces of cake while Flush barked out the correct number. "It is amusing to see him stir his little head at 'two' & then correct himself—and still more amusing to observe how, at every unqualified success, he turns round & looks at Arabel for applause." Spurred on by that success, Elizabeth next taught Flush how to read by saying the name of a letter and having him kiss the correct one. Her brothers enjoyed these sessions even more than Flush. "My brothers laughed the tears into their eyes . . . & were of opinion that if anybody else heard it, it might be used as straightforward evidence— (against not Flushie but me) of a 'non-compos-mentis' case."

It appeared as though Elizabeth had returned from Torquay in her familiar role as an invalid, the family's charming and childlike Ba. Nevertheless, she was too introspective and too honest to deny the shattering effect Bro's death had had on her. Gone was her naïve belief that all would go well in the world. Writing to Miss Mitford, she said, "My castle-building is at an end."

Elizabeth spent the next four years in her room at her father's house. Even with the comings and goings of her family and Wilson, most of her time was spent alone with Flush in her dark and secluded bedroom, "where the silence is most absolute." At times, her bedroom felt more like a prison than a retreat. "So profound is my solitude, & so complete my isolation from things & persons without. I lie all day, & day after day, on this sofa. . . . I might as well be in a wilderness—or a hermitage—or a convent—or a prison—as in this dark room, dark & silent."

Fresh air was thought to be dangerous for her, so the windows were sealed shut; in addition, a fire burned every day, leaving the room hot and smoky. To remind her of the world outside, Elizabeth asked that ivy be planted in a window box. It soon covered the window, and she spent hours staring at it: "Flush lies across my feet & my ivy waves in the wind." To avoid stirring up dust, the maids rarely cleaned, leaving spiders and their webs undisturbed in the corners, on the ceiling, and under the bed. Adding to the musty atmosphere, the scent of medicines, ointments, and eau de cologne pervaded the room.

Elizabeth's appearance was as gloomy as the setting. Pale and thin, she had dark circles under her eyes that looked like "two dark caves." Still in mourning for Bro and Sam, she dressed entirely in black: black velvet all winter and black silk for summer. Elizabeth was shocked when she read a description of herself that appeared in a book about British poets published at this time: "[It] shows me shut up in a dark room,—& frightens people away from me . . . as a sort of dictionary-monster, past bearing." The book's emphasis on her life as an invalid dismayed her, as did the *Quarterly Review*, which put her second on its list of the ten best British women poets, giving first place to Caroline Norton, whose work Elizabeth considered "feeble." She knew she needed to publish again in order to be taken seriously as a poet, but her creative spirit had deserted her.

Then the editor of *The Athenaeum* invited Elizabeth to write reviews for the journal. She began somewhat tentatively, but she was soon enthusiastically rereading her favorite Greek poets and producing detailed reviews of their works. This critical writing inspired Elizabeth to take up her own poetry again, which she did, producing a series of poems filled with the theme of loss. In "De Profundis," each stanza ends with a version of the refrain "And yet my days go on and on." The short poem "Grief" begins with the assertion "I tell you, hopeless grief is passionless." The poem describes the tearless anguish Elizabeth had experienced, ending with this line: "If it could weep, it would arise and go." The poem "Substitution" speaks more directly of her loss of Bro:

> When some beloved voice that was to you
> Both sound and sweetness, faileth suddenly,
> And silence, against which you dare not cry,
> Aches round you like a strong disease and new—
> What hope? what help? what music will undo
> That silence to your sense?

The pain of bereavement, although it had nearly cost her life in Torquay, started Elizabeth on the path toward adulthood. And Flush was her faithful companion on that journey.

During their hours alone together, Flush's antics broke into Elizabeth's depression. One time, she decided to find out what his reaction would be to seeing himself in a looking glass. At first, he ignored the mirror, which Elizabeth interpreted as his envy of "another" dog on her lap: "He can't bear . . . to look into a glass because he thinks there is a little brown dog inside every looking glass & he is jealous of its being so close to *me*." Elizabeth moved the mirror around her room so that Flush was forced to confront his image again and again. He became furious, "shivering with rage & barking & howling & gnashing his teeth at the brown dog in the glass."

Watching him come to terms with his reflection may have begun as a welcome distraction, but it led Elizabeth to profound insights about her life. Flush's anger reminded Elizabeth of her own outrage when her brothers were allowed to go to school, while she was expected to stay home to learn to run a household. She came to a startling conclusion: "Through the whole course of my childhood, I had a steady indignation against Nature who made me a woman." Eventually, Flush once again ignored his reflection. To Elizabeth, this meant he had followed the precept to "know thyself" and in doing so had achieved self-acceptance: "For Flush . . . has learnt by experience what that image means . . . & now contemplates it, serene in natural philosophy."

As Elizabeth gazed into the mirror at herself and Flush, she suddenly recognized, as Emily Brontë would also do, the unsettling similarity between lapdogs and women in Victorian England. Both were powerless, and both were dependent for their very existence on pleasing others. With something like the self-acceptance she attributed to Flush, Elizabeth bluntly stated, "Why, what *is* Flush, but a lapdog? And what am *I*, but a woman? I assure you we never take ourselves for anything greater."

In the silence of the sickroom, small acts signified the beginning of Elizabeth's stronger sense of self, such as her decision to let Flush sleep on her bed even though her doctor had forbidden it. Night after night, Flush would gaze longingly at Elizabeth and sigh as he stood on his hind legs, begging to be lifted up. Finally, his determination prevailed, and Elizabeth gave in. She was shocked by her act: "Think of his sleeping every night on my bed! I resisted a long while!" Elizabeth understood how out of character it was for her to flout her doctor's orders, and she proclaimed, "Some women might do such things—but no—I never could!"

Flush would also prove to be Elizabeth's ally in undermining her father's control over her. A Victorian patriarch, Mr. Barrett believed it was his duty to manage all the details of his adult children's lives, especially his daughters'. If they asked permission for the most innocent of outings—strawberry picking with Miss Mitford, for example—he invariably forbade it. His treatment of their distant cousin William Surtees Cook, who had fallen in love with Henrietta, was capricious. Sometimes Cook was treated warmly: He was invited to dinner and spent evenings with the family playing charades. Other times, Mr. Barrett forbade his visits despite Henrietta's pleading. Elizabeth never forgot "the dreadful scenes in which poor Henrietta was involved . . . how she was made to suffer—Oh, the dreadful scenes!—and only because she had seemed to feel a little." Although Elizabeth sympathized with Henrietta, she took her father's side, as she did in all family disputes. As a statement of her alliance with her father, she stayed in her room during Cook's visits, and he was never taken to meet her.

Mr. Barrett appreciated his oldest daughter's loyalty, and he also thought she was more spiritual and intellectual than her sisters. Thus, his domination of Elizabeth was subtler. Instead of railing and shouting at her, he monitored her activities, screened her visitors, and kept information from her if he thought it would upset her. With Flush as her ally, Elizabeth began to experiment with small acts of rebellion. Each evening, Mr. Barrett inspected Elizabeth's dinner tray to make sure she had eaten enough. Thanks to Flush, who happily devoured her unwanted food, her plate was always clean. Moreover, once she allowed Flush in her bed, Elizabeth was no longer alone when Mr. Barrett came to the room each night to kneel by the bed and pray with her. His evening visits to his daughter's room were another reminder of his authority over her, yet Flush's plump body hidden under the blankets would have undermined the solemnity of the nightly ritual and diluted its power.

Even as Elizabeth struggled to grow stronger, she still worried about her health. Her doctors often contradicted one another: one warned against fresh air, another promoted exercise. Some cautioned against too many visitors or too much writing, while others suggested travel abroad. As a result, Elizabeth fretted about every symptom, no matter how mild: "A cough is a matter of life or death with me—a hinge on which the door may turn either out or in." Her only exercise was wheelchair outings in the park with Wilson and Flush, so it is not surprising that she was easily fatigued. She continued to use opium, and whenever she felt disturbed or upset, she followed her doctors' advice and mixed it with brandy, thus tamping down unsettling emotions rather than experiencing them. (No record exists of the dosage she took, although the amount must have been small or she could not have continued her scholarly and literary pursuits.)

Some days, Elizabeth could not get up at all, and Flush would stay "in his eternal place on my bed," as still as the statues of dogs on royal tombs and, like them, an embodiment of loyalty and devotion. On days Elizabeth felt strong enough to leave her bed for the sofa, Flush was instantly at her side: "It is strange & dear of him— is it not?—that he should without beck or word, move from the bed to the sofa the moment I move, & back again with the same exactness?" However, when Elizabeth sat upright on a chair, to the "obvious inconvenience & dejection of my companion," Flush, also suffering the effects of little exercise, was now too fat to fit next to her.

When Elizabeth began allowing a few people to visit her, she begged Miss Mitford to bring her dog so that she could meet Flush's sire. Miss Mitford—a stout, white-haired woman in her sixties—somehow managed to transport her boisterous dog from the village of Three Mile Cross through London traffic to the Barrett home on Wimpole Street. In Elizabeth's cramped bedroom, the two male dogs growled and snapped as the women sipped tea and talked. Elizabeth was thrilled with the visit: "And although to be sure, the Flushies did break our talk into bits, I cannot repent having seen yours. He is in my mind evermore."

Although Elizabeth was exhausted after Miss Mitford's visit, she did not retreat to her bed but continued to marshal her strength. Then, in July 1842, at the age of thirty-six, Elizabeth recorded that she was able, for the first time since Bro's death, to stand upright unaided: "Think of my standing alone, with only one hand upon Flush—he standing quietly upon the sofa—only one hand leaning on Flush, to steady me." Now Elizabeth could leave her room, yet she discovered she was strangely reluctant to do so. Each time she attempted to venture out, she was overcome by anxiety. The sickroom had been a symbol of her role as a protected invalid; once she could leave it, expectations of her would change. What role would she have in the Barrett family if she were no longer a delicate, childlike woman?

It should come as no surprise that Flush, perfectly attuned to Elizabeth's moods, shared her anxiety. One day, they needed to leave the room for a few hours for one of its infrequent cleanings. When Elizabeth tried to cross the threshold, she staggered, which agitated Flush so that he shook violently. Eliz-

Elizabeth Barrett and Flush, 1843. *Watercolor by her brother Alfred Moulton-Barrett.*

abeth angrily labeled his behavior as "perverse" and confessed to Miss Mitford that Flush, who had been such an outgoing, curious puppy, had become "the prince of cowards."

Miss Mitford suggested they overcome Flush's fear (Elizabeth had not mentioned her own) by leaving the room in small steps. Following her advice, Elizabeth and Flush attempted limited excursions, beginning with trips to the downstairs parlor when only the family was present. In the drawing room, Flush would behave so outrageously that everyone's attention was focused on him rather than Elizabeth: "After an affectionate *devouring* scene upon the sofa in which I underwent a whole series of consoling kisses, he laid his head upon my shoulder and never left me until I went home again . . . upstairs!" Flush's theatrics helped Elizabeth tolerate the evenings downstairs, and after a few months, they were both able to leave the bedroom without difficulty. Elizabeth acknowledged that their shared weakness had deepened their attachment to each other: "There never was such a coward—not even his mistress! And with that bond of sympathy added to other still faster bonds, he and I are very near and dear." Just how dear he was to Elizabeth was about to be tested.

On September 13, 1843, while walking with Arabel, Flush was abducted by the infamous gang of dog stealers called "The Fancy." They simply grabbed him, threw him into a sack, and disappeared into the crowd. In nineteenth-century London, stealing pet dogs and demanding substantial ransoms for their safe return was a well-established and lucrative practice. A man could make several years' wages from one dog's ransom. In 1837, the London police identified more than 140 dog stealers. Dogs were lured with bait, usually liver mixed with myrrh or opium, or by a bitch in heat. If owners refused to pay the ransoms, their dogs' paws or even heads would be delivered to them. As Elizabeth exclaimed, "It is not *dogs* upon which they trade, but *feelings*. Wretched men!"

Mr. Taylor, ringleader of The Fancy, came in person to the Barrett home that night to demand a ransom for Flush's return. As

Mr. Taylor and Mr. Barrett exchanged angry words in the hallway, Elizabeth overheard everything. Mr. Barrett threatened to call the police if Flush was not immediately returned, and Mr. Taylor replied that they would never see the dog again. Mr. Barrett shut the door and returned to the dinner table without saying another word. Upstairs, Elizabeth gathered her own money and persuaded her brothers to deliver it to Mr. Taylor. She knew she was defying her father, but as she explained to Miss Mitford, "My despair overcame my sense of obedience." Mr. Barrett thought giving in to blackmailers was immoral, but Elizabeth felt differently. She believed that the welfare of a loved one, including a dog, overrode an abstract principle. The ransom paid, Flush was returned to Wimpole Street. Mr. Barrett chose to act as if nothing had happened.

Even though Elizabeth's brothers had delivered the ransom, they laughed at her tears over Flush's abduction and accused her of being childish. Elizabeth objected to their belief that a dog did not merit such loyalty: "It was excusable that I cried. As if Love (whether of dog or man) must not have the same quick sense of sorrow!" Elizabeth had shed few tears over her mother's and her brothers' deaths, but she was able to weep over the loss of Flush. Instead of accepting her family's judgment, Elizabeth put the question to a wider arena. She wrote numerous letters to her friends to find out whether they agreed with her actions on behalf of Flush. She described his abduction, her distress, and her decision to pay the ransom, and she asked the same questions over and over. "Did I tell you that I had lost my little dog, & recovered him after three days, by a deep bribery of the dogstealers? Do you know what it is, to love a dog & lose him—& is it in your philosophy to pardon a tear shed by woman in such a cause?"

The Fancy often stole the same dog many times, demanding ever-increasing ransoms, so it was not surprising when Flush was taken again a year later. This time, Elizabeth promptly sent her brothers to pay the ransom, but Flush was not returned. As days passed with no word from The Fancy, Elizabeth grew frightened, unable to sleep or to eat. Her brothers again admonished her, say-

ing that she should be
ashamed of making
such a fuss about a dog.
Even Miss Mitford
blithely offered Eliza-
beth a new puppy, one
that looked like Flush.
Elizabeth was shocked
by her friend's insensi-
tivity: "I am sure I
could not have borne
to see my Flushie re-
placed, *More Especially*
by a dog in any respect
like him. Oh no, no!—
That, I could never
have borne!"

Finally, the news
came that Flush was
alive and would be sent

Sketch of Flush, 1843. *Ink sketch by Elizabeth Barrett on the inside cover of her notebook.*

back. Elizabeth forgot her anger at Miss Mitford and wrote excitedly: "Dear Flushie! He will be at home in an hour. What a meeting we shall have! May God bless you, dearest friend! I am so
flushified, I can write of nothing else." Finally, a bedraggled Flush,
"drenched with rain, & a halter round his neck, just as if he had escaped hanging," was rudely deposited on the front stoop. Elizabeth
was horrified at his pitiable condition, especially when he whim-
pered at the sight of her. Flush remained "low and languid" for two
days before he regained his good spirits.

Elizabeth's response to Flush's abductions shows how much she
had changed since Torquay. The submissive daughter was becoming an autonomous, self-reliant adult. In ransoming Flush, she had
followed her own convictions with a determined will, to the point
of defying her father. She cried for Flush, expressing her feelings
instead of trying to blunt them, and she acted on Flush's behalf,

despite her brothers' derision and Miss Mitford's lack of understanding.

Elizabeth's internal transformation was also reflected in her new poems. No longer meditations on death, instead, they expressed her interest in politics and current events, as well as her newfound optimism about the future. Elizabeth was convinced that Flush had played a key role in her rekindled creativity because she understood that hopelessness had left her unable to write: "I [was] . . . so weary of my own being that to take interest in my very poems I had to lift them up by an effort & separate them from myself & cast them out from me into the sunshine where I was not—feeling nothing of the light which fell on them." Cut off from her own creativity, Elizabeth had fallen into self-loathing, which she concealed from everyone and which left her even more dependent on Flush's devotion.

Years later, when she looked back at this time, Elizabeth paid tribute to how much she owed her little dog: "Flush came nearer, & I was grateful to him . . . yes, grateful . . . for not being tired! I have felt grateful & flattered . . . yes flattered . . . when he has chosen rather to stay with me all day than go downstairs." The poem "Flush or Faunus" honors his role as Elizabeth's chief consoler:

> You see this dog. It was but yesterday
> I mused forgetful of his presence here
> Till thought on thought drew downward tear on tear
> When from the pillow where wet-cheeked I lay,
> A head as hairy as Faunus thrust its way
> Right sudden against my face,—two golden-clear
> Great eyes astonished mine,—a drooping ear
> Did flap me on either cheek to dry the spray!

The poem's somber classic tone, combined with the image of Flush using his ears to brush tears from Elizabeth's cheeks, reflects her attitude toward her dog. While she always acknowledged his importance, she was also aware of the more absurd aspects of their relationship. Even though she knew Flush was spoiled, Elizabeth admired his happy disposition, and she tried to convey his charm by making little sketches of him in the margins of letters and in her journal.

In August 1844, a two-volume collection of Elizabeth's new work, titled simply *Poems*, was published in London and America. The collection includes "To Flush, My Dog," a celebration of his beauty and liveliness:

> *Leap! thy slender feet are bright,*
> *Canopied in fringes.*
> *Leap—those tasselled ears of thine,*
> *Down in golden inches.*

The poem's major theme is Elizabeth's appreciation of Flush's loyalty in her darkest moments, as these lines illustrate:

> *This dog watched beside a bed*
> *Day and night unweary,—*
> *Watched within a curtained room,*
> *Where no sunbeam brake the gloom*
> *Round the sick and dreary.*

When one friend cautioned against including the Flush poem in the collection, Elizabeth rebuked him spiritedly: "Leave out Flush!!—Why for love's sake I could not do it. I shall make some alterations, & leave out a little, but the public must have an introduction to Flushie." *Poems* received respectful reviews and even sold fairly well, considering that, then as now, novels far outsold poetry collections. Once again, her cousin John Kenyon tried to persuade Elizabeth to take part in literary lunches, talks, and award ceremonies. She refused, preferring to stay in her room with Flush, answering the letters of admiration that arrived daily at 50 Wimpole Street.

Elizabeth used the subject of Flush, or dogs in general, as a barometer to determine the level of intimacy she would extend to new correspondents. When she asked the well-known painter Benjamin Robert Haydon what he thought of dogs, he was baffled and repeated her question: "You asked me if I had known attachment to Dogs?" On the other hand, James Martin, a rural justice of the peace, understood the significance of Elizabeth's questions: "You have got a dog, & so do I,—you love your Dog, & talk to him, & he understands you, & so do I to mine, & so does he me." Flush gave Elizabeth's readers an entry for writing to her. Thomas Westwood, an English poet, told Elizabeth he had wanted to write her for years but never had the courage until she published the poem about Flush: "I thought you might not consider it a hardship to bestow a moment or two on one, who will look quite as pleased to receive a few lines from you as Flush does when you pat him on the head."

Elizabeth Barrett and Flush, 1841. *Miniature by Matilda Carter.*

When Elizabeth's brother Alfred painted a watercolor of her, she insisted on posing with Flush in her arms. Wrapped in a red shawl, he appears absolutely certain that his place in the world is on Elizabeth's lap. Another portrait, a miniature by Matilda Carter, shows Flush again sitting on Elizabeth's lap, this time looking up at her with an expression of curiosity. The artist captured the remarkable similarity between the woman and the dog: Both have large brown eyes, and Elizabeth's hair is gathered on either side of her face in long curls, which look surprisingly like Flush's wavy spaniel ears!

Elizabeth honored Flush in her poems and in her letters, even though the intensity of her attachment was about to lessen. Flush would always be Elizabeth's beloved companion, but unknown to either of them, Robert Browning was about to move Flush from the center of Elizabeth's heart.

In January 1845, Browning was not yet a famous poet. He was just beginning to be taken seriously by literary London, with the notable exception of Miss Mitford. She did not admire his ardent poems or his fashionable dress, finding his distinctive yellow leather gloves especially distasteful. Elizabeth, on the other hand, was attracted both to Browning's poetry and to his appearance. She cut a picture of him from a literary journal and hung it in her bedroom, and she wrote a four-line tribute to him in her poem "Lady Geraldine's Courtship." He responded with a letter of appreciation, which Elizabeth answered immediately. Soon they were writing several times a week, then several times a day. Browning was determined to meet Elizabeth face-to-face, but she kept putting him off. He persisted until finally, five months after their first letters, Elizabeth agreed to see him.

When Wilson ushered Robert Browning into Elizabeth's room, he saw a pale woman dressed in black, wrapped in a shawl, and lying on a sofa with a suspicious dog at her feet. Elizabeth, who was thirty-nine, saw a short, younger (thirty-three), vigorous man, with dark, thick hair, piercing eyes, and a self-confident manner. He carried a bouquet of flowers just picked from

Robert Browning, 1858. *Oil portrait by Michele Gordigiani.*

his mother's garden, and he was, as usual, carefully and immaculately dressed and eager for conversation. They talked about poetry, he with a loud, confident voice; she hesitant, worried her thin voice would crack. In that first visit, they discovered they shared a passion for writing, language, and literature.

Elizabeth, who had allowed only a handful of people to visit her—Miss Mitford, John Kenyon, and a few others—now received Robert Browning once or twice a week. And on the days they could not meet, they wrote. Mr. Barrett knew of the visits of "Ba's poet" but not of their frequency. Only her sisters and Wilson knew, and only Flush was present during their meetings. Browning immediately understood and respected the depth of Elizabeth's devotion to her dog. Early on, he wrote, "I shall not attempt to speak and prove my feelings,—you know what even Flush is to me thro' you."

Browning lived with his sister and his parents, the latter providing financial support so that he was able to devote his life to poetry (another reason Miss Mitford refused to take him seriously). Once he met Elizabeth, however, he lost interest in dinner parties, soirées, and weekends in the country. Soon, the two were addressing each other as "dear friend"; then Robert progressed to calling Elizabeth "Ba," the intimate nickname that only her family used. Robert imagined himself lying in Flush's place at Elizabeth's feet: "Like Flush, with all manner of coral necklaces about my neck, and two sweet mysterious hands on my head, and so be forced to hear verses on me, Ba's verses."

Elizabeth's sexuality had been dormant for years. Now, however, she exploded with desire and energy as she compared herself to Flush: "I must & will see you tomorrow—I cannot do otherwise. It is just as if Flush had been shut up in a box for so many days." Occasionally, Elizabeth was so overcome by the emotions Robert stirred in her that she reverted to her habit of using Flush to conceal her feelings. Once Robert wrote an especially loving letter, and she answered him with a description of Flush's dainty eating habits. But as soon as she realized what she was doing, she stopped and spoke directly to Robert, admitting how powerfully his letter had affected her: "So, when you write me such a letter, I write back to you about Flush. Dearest beloved, but I have read the letter & felt it in my heart, through & through! & it is as wise to talk of Flush foolishly, as to fancy that I could say *how* it is felt—this letter!"

Elizabeth and Robert used Flush as a symbolic go-between to help them express their feelings in conversations and letters. If Robert thought Elizabeth needed more fresh air, he told her indirectly, through Flush: "The day is fine . . . you will profit by it, I trust. 'Flush, wag your tail and grow restless & scratch at the door!' " When Elizabeth worried how others might judge their relationship, Robert reassured her by explaining that people would simply see them "with Flush's eyes"—in other words, with the sympathy that the couple ascribed to Flush.

In all this bantering about Flush, the two seemed to have forgotten the real Flush: a full-grown, spoiled dog accustomed to Elizabeth's total attention. Then he bit Robert. Elizabeth was horrified, and as soon as he left, she slapped Flush's ears, the first time she had ever touched him with anything but kindness. When she wrote Robert that evening, Elizabeth at first minimized what had happened, saying Flush had bitten Robert because he had been carrying an umbrella. Then her tone shifted as she described her punishment of Flush and his reaction to it: "I slapped his ears & told him that he never should be loved again: and he sat on the sofa (sitting, not lying) with his eyes fixed on me all the time I did the flowers, with an expression of quiet despair in his face. At last I said, 'If you are good, Flush, you may come & say that you are sorry' . . . at which he dashed across the room &, trembling all over, kissed first one of my hands & then another & put up his paws to be shaken, & looked into my face with such great beseeching eyes, that you would certainly have forgiven him just as I did."

In contrast to Elizabeth, Robert was patient with and tolerant of Flush's aggressiveness. He had learned this lesson as a child when his own dog had bitten him as he kissed his mother. Perhaps remembering that incident, Robert explained Flush's motives to Elizabeth: "Oh, poor Flush,—do you think I do not love and respect him for his jealous supervision,—his slowness to know another, having once known you?" The crisis seemed to be over, and Flush had resumed his role of devoted companion when, three weeks later, he bit Robert again. This time, Elizabeth threatened to muzzle him, but again, Robert intervened, saying Flush merely acted the way that "dogs who are dogs do." He disagreed with the idea of a muzzle, saying it would only turn Flush's "transient suspicion of me . . . into absolute dislike,—hatred!" Instead, he began to bring Flush's favorite cakes as a way to win him over.

By the summer of 1846, at the age of forty, Elizabeth was happily in love. She was physically stronger than she had been since childhood, and she celebrated by exploring the parks and shops of London with Arabel and Flush. She boasted to Robert that one night she even ventured outside alone: "Therefore I put on my bonnet, as a knight of old took his sword, . . . aspiring to the pure heroic . . . & called Flush, & walked down stairs & into the street, all alone—*that* was something great!—And, with just Flush, I walked there, up & down in glorious independence."

She and Robert began to dream about a life together in Italy, the country so often celebrated by Keats, Byron, and Shelley, poets they both loved. For the past few years, Elizabeth had made plans to spend winters in Italy, but they always came to naught either because of her own hesitation to leave home or because of Mr. Barrett's reluctance to let her go. As the couple wove poetic stories about what Italy would be like, Robert invariably assigned a role to Flush: "Think of you and me . . . why, we shall walk arm in arm; would Flush object to carry an umbrella in his mouth?"

The couple knew that Mr. Barrett was opposed to any of his children, son or daughter, marrying. Some biographers speculate that the prohibition arose from Mr. Barrett's belief that he carried mixed blood as a result of his family's history of slave ownership, while others attribute it to his loneliness after his wife's death. Or it may have been that he simply could not condone the choices that his children made. He rejected Henrietta's suitor William Surtees Cook because he had no source of income outside of his soldier's pay. (They eventually married without Mr. Barrett's permission.) According to one of Mr. Barrett's nephews, his uncle had objected to Robert Browning because he considered him to be working-class.

Elizabeth knew that if she married Robert, her father would cast her out of his home and out of his heart, so certain was she that Mr. Barrett would never approve of his forty-year-old invalid daughter's marrying a poet six years younger than she. Robert wanted to meet Mr. Barrett to ask formally for his blessing, but Elizabeth was too wary of her father's wrath to consider such a step.

When the couple turned from daydreaming to making concrete plans for marrying and leaving England, Elizabeth tried to convey to Robert how frightened she was of her father's reaction. She did so by telling him that if Flush were left behind, Mr. Barrett would use her dog as a scapegoat for his anger toward her: "But you will let him [Flush] come with us to Italy, instead—will you not dear, dearest? In good earnest, will you not? Because, if I leave him behind, he will be hanged for my sins in this house." Robert assured Elizabeth that Flush would never be forsaken.

Elizabeth continued to make plans, confiding in her sisters but relating only a few necessary details to Wilson, who had agreed to take part in the wedding and to accompany Elizabeth to Italy. When Miss Mitford made the forty-five-mile journey to London to visit her, Elizabeth told her nothing. Later, she boasted to Robert that she had verbally "fenced" throughout the visit, so that she would not inadvertently reveal their plans to the woman who had been like a mother to her. Her deception of Miss Mitford shows how determined Elizabeth was to begin a new life with Robert, even though it meant leaving her family and her dear friend.

Elizabeth's preoccupation with her secret plans was interrupted when Mr. Taylor's Fancy took Flush for the third time, on September 1, 1846. Elizabeth and Arabel were shopping on Vere Street when Flush suddenly vanished. Elizabeth immediately informed Robert: "Here is a distress for me, dearest! I have lost my poor Flush—*lost* him!" Elizabeth was upset but confident that Flush

would be quickly ransomed and returned. She continued her note
to Robert with a description of the new boots she had bought for
their journey and reviewed the schedule for their departure.

Robert, distracted by a headache and the flu, was unruffled:
"Poor Flush—how sorry I am for you, my Ba! But you will recover
him." Then Robert lectured Elizabeth against paying a ransom because to do so would encourage dognapping. He sounded just like
Mr. Barrett, but then he went further than Elizabeth's father had
ever done. Robert declared that he would not pay a ransom even if
it meant Flush would be killed: "You think I should receive Flush's
head? Perhaps so, God allows matters to happen!" As soon as he
posted the letter, Robert realized he had made a terrible mistake.
He did not wait for Elizabeth's answer but immediately wrote a second letter apologizing for the first. He attributed his callousness to
illness, claiming he had not been himself when he wrote the letter.
He conceded: "I ought to have told you (unless you divined it, as
you might) that I would give all I am ever to be worth in the world,
to get back your Flush for you."

Because of Robert's illness, the couple had not seen each other
for several days. If they had been able to meet in person, they might
have resolved their differences over what they had come to call "the
Flush-argument." Instead, the dispute escalated. Elizabeth asked
Robert what he would do if the "banditti" kidnapped her in Italy.
Would he refuse to pay a ransom even if they cut off one of her ears
and sent it to him? She told him succinctly, "I am *your* Flush, & *he*
is mine." She would expect Robert to pay a ransom for her, just as
she would pay whatever it cost to recover Flush.

By now, Elizabeth was very angry, disappointed at Robert's lack
of empathy, anxious about her impending marriage, and increasingly worried about Flush. She had sent her brother Henry to pay
Mr. Taylor, but there was no sign of her dog. When five days had
passed, Elizabeth decided it was time to take things into her own
hands, so she and the loyal Wilson set out by cab to search for
Flush. They ignored the pleas of Henry, who begged them not to
go because he was afraid they would be murdered.

Elizabeth's quest for Flush at this point assumes a mythic dimension, for no less was required of her (and poor Wilson) than a descent into the underworld—the slums of Whitechapel, where Jack the Ripper stalked, killing prostitutes. Like the frantic Demeter searching for her daughter, Persephone, Elizabeth looked everywhere for Flush. She and Wilson traveled to an area just outside London called the Rookery, a refuge for thieves, prostitutes, and outlaws because it was beyond the city's legal boundary. Elizabeth saw, heard, and smelled the world of the slums, a world she would re-create in her epic poem *Aurora Leigh*:

> . . . *A sick child, from an ague-fit,*
> *Whose wasted right hand gambled 'gainst his left*
> *With an old brass button in a blot of sun,*
> *Jeered weakly at me as I passed across*
> *The uneven pavement; while a woman, rouged*
> *Upon the angular cheek-bones, kerchief torn,*
> *Thin dangling locks, and flat lascivious mouth,*
> *Cursed at a window—*

She and Wilson did not confront the thieves directly because Elizabeth knew from experience that arguing with men would do no good. Instead, they approached Mrs. Taylor, wife of the dog stealer, and appealed to her, begging her to help them get Flush back. The collaboration among the women from three different classes of Victorian society was successful, and Mrs. Taylor persuaded her husband to return Flush that night.

Rescuing Flush showed Elizabeth that she had the courage to act on her convictions, no matter where they led her or who opposed her, even Robert. She would draw on the same qualities of courage and determination in the next weeks as she took the steps that would forever change her life.

On the morning of September 12, 1846, just five months after they met, Elizabeth and Robert were secretly married in Marylebone Parish Church. After the quiet ceremony, the bride and groom took separate cabs back to their homes. In the following days, Elizabeth struggled to write farewell letters, including one to Miss Mitford in which she addressed her friend's hurt feelings: "Against you,—in allowing you no confidence, I have not certainly sinned, I think—so do not look at me with those reproachful eyes." And of course, she included a reference to Flush, who remained a strong link between the two women: "You will understand how it was to hear the words that Robert loved me. How I must have felt in hearing them—I who loved Flush for not hating to be near me . . . I who by a long sorrowfulness and solitude, had sunk into the very ashes of self humiliation."

On September 19, a week after their wedding, Elizabeth posted Miss Mitford's letter, as well as separate ones to each member of her family. Then, as the Barretts sat down to their afternoon meal, Elizabeth, without a word of farewell, left home forever. Accompanied by Wilson, who carried Flush, Elizabeth walked the few blocks to Hodgson's bookstore, where Robert waited. They took a cab to Vauxhall station, then the train to Southhampton, where they boarded the night ferry and crossed the English Channel to France. They rested in Rouen for a few hours, because, as Elizabeth noted, they all were "exhausted either by sea or sorrow." Then they continued their journey.

On their way to Paris, an incident occurred that made it plain Robert had taken Flush's place as his wife's closest companion. Stopping for a picnic, the couple came upon a stream and waded through the "boiling water to a still rock in the middle of it." Flush was determined to follow Elizabeth as he had always done—from Torquay to London, from sickroom to drawing room, from London to France: "Flush proved his love of me by leaping (at the cost of wetting his feet & my gown) after me to the slippery stone, & was repulsed three times by R. poor Flushie!" Whatever Robert's reason for "repulsing" Flush—perhaps he was worried about the little dog's safety or impatient with his determination to stay close to Elizabeth—he was now clearly first in Elizabeth's heart.

When the Brownings arrived in Paris, they acted like any other honeymooners: They walked along the Seine, toured the Louvre, and dined in restaurants (which Elizabeth had never done before). She wrote her sisters how happy she was, that she and Robert "sit through the dusky evenings watching the stars rise over the high Paris houses and talking of childish things." In her farewell letters to her family, she had given them a post office address in Orléans where they could write to her. For that reason, beneath her joy in Paris lay a terrible dread about the letters she knew would be waiting for her.

When they at last arrived in Orléans and collected their mail, Elizabeth asked Robert to wait outside their hotel room so that she could be alone. Then, with Flush on her lap, feeling as if she were looking at her "death warrant," Elizabeth opened her father's letter. In "hard and unsparing" terms, he informed his daughter that she was disinherited and that he no longer held any affection for her. Next came George's letter, written on behalf of all Elizabeth's brothers: Equally harsh, it denounced her for publicly disgracing the Barrett family name. (Although the brothers eventually softened, Mr. Barrett never saw Elizabeth again. When he died, all the letters she had written him after her marriage were discovered unopened in his desk.) Finally, there were sympathetic words, albeit a bit reproachful, from Miss Mitford, who said she would have been honored to stand up for Elizabeth at her wedding. But the letters from Henrietta and Arabel, who had to deal with their enraged father and brothers, held nothing but joyful congratulations to their sister and to Robert.

Once they reached Italy, Elizabeth knew that she and Flush had left behind the gray world of the Wimpole Street sickroom forever. They had escaped Mr. Barrett's rules, Victorian England's morality, leash laws, and dog stealers. Elizabeth now wore gauzy shifts instead of heavy black mourning dresses, let her hair loose from its tight coils, and walked barefoot on the marble floors of their new home in Florence.

After searching for months, Elizabeth and Robert had fallen in love with the Palazzo Guidi. No longer a palace, it had been divided into two apartments, one of which the Brownings leased. Their half was a suite of eight spacious rooms with high windows and a narrow terrace. Elizabeth named it "Casa" Guidi because she wanted to transform "a mere palace into a home." (Today, as part of the Landmark Trust, Casa Guidi has been restored and is open to the public.) Along the terrace were pots of orange trees and myrtle that filled the rooms with their fragrance. Elizabeth kept the windows wide open and delighted in watching parades and political demonstrations from the balcony. Caught up in the new spirit of nationalism, she began writing *Casa Guidi Windows*, a political poem about Italy's reunification.

Flush also relished the sights, sounds, and smells of Italy. Because Elizabeth no longer needed his constant attention, the little spaniel was free to reenter the world of dogs. He shed his collar and leash and came and went freely. He suffered terribly from fleas, and so Robert shaved his coat, which effectively removed the last traces of Flush's former identity as a purebred Cocker Spaniel. Elizabeth missed his curls, but she was proud that he now fit in with the other dogs that wandered the streets of Florence: "My Flush is as well as ever, and perhaps gayer than ever I knew him. He runs out in the piazza whenever he pleases, and plays with dogs when they are pretty enough, and wags his tail at the sentinels and civic guard, and takes the Grand Duke as a sort of neighbor of his."

Elizabeth's letters to Henrietta and Arabel focused on her happiness, although, at times, she missed her sisters terribly. Then, following her old custom, she wrote about Flush to help convey her feelings. She admitted to Arabel that she depended on him for company on nights when heat and homesickness prevented her from sleeping: "Flush & I can't sleep, & are given to wandering from one room to another." Arabel responded in kind by saying she often dreamed of Flush and missed their walks together rather than confessing directly how lonely she was for her sister. Elizabeth rarely mentioned her years as an invalid or the depression she had experienced, but when she did, it was through Flush: "I have Flush with me here, and he adapts himself to the sunshine as to the shadow, and when he hears me laugh lightly, begins not to think it too strange."

Elizabeth reported that Flush was growing "very fond of Robert, as indeed he ought to be." Secure in her marriage, Elizabeth enjoyed watching the connection develop between her dog and her husband. She wrote that Robert took Flush for his daily walks "to the Cascine [a park along the Arno River] where he always dances for joy of the long grass & thick underwood . . . or to Bellosguardo up the hills where Milton went to visit Galileo, & which (probably for that reason) is a favorite walk of Flush's."

Elizabeth shed the fretful anxiety she had once felt about her little dog. On the Brownings' first wedding anniversary, Flush ran after a little spotted female and stayed away all night. Elizabeth admitted that at first, she reverted to "sighing over all these vicissitudes in the most melancholy of moods," but then she adopted Robert's relaxed attitude over Flush's absence. When the exhausted dog appeared the next morning, Robert teased Elizabeth about Flush's behavior, "quite disgraceful for a respectable dog like him." Elizabeth laughed, although in London, she had been annoyed when Robert tried to convince her that Flush was no different from other "dogs who are dog-like."

On March 9, 1849, at the age of forty-three and after two miscarriages, Elizabeth gave birth to a healthy son, whom they named Robert Wiedemann Barrett Browning, or Pen for short. (Wiedemann was Robert's mother's maiden name.) Flush reacted in a predictable way to this threat to his security by barking frantically at the intruder. When that did not work, he gave up and withdrew in despair before finally capitulating to the inevitable: "For a whole fortnight he fell into deep melancholy and was proof against all attentions lavished on him. Now he begins to be consoled a little and even condescends to patronize the cradle."

Soon after Pen's birth, Robert received word that his mother, whom he dearly loved, had died. Feeling he could not leave his wife and newborn son, Robert did not attend the funeral. In the ensuing months, he struggled with a depression much like the one Elizabeth had suffered after Bro's death. His plight moved her to show her husband the love poems she had been secretly writing ever since their courtship began. Published the next year as *Sonnets from the Portuguese* (the title an effort to disguise the poems' intensely personal nature), the forty-three sonnets include "How do I love thee? Let me count the ways." The poems did not cause much of a stir at the time, although they comforted Robert greatly. Today, *Sonnets from the Portuguese* are the best-loved of Elizabeth Barrett Browning's poems.

Also in 1850, Elizabeth began *Aurora Leigh*, her epic poem about a woman who surmounts the obstacles of the Victorian period to become a respected and successful writer. (*Aurora Leigh* would be published in 1856 to great acclaim and would influence generations of women writers, including Emily Dickinson and Virginia Woolf.) Every morning, Elizabeth and Robert retreated to their separate studies to write, while Wilson took Pen and Flush to the park.

Boy and dog were slowly developing their own relationship, which, according to Elizabeth, was one-sided: "The affection between Baby & him is not equal, Baby's love for him being far stronger. He, on the other hand, looks down upon Baby." Pen showered the aging dog with hugs and kisses, which Flush would tolerate for a while before walking away, seemingly offended by such excessive displays of affection. Elizabeth was touched when Pen included Flush in his nightly prayers: "I have never taught the child any prayers, so he prays out whatever is in his little heart, and Flush being there, comes in for blessing, as why should he not?" When Arabel wrote that she was worried Elizabeth was overlooking Flush because of Pen, Elizabeth was indignant: "I wonder at your imaginations about Flush. How ungrateful & fickle you think me! Why Flush has as much love & perhaps more attention than ever."

Flush was a tangible link between Elizabeth's former life and her life in Italy. She found it reassuring to believe that he continued to see her as the same person she had always been, despite marriage, Italy, and Pen: "He calls me Miss Barrett still." And when Elizabeth looked at the overweight, aging dog, she could still see Flush's endearing charm: "[He] has all his old ways." But at fourteen, Flush wheezed when he walked and had developed an old-dog smell. A brief image of him appears in one of Robert's poems as "an old dog, bald and blindish," accompanying the poet on his evening walks. One of Elizabeth's friends in Florence recalled, "By the time I knew Flush he was an old mangy creature, an uncomfortable fellow-passenger in a vettura."

Elizabeth Barrett Browning and Robert Wiedemann (Pen) Barrett Browning, 1860.

To children, however, Flush was still an appealing little dog. A child who played with Pen at Casa Guidi remembered Flush as "a beautiful brown dog, with golden eyes." During tea, she noticed that Flush took the bread and butter he was offered, but he kept his eyes on the plum cake: "I recollect that Mrs. Barrett Browning whispered to me that if I looked under the divan I would find the bread and butter hidden there. She explained that Flush was far too polite a dog to refuse anything offered to him; but from personal observation she knew that he would not eat bread and butter when he saw any chance of getting plum-cake. Pen and I crept on all fours and looked under the divan; yes, there were all the slices of thin bread and butter in a row, and untouched."

In June 1854, Flush died peacefully and was buried in the vaults of the Casa Guidi. Keeping the sad news from Miss Mitford, who was gravely ill, Elizabeth wrote to Arabel: "Another thing which has saddened me much these last days is Flush. . . . He is gone, Arabel. He died quite quietly—I am sorry to say Penini found him and screamed in anguish. There was no pain, nothing to regret in that way—our grief for him is the less that his infirmities had become so great that he lost no joy in losing life. He was old you know—though dogs of his kind have lived much longer—and the climate acted unfavourably upon him. He had scarcely a hair on his back—everyone thought it was the mange, and the smell made his presence in the drawing room a difficult thing. In spite of all however, it has been quite a shock to me and a sadness. A dear dog he was."

For the thirteen years they spent together, Elizabeth kept the promise she had made to Flush: "He & I are inseparable companions, and I have vowed him my perpetual society in exchange for his devotion." Seven years later, on June 29, 1861, Elizabeth herself died, held in Robert's arms.

Chronology

ELIZABETH BARRETT BROWNING

1806   March, birth of Elizabeth Barrett Browning.

1818   [July, birth of Emily Brontë.]

1826   *Essay on Mind, with Other Poems* published.

1828   October, death of Mary Barrett, Elizabeth's mother.

1830   [December, birth of Emily Dickinson.]

1833   Elizabeth's translation of Aeschylus's *Prometheus Bound* published.

1838   June, *Seraphim and Other Poems* published.
        August, Elizabeth goes to Torquay for her health.

1840   July, Elizabeth's brother Bro drowns.

1841   January, Miss Mitford sends Flush.
        September, Elizabeth and Flush return to London.

1843   September, Flush stolen.

1844   Flush stolen for the second time.
        Poems published.

1845   January, Robert Browning first writes to Elizabeth.
       May, he visits for the first time.

1846   September 1, Flush stolen for the third time.
       September 12, Elizabeth and Robert marry secretly.
       A week later, they leave for Italy.

1848   [December, death of Emily Brontë.]

1849   March, birth of Elizabeth and Robert's son, Robert
       Wiedemann (Pen) Barrett Browning.

1850   *Sonnets from the Portuguese* published.

1851   *Casa Guidi Windows* published.

1854   June, death of Flush.

1856   *Aurora Leigh* published.

1861   June 29, death of Elizabeth Barrett Browning, age
       fifty-five. She is buried in the "English" Cemetery
       in Florence.

EMILY BRONTË
and KEEPER

"The tawny and lion-like bulk . . . is ever
stretched beside her. . . . One hand of the mistress
generally reposes on the loving serf's rude head,
because if she takes it away he groans
and is discontented."

EMILY BRONTË

On England's Yorkshire moors in the mid-1840s, the villagers of Haworth often paused in their work at the sight of Emily Brontë, the parson's daughter, striding across the heath with a massive dog at her side. Years later, they could still remember the tall woman and her dog appearing suddenly out of the fog. No warning of their approach could be heard except for the dog's odd breathing, a wheezing whistle, the result of an injury from one of his fierce brawls with the local dogs. Emily would nod a greeting and pause to hear the latest tales of quarrels, thievery, or ghost sightings. The dog, Keeper, stood completely still—his eyes on his mistress—until the moment she stirred, when he instantly followed her. A strange pair they were, uncanny and frightening, like the old stories of the goddesses and their dogs. Yet there was gentleness between them.

Emily Brontë's relationship with Keeper may have been the closest one she ever had outside her family. Unlike Elizabeth Barrett Browning, who wrote numerous letters filled with details about Flush, Emily Brontë left behind little private writing, let alone an account of her life with Keeper. After her death, almost all her pa-

Emily Jane Brontë, ca. 1833–34. *A fragment cut from* The Gun Group, *an oil painting of the Brontë siblings by Branwell Brontë.*

pers were destroyed, most likely by Charlotte Brontë in an attempt
to protect her sister's privacy. The only writing that remains, aside
from her published work, consists of a few short notes, four diary
papers, several essays, and some pages from her household account
book. Like everything else about Emily Brontë, the story of her relationship with Keeper is mostly speculation, based on recollections
of those who knew her and on what she said about dogs in her essays and poems and in *Wuthering Heights*, her only novel. The most
vivid portrait of Emily and Keeper comes from Charlotte Brontë's
novel *Shirley*, which was completed after Emily's death. Charlotte
said the character of Shirley was intended as a tribute to her sister,
so the scenes of Shirley with her dog Tartar can be taken as Charlotte's memories of Emily with Keeper.

Emily, the fifth Brontë child, was born in 1818. Mrs. Brontë, already suffering from the cancer that would take her life, had little
strength to care for her newborn daughter. During Emily's first
year, her mother again became pregnant. She was exhausted,
bedridden, and never recovered from the difficult birth of her
youngest child, Anne. The servants recalled her crying out in pain
while her husband, inconsolable and helpless, isolated himself in
his study. As Mrs. Brontë grew worse, her sister, whom the children
called Aunt Branwell, came to help but was quickly overwhelmed
by the needs of six young children. Aunt Branwell concentrated on
the infant Anne and three-year-old Branwell, her namesake and the
only boy, leaving Charlotte and Emily in the care of the older girls,
Maria and Elizabeth, still children themselves. The uncertainty and
upheaval in the close quarters of the Haworth Parsonage must have
bewildered and frightened Emily, a toddler who needed the security of a loving adult.

Five months after Emily's third birthday, her mother died and
was buried under the stone floor of the church, which stands just
beyond the parsonage. Left to their own resources while their father grieved and their aunt tried to organize the household with the
help of Maria and Elizabeth, the four younger children drew close

together. Charlotte, Branwell, Emily, and Anne spent hours on the moors, exploring the vast treeless hills and discovering where heather and harebells grew. They all loved the moors; for Emily, they became a kind of substitute for a caring mother, an image that appears later in her poetry:

> The linnet in the rocky dells,
> The moor-lark in the air,
> The bee among the heather-bells
> That hide my lady fair:
>
> The wild deer browse above her breast;
> The wild birds raise their brood,
> And they, her smiles of love caressed,
> Have left her solitude!

Although Mr. Brontë would always require hours away from the prattle of his children, in the months after his wife died, he resolutely emerged from his study and set about directing their education. Using books from his own library and borrowing others from friends and nearby lending libraries, he gave them lessons in history, mathematics, and literature. The parish organist was recruited for music lessons; Emily, in particular, became an accomplished pianist. In addition, Mr. Brontë regularly hired local artists to come to the parsonage for private drawing lessons. It was always assumed that Branwell would someday go away to school, but Mr. Brontë worried about his daughters' futures. When he learned of a boarding school that offered a reduced rate for the daughters of clergy, he decided to send the four oldest girls there.

Thus, before she was six, Emily went away to the Clergy Daughters' School at Cowan Bridge, which would become infamous as the Lowood School in *Jane Eyre*, where Charlotte described its bitter cold, squalid atmosphere, and inedible food. Cowan Bridge kept an entrance book in which initial assessments of the students were noted. For Charlotte, the entry states, "Reads little—Writes pretty well." On the other hand, Emily, listed as "5¾ years old," seems to have made a better first impression. Her entry says, "Reads very prettily."

Emily, who was probably the youngest child in the school, initially thrived on the attention she received. A teacher recalled her as "a darling child . . . quite the pet nursling of the school." Soon, though, her brief happiness as a darling pet was overshadowed by the cruelty at Cowan Bridge. Emily witnessed the humiliating and merciless punishments meted out to the older girls, including her oldest sister Maria, for the slightest infraction of rules. If their clothing or rooms were untidy, they suffered the humiliation of having to stand barefoot in front of the other students; if late for class, they were publicly struck; and no matter how ill, they were forced to spend hours kneeling in the icy chapel.

Then Maria, whose sweet disposition had made her a gentle surrogate mother for the Brontë children, contracted typhoid fever. Emily and Charlotte watched helplessly as their eleven-year-old sister suffered quietly in the cold dormitory until finally she was sent home to die. A few months later, Elizabeth fell ill and was also sent home. Charlotte and Emily, terrified, were left behind at the school until their frantic father came and fetched them. They reached home in time to witness ten-year-old Elizabeth's death.

Once again, the children took part in a funeral service, this time kissing their sister goodbye for the last time. Again, they followed their father as he led the funeral procession out the front door, through the scraggly garden, and into the cold stone church. They watched as Elizabeth's coffin was lowered into the vault that held their mother and Maria. A poem of Branwell's captures the emotions of the children that day:

> *Down, down, they lowered her, sad and slow,*
> *Into her narrow house below:*
> *And deep, indeed, appeared to be*
> *That one glimpse of eternity,*
> *Where cut from life, corruption lay,*
> *Where beauty soon should turn to clay.*

How much of Emily's reticent nature as an adult was due to her temperament and genius and how much was caused by these early losses can never be known. Nevertheless, some of her character traits suggest she was seriously affected by the deaths of her mother and sisters. She was prone to unbearable anxiety whenever she left home, and she never made any effort to connect at an intimate level with anyone outside her family. People who met Emily remarked on her complete indifference to others, in contrast to her keen interest in animals. Even as a very young child, she was more at ease with animals than with people. A servant recalled four-year-old Emily with "the eyes of a half-tamed creature" as caring "for nobody's opinion, only being happy with her animal pets." Elizabeth Gaskell, Charlotte's friend and the author of her first biography, said that while Charlotte felt affection for animals, Emily was passionate about them. In *The Life of Charlotte Brontë*, Gaskell quotes a neighbor's assessment of Emily: "She never showed regard to any human creature; all her love was reserved for animals."

The four surviving children turned to one another for comfort, and in the way that children deal with grief, they spent hours in imaginative play, enacting over and over again tales of loss and reunion. Inspired by a set of toy soldiers Mr. Brontë had given Branwell, they created involved, collaborative chronicles, with plots drawn from contemporary newspapers and settings influenced by the landscape paintings that lined the parsonage walls. To shield their stories from adult eyes, the children, using quill pens and minuscule handwriting, wrote them in tiny booklets. They invented a faraway land called Angria, with palm trees and warm ocean breezes, where they could control everything, including who lived and who died. They wrote elaborate plots, produced detailed illustrations, and then acted out the battles, daring rescues, and loving reunions. Their sustained playacting and writing created an intense intimacy best described by Charlotte: "We wove a web in childhood / A web of sunny air."

Although the children all immersed themselves in the parts they were playing, only Emily seemed unable—or unwilling—to keep a clear line between what was real and what was imaginary. When she was caught up in a role, Emily would sometimes display an impulsive, violent streak that she usually kept under strict control. Once, acting the part of King Charles, she leaped out a bedroom window onto a nearby tree, cracking a branch and almost destroying her father's favorite cherry tree. On another occasion, she raged in such a tantrum that Branwell wrote a jingle accusing her of bellowing like a bull, swilling alcohol, and drawing a knife on him. Branwell was given to exaggeration, yet on this occasion, he was clearly awed by Emily's outburst.

Eventually, Emily and Anne grew tired of the constant military campaigns of Angria, its grand palaces and exotic customs. With Anne faithfully following her, Emily, now aged thirteen, broke away from Branwell and Charlotte and established a new imaginary world named Gondal. Although Charlotte and Branwell left behind notebooks and drawings of Angria, only scattered poems, lists of names, and a few sketches remain of Anne and Emily's Gondal. And yet, from these bits and pieces and from the several Gondal poems that were eventually published, it is possible to reconstruct to some degree Emily's first portrayal of her inner world. Gondal was based on solid Yorkshire geography with realistic details of everyday life, such as meals of mutton, potatoes, and puddings. As the following stanza indicates, it was also filled with romantic Scottish elements drawn from one of Emily's favorite writers, Sir Walter Scott:

> *High waving heather, 'neath stormy blasts bending,*
> *Midnight and moonlight and bright shining stars:*
> *Darkness and glory rejoicingly blending,*
> *Earth rising to heaven and heaven descending,*
> *Man's spirit away from its drear dungeon sending,*
> *Bursting the fetters and breaking the bars.*

In striking contrast to Angria's warlike leaders, Gondal was ruled by a valiant queen, Augusta Geraldine, a reflection of Emily's fascination with Mary, Queen of Scots. Like her, Augusta Geraldine led a life of suffering, isolation, and exile. One of Emily

Brontë's best-known poems, now titled "Remembrance," was originally written as an elegy for the queen's lover:

> Cold in the earth-and the deep snow piled above thee!
> Far, far removed, cold in the dreary grave!
> Have I forgot, my Only Love, to love thee,
> Severed at last by Times's all-wearing wave?

Although Anne would become disenchanted with Gondal, and Branwell and Charlotte would outgrow Angria, Emily never left her imaginary world behind. She continued to write Gondal poems for the rest of her life, and her novel *Wuthering Heights* would deepen and expand themes first explored in Gondal. Even more than her brother and sisters, Emily felt at home in the world of her imagination. Beyond that, her writing helped her develop a stoic attitude toward the hardships of life. Her best-known poem, read at Emily Dickinson's funeral, begins: "No coward soul is mine, / No trembler in the world's storm-troubled sphere!"

By the time she was fifteen, Emily had grown into a striking young woman. Charlotte's friend Ellen Nussey, the only regular visitor to the parsonage, was initially put off by Emily's aloof manner but was captivated by her appearance: "Emily Brontë had . . . a lithesome, graceful figure. She was the tallest person in the house, except for her father. . . . She had very beautiful eyes—kind, kindling eyes; but she did not often look at you; she was too reserved. Their colour might be said to be dark grey, at other times dark blue, they varied so." Ellen said that even though Emily wore her hair like Charlotte's in an "unbecoming tight curl and frizz," all eyes followed her: "A tall long-armed girl, full grown, elastic of tread; with a slight figure that looked queenly in her best dresses, but loose and boyish when she slouched over the moors, whistling to her dogs, and taking long strides over the rough earth."

Ellen provides rare glimpses of Emily at ease with her sisters. One afternoon, they climbed to a hidden place deep in the moors where several springs joined together, which Anne and Emily had named the Meeting of the Waters. There Emily reclined on a large stone with her hand in the spring and played with the tadpoles, "making them swim about, and then, moralizing on the strong and the weak, the brave and the cowardly, as she chased them with her hand." Emily's view of nature as a brutal life-and-death struggle, here lightly recounted as she plays with tadpoles, would emerge full-scale in *Wuthering Heights*. Later that evening, Ellen watched as Emily, engrossed in one of her father's Irish tales, "stooped down to hand her porridge-bowl to the dog." As Grasper eagerly licked the bowl, Ellen noticed that Emily was oblivious to such a casual blurring of boundaries between her and the dog.

A small Irish Terrier, Grasper was with the Brontë family from 1830 to 1834, judging from the Haworth dog-tax records. Emily's fondness for him can be seen in the small pencil drawing she made, which she titled "Grasper—from life. January 1834" and signed "Emily Jane Brontë." She sketched Grasper's coarse coat with a pencil, and she carefully detailed his leather collar with its brass label inscribed with the Brontë name and address. She drew Grasper in profile, capturing the bright, alert gaze of the terrier combined with a docile expression, which gives the impression of a spunky dog who wished to please. The drawing is the last record of Grasper, who was apparently gone before Keeper arrived.

Despite her affection for Grasper, Emily's early Gondal poems suggest that, even as an adolescent, she did not have a sentimental attitude toward dogs. She accepted them as devoted companions, but she never let go of the fact that they can be instinctive predators, as shown in this poem fragment:

> And hungry dogs, with wolf-like cry,
> Unburied corpses tear
> While their gaunt masters gaze and sigh
> And scarce the feast forbear.

In picturing dogs as carrion eaters, Emily presents a seldom-mentioned characteristic of dogs, one partly responsible for the unclean and degraded reputation they have in some cultures. In

"Grasper from life," 1834. *Pencil sketch by Emily Brontë.*

times of famine or disease, roaming packs of pariah dogs would devour human corpses. As a result, some ancient religious texts contain purification rituals that one must undergo after coming into contact with a dog. In Emily's poem, the dogs revert to primitive behavior because their owners are too exhausted to restrain them. As would be evident in *Wuthering Heights*, Emily considered dogs as separate, independent creatures with their own drives and instincts. She felt exactly the same way about people and would observe them closely, as an outsider, and she never seemed shocked by what either species was capable of doing.

The day before her seventeenth birthday, Emily made a sec-

ond attempt to leave home to attend school. Nine years had
passed since Cowan Bridge, and Mr. Brontë decided it was time
for her to resume her formal education. He arranged for her to
accompany Charlotte to Roe Head School, where Charlotte had
been a student and was now hired as a teacher. Within a few
months, his plans for his daughters fell apart. Charlotte quickly
realized that she hated teaching: "Am [I] to spend the best part of
my life . . . forcibly suppressing my rage at the idleness, the apa-
thy . . . and the most asinine stupidity of those fat-headed oafs?"
And Emily discovered that she knew more of literature, music,
and philosophy than her teachers at Roe Head, a tribute not only
to her intelligence but also to Mr. Brontë's teaching.

Beyond mere boredom at school, Emily felt suffocated by the
constraints of following a schedule after nine years of freedom.
Within weeks, she stopped eating and grew increasingly quiet and
subdued. Charlotte, remembering what had happened to Maria
and Elizabeth, reacted instantly: "Her health was quickly broken;
her white face, attenuated form, and failing strength threatened
rapid decline. I felt in my heart that she would die, if she did not
go home, and with this conviction obtained her recall." Emily
lasted three months at Roe Head; then Anne quietly took her
place.

Emily spent the next three years at the parsonage, content
and happy. Branwell was also at home, experimenting with por-
traiture by inviting local dignitaries to sit for him. Mr. Brontë was
valiantly trying to keep abreast of his growing parish, sometimes
performing as many as twenty baptisms in one day. Helping with
household tasks, Emily still had enough time and freedom to
write poetry. Fragments of poems, such as this one scribbled on a
scrap of paper, show that she continued to combine Gondal settings, such as Lake Wernas, with landscape from the Yorkshire
moors:

> *Cold clear and blue the morning heaven*
> *Expands its arch on high*

> *Cold clear and blue Lake Wernas water*
> *Reflects that winter sky.*

In September of 1838, Emily set off once again, this time hoping to succeed as a teacher at Law Hill, a girls' boarding school about ten miles from Haworth. Emily had accepted the position to supplement her father's income, still meager in spite of his having been the curate for more than eighteen years. Although she dreaded leaving home, she felt it her duty to contribute to the family's finances. Charlotte was now working as a governess, and Branwell had moved to a nearby town to set up a studio as a professional artist. Only Anne was unable to work because she had fallen ill at Roe Head and was still recuperating.

Even though Emily was determined to succeed, she was soon overwhelmed by the working conditions at Law Hill, which employed three teachers to oversee forty energetic girls. Charlotte worried about Emily, predicting that the "hard labour from six in the morning until near eleven at night, with only a half-hour exercise between" would prove too much for her younger sister: "I fear she will never stand it." As grueling as the schedule was, the lack of privacy and being confined indoors were even harder for Emily to bear. The poems she wrote at Law Hill evoke her yearning for the Yorkshire moors:

> *For the moors, for the moors where the short grass*
> *Like velvet beneath us should lie!*
> *For the moors, for the moors where each high pass*
> *Rose sunny against the clear sky!*
>
> *For the moors, where the linnet was trilling*
> *Its song on the old granite stone—*
> *Where the lark—the wild sky-lark was filling*
> *Every breast with delight like its own.*

Emily returned home for the Christmas holidays, but the brief time with her family and the freedom of the moors only made the return to Law Hill more unbearable. She became so depressed that she could no longer write, and without that outlet, Emily completely broke down. Unable to eat or sleep, she was compelled to resign. She had lasted less than six months at Law Hill and made little impression while there. One student, though, remembered that in Emily's farewell announcement to the class she said that the only individual she had cared about in the whole place was the house dog.

Discouraged, Emily returned home, climbing the steep Main Street to the parsonage, perched only a few feet above the shops and pubs of Haworth. Once she entered the lane beside the graveyard, she was almost home. At that point, she could hear the warning growls of her father's new guard dog, the ferocious Keeper. Certainly her family would have written Emily about the new dog, but nothing could have entirely prepared her for the sight of Keeper, so different from the friendly little Grasper.

The townsfolk described Keeper as a "savage brute," a dog with a reputation for violence. His brass collar, now displayed in the Brontë Parsonage Museum, leaves no question that Keeper was huge. Marauding Luddites might have been the reason Mr. Brontë chose a formidable guard dog instead of another small terrier like Grasper. Luddites were hand workers—wool combers and weavers—whose livelihoods had been eliminated by encroaching industrialization. They frequently raided at night, smashing the new factory machinery and threatening anyone they considered to represent authority, even a clergyman. To protect his family, Mr. Brontë slept with a brace of loaded pistols by his bed. These he would fire off each morning to discharge the ammunition, aiming out his bedroom window at the church spire. The neighbors, who already considered Patrick Brontë eccentric, insisted it was his way of letting everyone know the family had survived unharmed through the night.

Keeper was a good choice for a guard dog. Even though he was not purebred, he was obviously descended from Mastiffs, which can be traced back to ancient Assyria and Babylonia, where they were originally bred to hunt lions and to guard sheep from wolves. Later they were trained to be war dogs. British Mastiffs, in particular, inspired dread in those who faced them in battle. One account, dating back to about A.D. 50, speaks of them as monsters: "Vaste, huge, ugly and stobborne, of a Hevy and Burthenous Body and therefore of but little Swiftnesse, terrible and frightful to Behold." Keeper's specific background remains obscure, and it is unclear who gave him the name that would prove to be so fitting. *Keeper* means "one who keeps, one who stands guard over another." And in the ten years Keeper would spend with Emily, that is the role he would consistently play for her.

Emily easily settled back into life at the parsonage. Branwell, after failing as a portrait painter, had also returned home, and so Emily was once more the housekeeper for her father, Branwell, and Aunt Branwell. What feelings Emily may have had as she watched Anne, the baby of the family, uncomplainingly set out to become a governess are not known. Emily was, however, clearly aware from Charlotte's bitter letters that her older sister detested being a governess: "A private governess has no existence, is not considered as a living and rational being except as connected with the wearisome duties she has to fulfill." Neither Charlotte nor Anne ever expressed resentment at Emily's being able to stay at home. According to Anne, they appreciated her contribution: "We . . . all are doing something for our own livelihood except Emily, who, however, is as busy as any of us, and in reality earns her food and raiment as much as we do."

Emily baked bread, cleaned, and did laundry with the help of the servant, Tabby Ackroyd, who had been with the family since the children were infants and would remain with the Brontës until her death. In the afternoons, Emily sometimes shot pistols with her father at targets he set up in the backyard, or she tended the neglected flower beds in front of the house. After the evening meal, she liked to retreat to her books, studying German philosophy or translating Horace. Often she played the piano, especially pieces by

Beethoven, her favorite composer. About this time, she may have begun preliminary work on *Wuthering Heights*. Much of the scenery as well as the manor houses in the novel seem to be based on the countryside around Law Hill, which she had just left. Furthermore, Law Hill was a working farm as well as a boarding school, so that details of farm life, vividly rendered in the novel, might well have been written while they were still fresh in Emily's mind.

Emily also took over the care and affections of Keeper. Like Grasper, he had been licensed as Mr. Brontë's dog but soon became Emily's, accompanying her whenever household errands took her into the village. There, he was often challenged by the local dogs, which resulted in numerous fights. Perhaps to justify their animals' poor performance against the ferocious Keeper, the townsfolk debated among themselves about his breeding. Even a casual visitor to Haworth joined the discussion, pointing out that Keeper represented every type of British dog, including the unfortunate turnspits, that spent their lives walking in circles and turning the roasting rods on which game was cooked. The visitor thought Keeper was "a conglomerate, combining every species of English caninity from the turnspit to the sheepdog, with a strain of Haworth originality superadded."

That Emily Brontë relished watching Keeper's battles seems certain from the zestful descriptions of dogfights that appear in *Wuthering Heights*. The character Cathy Linton meets young Hareton, whom she will eventually marry, when their dogs commence "a smart battle." Their efforts to separate the dogs "formed an introduction," a notable departure from the stilted way that young lovers usually meet in Victorian novels. When Cathy's dog Charlie, a fierce Pointer, is defeated in another battle, Cathy finds him with a swollen head and a bleeding ear. More upset about his defeat than his injuries, Cathy walks him home with her other dogs, all of them, girl and dogs, "limping, and hanging their heads . . . sadly out of sorts."

In addition to his prowess in dogfights, Keeper was known for his fierce temperament. When he had first come to the Brontë home, the family was cautioned that although Keeper was faithful, if he were ever hit, he would grab the throat of the person who did it and hang on "till one or the other was at the point of death." Such a dire warning indicates that Keeper's early years had been harsh ones that left him wary of people. Charlotte described how he would stand watching her like "a devouring flame." His size and seriousness impressed observers, who often commented about how big and grim he was. Keeper was identical to Tartar, described in Charlotte's novel *Shirley* as a "rather large, strong, and fierce-looking dog, very ugly," with a peculiar growl that sounded like a "strangled whistle." Even though Keeper inspired fear, he intrigued people—the same response Emily herself inspired. Mrs. Gaskell, in her biography of Charlotte Brontë, said of Emily, "[She] must have been a remnant of the Titans—a great-granddaughter of the giants who used to inhabit the earth."

These two strong characters—the formidable, resolute woman and the huge, fearsome dog—engaged in a power struggle that captured the attention of all who witnessed it. Although Emily might have tolerated and even enjoyed the spectacle of Keeper battling other dogs when she was with him, for him to do so on his own provoked her anger. John Greenwood, the Haworth stationer, recalled one occasion when Emily dragged Keeper out of a dogfight: "Keeper and another great powerful dog out of the village were fighting down the lane. She was in the garden at the time, and the servant went to tell her. . . . She never spoke a word, nor appeared the least at a loss what to do, but rushed at once into the kitchen, took the pepper box, and away into the lane where she found the two savage brutes each holding the other by the throat in deadly grip, while several other animals, who thought themselves men, were standing looking on like cowards as they were, afraid to touch them—there they stood gaping, watching this fragile creature spring upon the beasts—seizing Keeper 'round the neck with one arm, while with the other hand she dredges their noses with pepper, and separating them by force of her great will, driving Keeper, that great powerful dog, before her into the house, never once noticing the men, so called, standing there thunderstruck at the deed."

Even though the family knew Keeper could be dangerous, he was allowed free run of the parsonage. Because he intimidated people, they made allowances for him, just as they would always do for Emily. Although Aunt Branwell had permitted Grasper in the parlor only on special occasions, she let Keeper come inside whenever he wished because she was so frightened of him that she dared not discipline him. Mrs. Gaskell believed that Emily loved Keeper precisely because of his "fierce, wild intractability."

Emily may well have seen in Keeper a reflection of her own nature. She, too, refused to be dominated or to accommodate others' expectations. Emily was the only Brontë daughter who rarely attended church services, despite her father's position. To her sisters' dismay, she wore hopelessly old-fashioned mutton sleeves, even though they provoked laughter. Like Keeper, Emily was virtually indifferent to physical pain. Once, when she was giving water to a stray dog, he suddenly bit her. Realizing the dog might have rabies, Emily grabbed a red-hot poker and cauterized the wound herself without calling for help; she did not even mention the incident until Charlotte asked about the scar.

Notwithstanding her physical strength and remarkable intelligence, choices in life were limited for Emily. In contrast to Branwell—who experimented with being a writer, a portrait painter, a tutor, and a railroad employee—Emily and her sisters had few options. In nineteenth-century England, a woman from a family with neither money nor connections could marry, become a teacher or governess, or possibly emigrate. Emily was too odd to attract a husband, too independent to teach or be a governess, and too anxious to tolerate the loneliness of emigration. Even her position as the family housekeeper was tenuous. Once her father died or retired, the next curate and his family would take over the parsonage. Emily's poems from this time are filled with images of imprisonment and a recurring theme of longing for freedom. Yet the poems still speak with a ringing voice that echoes Keeper's "fierce, wild intractability."

Riches I hold in light esteem
And Love I laugh to scorn,
And Lust of Fame was but a dream
That vanished with the morn—

And if I pray, the only prayer
That moves my lips for me
Is—"Leave the heart that now I bear
And give me liberty."

Emily must have experienced vicarious pleasure from Keeper's freedom. He ambled through the village unafraid of any dog, roamed the vastness of the Yorkshire moors, and sauntered in and out of the parsonage at will. At that time, dogs were rarely neutered, so Keeper most likely enjoyed sexual freedom as well. Ellen Nussey often witnessed Emily's pride in Keeper's untamed spirit: "Sometimes Emily would delight in showing off Keeper—make him frantic in action, and roar with the voice of a lion. It was a terrifying exhibition within the walls of an ordinary sitting-room."

A similar dynamic takes place in *Wuthering Heights* between the heroine, Catherine Earnshaw, and a guard dog named Skulker, a frightening animal with a "huge purple tongue hanging half a foot out of his mouth, and his pendant lips streaming with bloody slaver." Skulker discovers Catherine, at the time a young girl, on his property and bites her ankle. Hearing her screams, the family rushes out and carries her inside to tend to her wound. As she lies on a sofa recuperating, she has Skulker brought to her. With arrogant self-confidence, Catherine chastises the cringing dog. Soon he sits meekly by her side as she alternates between feeding him treats from her plate and pinching his nose—a combination of kindness and cruelty that may have characterized Emily's initial treatment of Keeper. Emily encouraged Keeper's wildness, but at the same time she was determined to dominate him. She may have resented the fact that her dog possessed more freedom than she could ever have.

Emily's conflicted emotions exploded in one confrontation,

which was witnessed by Charlotte and their servant Tabby. According to Mrs. Gaskell, Keeper had a habit of sleeping on the parsonage beds, which were covered in white counterpanes. This infuriated Emily, well aware of the hours of labor it took to keep the bed linens white. One evening, Tabby discovered Keeper on a bed. Too frightened to confront the dog herself, she told Emily, who immediately ran upstairs.

Mrs. Gaskell describes what happened next in graphic detail: "Down-stairs came Emily, dragging after her the unwilling Keeper, his hind legs set in a heavy attitude of resistance, held by the 'scruff of his neck,' but growling low and savagely all the time. . . . She let him go, planted in a dark corner at the bottom of the stairs; no time was there to fetch stick or rod, for fear of the strangling clutch at her throat—her bare clenched fist struck against his red fierce eyes, before he had time to make his spring . . . she 'punished him' till his eyes were swelled up, and the half-blind, stupefied beast was led to his accustomed lair to have his swelled head fomented and cared for by the very Emily herself."

Hints of Emily's temper had appeared in accounts of her as a child, but her beating of Keeper is still shocking. How to explain such treatment of a devoted dog? For one thing, Emily was responding to what she considered a serious transgression. At that time, country dogs were ordinarily kept outside and came in only on special occasions. Some were allowed in the kitchen and beside the hearth, like the dogs in *Wuthering Heights*, but they were never permitted upstairs in the bedrooms. By lying on the beds, Keeper was violating an important boundary. Even though Emily had been comfortable with an earlier blurring of the human-dog boundary when she shared a bowl of porridge with Grasper, she had done so according to her wishes, not his.

At a deeper and more personal level, Emily might have been using Keeper as a scapegoat, displacing her own frustrated anger onto him, a practice that unfortunately is still common today. Dogs have always been convenient targets: They live close to humans, they are usually subservient, and they cannot speak. Circumstances had forced Emily into a constricted existence. Like other talented women of her time and class, she discovered that writing gave her some control over her life, but her pent-up anger and rage remained a frightening force within her. Keeper was strong and independent, character traits that Emily shared. Just as desperate parents will beat a rebellious child who reminds them of themselves "for his own good," Emily may have felt that by subduing Keeper, she could also subdue her own stubbornness and pride.

To some extent, Emily's treatment of Keeper mirrors the cycle of violence that characterizes domestic abuse, in which episodes of cruelty are followed by excessively loving behavior. After Emily beat Keeper, she washed the wounds that she herself had inflicted. This pattern of nurturing after violence also occurred when Keeper was injured in dogfights and Emily cared for him, moments captured by Charlotte in her description of Shirley and Tartar: "She had not a word for anybody during the rest of the day; but sat near the hall fire till evening watching and tending Tartar who lay all gory, stiff, and swelled, on a mat at her feet. She wept furtively over him sometimes, and murmured the softest words of pity and endearment, in tones whose music the old, scarred canine warrior acknowledged by licking her hand or her sandal alternately with his own red wounds."

This image of Emily weeping and whispering to Keeper and his affectionate response is key to understanding how the two resolved their power struggle. Although Keeper may have growled at Emily when she dragged him down the stairs, the powerful Mastiff did not attack her. In the face of her anger, he remained quiet and submissive. His loyalty and devotion led Emily to soften her stance toward him. Moreover, because Emily had known so little mothering, caring for Keeper was comforting for her as well. Gradually, their relationship was transformed into one of mutual respect.

Ellen Nussey noted that evenings in the parsonage sitting room were tranquil once Emily no longer teased Keeper to make him bark. Instead, she spent hours "kneeling on the hearth, reading a book, with her arm round him." To explain the intense connection she now observed in the pair, Ellen resorted to anthropomor-phism: "Poor old Keeper, Emily's faithful friend and worshipper, seemed to understand her like a human being." Ellen discovered she could even earn a rare smile from Emily if she sat uncomplain-ing while Keeper rested his heavy head on her lap. Charlotte was also touched by the tableau that Emily and Keeper presented on those quiet, firelit evenings: "The tawny and lion-like bulk . . . is ever stretched beside her; his negro muzzle laid on his fore paws, straight, strong, and shapely as the limbs of an Alpine wolf. One hand of the mistress generally reposes on the loving serf's rude head, because if she takes it away he groans and is discontented."

Keeper's importance to Emily can be seen in her casual men-tions of him in the diary papers that she and Anne exchanged every four years on their birthdays. Begun in 1837, when Emily was nine-teen, these were private musings in which the sisters reported the important events of the past four years and expressed their hopes for the future. They are the only spontaneous writing of Emily to survive, and as such, they show a side of her not found in her poems and novel. In these short papers, the affection between the two younger sisters shines through, as does their happiness when they were able to spend time together at home. Emily's second diary paper, written on a rainy Friday night in July of 1841, lists the whereabouts of all the inhabitants of the parsonage, including each animal: "I am seated in the dining room alone. . . . Papa is in the parlour. Aunt upstairs in her room. . . . Victoria and Adelaide [Emily's geese] are ensconced in the peat-house—Keeper is in the kitchen—Nero [Emily's tame hawk] in his cage." Emily is describ-ing a typical evening with Keeper warm and dry in the kitchen, her domain.

Keeper and Emily spent most of the day in each other's com-pany. Neighbors passing by the parsonage's open kitchen door re-membered the sight of Emily kneading bread dough, her German books propped up in front of her and Keeper asleep at her feet. If the two were not in the kitchen, they were on the moors, Emily's fa-vorite place to read, write, and draw. One watercolor, titled

Keeper—From Life, which now hangs in the Brontë Parsonage Museum, shows his distinctive black markings and his short, silky tan coat. Keeper's shoulders look massive, but his half-opened eye seems friendly as he lies in the grass, his head on his paws with

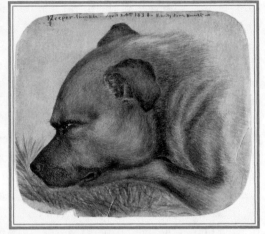

"Keeper from life," 1838. *Watercolor by Emily Brontë.*

one ear turned back, as if listening to Emily. Very slowly—for trust and attachment did not come easily to either one—their bond deepened.

This period of contentment came to an end in 1842, when Charlotte persuaded Emily, then twenty-four, to go with her to Brussels. Determined to escape the humiliating and exhausting life of a governess, Charlotte decided that she and her sisters would open their own boarding school at the parsonage, and she became convinced that offering advanced training in foreign languages would increase the school's chance of success. From friends, Charlotte learned of the Pensionnat Heger, run by Monsieur and Madame Heger, which specialized in foreign-language instruction and provided reasonable rates for English boarders. She persuaded Aunt Branwell to pay the tuition and was ready to leave for Brussels when Mr. Brontë announced that he would not allow her to go abroad alone. The family needed Anne's income as a governess, so she could not accompany Charlotte. Perhaps Emily felt guilty about all the years she had been able to spend at home; at any rate, she agreed without argument to spend a year in Brussels with Charlotte.

Although Emily had never been abroad, she showed no interest in sightseeing or any curiosity about the other students. Back in Haworth, Charlotte's friends were astonished that Emily had agreed to go to Brussels, and they wondered how she must be doing: "Tell me something about Emily Brontë. . . . Imagine Emily turning over prints or 'taking wine' with any stupid fop & preserving her temper & politeness!" They need not have wondered, for Emily made no effort to be sociable. A British family who invited the sisters for Sunday dinners was sympathetic toward Charlotte's awkward efforts at conversation but annoyed by Emily, who "hardly ever uttered more than a monosyllable." One fellow student recalled her impression of Emily: "I simply disliked her from the first, her tallish ungainly ill-dressed figure . . . always answering our jokes with 'I wish to be as God made me.' "

At the Pensionnat Heger, Emily suffered terribly from homesickness, but she did not give in to it. Instead, according to Charlotte, her sister "worked like a horse" at her studies. Emily's intelligence impressed M. Heger, the headmaster: "She should have been a man—a great navigator. Her powerful reason would have deduced new spheres of discovery from the knowledge of the old; and her strong imperious will would never have been daunted by opposition or difficulty." When M. Heger instructed Emily and Charlotte to copy the works of other writers as a way of learning French, Emily objected because she did not want her creativity to be curbed. Although M. Heger insisted she follow his direction, he was struck by Emily's original mind: "Her faculty of imagination was such that, if she had written a history, her view of scenes and characters would have been so vivid, and so powerfully expressed, and supported by such a show of argument, that it would have dominated over the reader, whatever might have been his previous opinions, or his cooler perceptions of its truth."

Emily's essays, written in French under M. Heger's direction, include one titled "Letter from One Brother to Another," which suggests Emily's yearning for the moors and Keeper. She describes a man coming home after a long journey: "Yesterday at evening I arrived at the old gates of the park; it was a night of storm and pouring rain but through the darkness I distinguished from afar the light of the windows, which cast long rays between the branches of the trees and guided me to the door. . . . [He enters the house.] Something stirred in the room. It was a large dog that arose from a corner and approached to examine the stranger; he did not find a stranger. He recognized me, and he attested his recognition by the most expressive caresses."

Keeper surely suffered during the nine months of Emily's absence. He was left in the care of Mr. Brontë, who was preoccupied with his pastoral duties, and of Aunt Branwell, who gave away Emily's geese, Victoria and Adelaide, and let her tame hawk Nero loose to fend for itself. Since Aunt Branwell was afraid of Keeper, she was unlikely to have allowed him inside the parsonage without Emily there. So Keeper, accustomed to sleeping at Emily's feet in front of the fire, must have lived outside while he waited for her during the months she was away.

In November of 1842, Aunt Branwell died unexpectedly, and Charlotte and Emily were immediately summoned home. After the funeral, Charlotte decided to return to Brussels, ostensibly to finish her studies, but in reality because she had fallen in love with M. Heger. Anne went back to the Robinson family, where she had been governess for the past two years. Branwell was soon to join her because Anne had persuaded the Robinsons to hire him as tutor to the oldest boy. Desperate for work, Branwell was grateful for Anne's help. He had failed as a portrait painter, and then he had taken a job with the railway but was dismissed for negligence. Emily did not return to Brussels; in fact, she would never leave home again.

Emily happily returned to her housekeeping and gardening tasks, and she once again roamed the moors with sketchbook in hand and Keeper for company. Beneath the surface, however, she had changed. Although Emily had always enjoyed writing, she now began to exhibit a mature interest in her work. Perhaps influenced by M. Heger's high regard for her, she set to work gathering all her poems together, including those hastily composed on scraps of paper. After reading them closely, she selected about seventy-five, which she carefully transcribed and edited. Next, she separated the Gondal poems from the others, her first attempt at doing so. She filled two manuscript books, one inscribed "Gondal Poems" and the other simply "E.J.B." It seemed as though Emily was ready to move forward into themes and subjects far beyond the familiar world of Gondal.

Then, on New Year's Day 1844, Charlotte, after finally realizing that the happily married M. Heger did not return her passionate feelings, came home in despair. She spent her days writing anguished letters to M. Heger and making increasingly desperate plans for a school in the parsonage. (Charlotte would write about her heartbreak in the novel *Villette*. Eventually, she would marry Arthur Bell Nicholls, one of her father's curates.) The following June, Anne suddenly appeared at the parsonage. She had resigned her post as governess, saying only, "I have had some very unpleasant and undreamt of experience of human nature." Although Anne did not tell her sisters what had happened, Emily and Charlotte learned the facts soon enough when Branwell returned in disgrace, dismissed for having an affair with Mrs. Robinson, the mother of his charges.

Emily relates none of these events in her 1845 diary paper, except for a brief mention of Branwell, "who I hope will be better and do better." Her indifference to her siblings is striking: "I am quite contented for myself . . . seldom or ever troubled with nothing to do and merely desiring that everybody could be as comfortable as myself and as undesponding and then we should have a very tolerable world of it." The diary letter focused primarily on her animals and the latest events in Gondal. When Emily had divided her poems into two notebooks, she was apparently trying to differentiate what she called the "world within" from the "world without." Now, however, Emily reverted to spending hours in her fantasy kingdom. Her renewed preoccupation suggests she was dealing with the stressful events in the Brontë household by retreating even further into her inner world.

The seductive appeal of those imaginary kingdoms is clear in

Charlotte's account of how difficult it had been for her to stop writing about Angria. As the plots of the chronicles became ever more passionate and violent, Charlotte had confessed to a friend, "If you knew my thoughts; the dreams that absorb me; and the fiery imagination that at times eats me up . . . you would pity and I dare say despise me." When she was twenty-three, Charlotte finally decided she had to stop. In her diary, she wrote "Farewell to Angria," which captures the vivid atmosphere that Emily refused to leave: "I long to quit for awhile that burning clime where we have sojourned too long—its skies flame, the glow of sunset is always upon it. The mind would cease from excitement and turn now to a cooler region where the dawn breaks grey and sober, and the coming day for a time at least is subdued by clouds."

Not only did Emily remain in "that burning clime," but her diary papers also reveal little differentiation between the "world within" and the "world without." In her first diary letter, written in 1837, when she was nineteen, Emily moved without pause from the descriptions of the Brontë kitchen to news from Gondal to current events in England: "Tabby in the Kitchen—the Emperors and Empresses of Gondal and Gaaldine preparing to depart from Gondal to prepare for the coronation which will be on the 12th of July—Queen Victoria ascended the throne this month."

The second diary letter, written in 1841, shows that she continued to blur distinctions between real and imaginary events. She described an excursion she and Anne took to the city of York, mentioning little of what they saw or did, instead focusing on the scenes from Gondal they acted out during the carriage ride. Her detailed account sounds as if it were about real people and events: "We were . . . Catherine Navarre and Cordelia Fitzaphnold escaping from the palaces of Instruction to join the Royalists who are hard driven at present by the victorious Republicans."

By the third and final diary papers, written in 1845, Anne no longer had much enthusiasm for Gondal, stating, "The Gondals are at present in a sad state." Emily was oblivious of Anne's feelings, exclaiming, "The Gondals still flourish bright as ever . . . we intend sticking firm by the rascals as long they delight us which I am glad to say they do at present." The diary papers show that, even at twenty-seven, Emily Brontë could not give up the magical world that she and her brother and sisters had first created as a way of coping with the deaths of their mother and sisters.

As the family struggled with money worries, Mr. Brontë's failing eyesight, and Branwell's growing addiction to opium and gin, a new dog offered welcome distraction. In appreciation for her years of service as their children's governess, the Robinson family had given Anne a lovely King Charles Spaniel with a long, silky black-and-white coat. Perhaps they hoped the valuable little dog, named Flossy, would make up for their dismissal of Branwell.

Flossy fit into life at the parsonage as if she had always been part of it. Keeper immediately befriended her, an impressive sign of how much he had changed. When he had first come to the Brontës', he would have challenged any dog coming into his territory, especially a submissive lapdog like Flossy. Charlotte's friend Ellen Nussey noticed how companionable the dogs were, and that the

Flossy, ca. 1843. *Watercolor by Emily Brontë.*

two of them, so different in appearance and temperament, liked to spend time together. Here she describes one of their daily rituals: "Keeper and Flossy were always in quiet waiting by the side of Emily and Anne during their breakfast of Scotch oatmeal and milk, and always had a share handed down to them at the close of the meal." Emily sketched Flossy asleep on the sofa in the parlor— there were no beatings when Flossy slept on the furniture—while Keeper lay on the floor at Emily's feet.

Even though the circumstances of Anne's return were painful, she and Emily enjoyed spending time together once again. Their dogs gave them an excuse to leave the gloomy atmosphere of the parsonage and go on long walks. The two sisters revisited their favorite spots on the moors and must have laughed at the sight of Flossy trying to keep up with Keeper. Emily's sketchbook contains several quick studies of Flossy sleeping, the curled-up dog recognizable by her distinctive spaniel ears. A watercolor of Flossy chasing a goshawk across the moors captures the spaniel's beauty: her thick glossy coat, the feathering on her legs and plumed tail, and

Keeper, Flossy, and Tiger, 1843. *Photograph of a watercolor by Emily Brontë. The location of the original is unknown.*

her warm brown eyes. The painting conveys the ecstasy a dog feels when doing the job it was bred to do, and Emily knew spaniels were bred to hunt, not sit on people's laps. One sunny afternoon, Emily sketched Keeper, Flossy, and the cat Tiger lying under a tree together. Keeper, the dog that had once been known for his ferocity, now lay quietly contemplating the countryside with Flossy curled up by his side and Tiger sitting by his head.

When Flossy gave birth to a litter of puppies, they provided a diversion for the whole family and especially for Charlotte, lifting her out of her depression over M. Heger and distracting her from anxiety about the future. (The puppies' sire was not named; Keeper was apparently not considered a possibility.) The sisters gave one puppy—unimaginatively named Flossy Junior—to Ellen Nussey. Letters between Charlotte and Ellen contained stories about the destructive puppy, now referred to as "that infamous little bitch." Flossy Junior ate a neighbor's favorite hat and then embarked on what Charlotte labeled "The Catastrophe," ripping up Ellen's cherished bertha, which is a painstakingly embroidered lace collar worn over an evening dress.

Even Emily joined in the correspondence, although at a distance, letting Charlotte insert comments from her into the letters: "Emily was wondering the other day how poor little Flossy [Junior] gets on." She did not revert to the exasperated-but-indulgent tone typical of Charlotte and Ellen's discussions about the puppy. Instead, she gave practical, even stern, advice. She expressed concern when she learned Flossy Junior was pregnant because she said the dog was far too young. When Flossy Junior gave birth to a large litter, Emily bluntly suggested that all the puppies but one be killed, "for if kept they will pull their poor little mother to pieces."

No matter how entertaining the dogs were, Charlotte could not ignore the fact that only Mr. Brontë was earning a wage, and his salary was not enough to support the family. She had given up her plans for opening a school, having finally come to terms with the unlikelihood of its success. Family finances were at a crisis point. One afternoon, Charlotte discovered Emily's notebooks of poems and was so taken with their "peculiar music—wild, melancholy, and elevating"—that she decided the sisters should collaborate on a book of poetry. Although Emily dreaded the exposure of publication, she agreed to Charlotte's plan and revised her poems, carefully eliminating all references to Gondal.

Using the male pseudonyms Currer (Charlotte), Ellis (Emily), and Acton (Anne) Bell, the sisters paid to have their book published with their modest legacies from Aunt Branwell. *Poems* appeared in May 1846 and received anonymous reviews by *The Critic* and *The Athenaeum*. Both were more interested in speculating about the identities of the mysterious authors than in commenting on the quality of the poems, but the *Athenaeum* reviewer went on to praise "Ellis" as "an inspiration which may yet find an audience in the outer world. A fine quaint spirit . . . which may have things to speak that men will be glad to hear, and an evident power of wing that may reach heights not here attempted."

Indeed, Emily's twenty-one poems far surpass her sisters' contributions. One of the best known is "The Prisoner," which has been interpreted as a description of mystic revelation or poetic inspiration:

> He comes with western winds, with evening's wandering airs,
> With that clear dusk of heaven that brings the thickest stars;
> Winds take a pensive tone and stars a tender fire
> And visions rise and change which kill me with desire—

> .   .   .   .

> But first a hush of peace, a soundless calm descends;
> The struggle of distress and fierce impatience ends;
> Mute music soothes my breast—unuttered harmony
> That I could never dream till earth was lost to me.

Poems sold only two copies, but Charlotte now knew how to bring a book to publication, and she had learned that poetry, no matter how well reviewed, was not profitable. Undaunted, the sisters turned to writing novels: Charlotte, *Jane Eyre*; Anne, *Agnes Grey*; and Emily, *Wuthering Heights*.

While writing *Wuthering Heights*, EMILY was living with two unpredictable, violent—although very different—men: the fictional Heathcliff and her brother, Branwell. Heathcliff dominates the novel. His obsessive love for Catherine Earnshaw, his acts of cold cruelty, and his outbursts of rage repel yet fascinate readers. Charlotte gave a succinct assessment of Heathcliff: "Whether it is right or advisable to create things like Heathcliff, I do not know: I scarcely think it is."

Just as Heathcliff became the focus of *Wuthering Heights*, Branwell's steady deterioration overshadowed everything else in the parsonage. He had been drinking heavily and using opium ever since his dismissal from the Robinson family. When he learned that Mr. Robinson had died, Branwell expected to marry Mrs. Robinson. Instead, the now-wealthy widow sent her coachman to tell Branwell that she would lose her inheritance if she had any further contact with him. Stunned by her rejection, Branwell spent his time at the Black Bull complaining about the unfairness of his life and borrowing money to pay for gin, the cheapest drink available. The signs of Branwell's dissolution, especially his pronounced delirium

tremens, increasingly alarmed Mr. Brontë. Worried that Branwell might harm himself, Mr. Brontë insisted his son sleep in the same bed with him so that he could protect him.

As Branwell grew ever more self-pitying and incoherent, Charlotte and Anne distanced themselves from him. Emily's feelings for her brother were less judgmental than her sisters'. She had once been drawn to Keeper because of

Self-portrait, ca. 1840. *Pencil sketch by Branwell Brontë.*

his violent reputation, and she was now absorbed in creating the intransigent Heathcliff. Her interest in Branwell's dissolution seems part of her fascination with every aspect of life, no matter how pathetic or terrifying. Although Charlotte was horrified when she discovered that Branwell was cadging money from their father, Emily simply remarked that he was a "hopeless being." Perhaps she remembered his energy and high spirits as a boy, the love of the moors he had shared with his sisters, and the portrait he had painted of them when they were all in their teens (today in London's National Portrait Gallery). There is a hint of pity for Branwell in a Gondal poem written when he first began to disappoint the family:

> *Well some may hate, and some may scorn,*
> *And some may quite forget thy name,*
> *But my sad heart must ever mourn*
> *Thy ruined hopes, thy blighted fame.*

To the villagers, Emily seemed protective of Branwell. They remembered her running down the short lane from the parsonage to the Black Bull to warn him when their father was coming. Keeper must have given Emily the fortitude she needed to enter the pub, where she would have had to face Branwell's anger and his friends' derision. Often she would lead him home and carry him up to his bed. If Branwell returned on his own from the pub, he would want to talk. Emily, who was always up late, would sit with Keeper at her feet and listen to her brother's drunken ramblings. On the night he set fire to the curtains, Emily quickly and quietly doused the flames so as not to waken her father and sisters.

Despite the turmoil caused by Branwell, Emily worked steadily on *Wuthering Heights*, becoming as immersed in the novel as she had once been in the imaginary kingdom of Gondal. As she grappled with the complicated plot and often-grotesque characters, Keeper helped Emily stay anchored to the world of everyday life. Most dog owners depend on their dogs to keep them connected to the natural world. Taking a dog for a daily walk allows one to experience the changing seasons and the vicissitudes of weather. But

Emily Brontë, who wasted away if not free to wander the moors, did not need Keeper to connect her to nature. Instead, she needed him to help her stay grounded with daily routines, which she tended to forget when she was absorbed in writing.

In one of her diary papers, Emily admitted she was distracted without a "regularity paper," her term for a schedule: "I have a good many books on hand—but I am sorry to say that as usual I make small progress with any—however I have just made a new regularity paper! And I mean to do great things." Even though she had chafed at the schedules imposed on her at Roe Head and Law Hill, she needed structure for her life while she was writing *Wuthering Heights*. And Keeper provided that structure. Emily had to take care of him—feed him, give him water, and exercise him—no matter what was happening in the nightmare world she was creating.

WUTHERING HEIGHTS, EMILY BRONTE'S ONLY sustained piece of writing, has often been used to try to learn more about this very private woman. Even if the focus here is especially on the depiction of dogs in the novel, there still emerges a disturbing sense of the bleakness of Emily's inner world. The opening of *Wuthering Heights* (the title is the name of Heathcliff's home) takes place in a kitchen, which is described in careful detail, including pewter platters, an immense oak cupboard, and a dog sleeping on the hearth, an archetypal image of peace and security. Yet this dog, "a huge, liver-coloured bitch pointer, surrounded by a swarm of squealing puppies," bares wolflike fangs and snarls when a visitor approaches her. Suddenly, Heathcliff enters the kitchen and kicks the dog, explaining, "She's not accustomed to be spoiled—not kept for a pet."

This outburst, the reader's introduction to Heathcliff, sets up the struggle between dominance and submission that underlies the entire novel and characterizes not only the interactions among people but also between people and animals. In an essay for M. Heger, Emily said that the link between owners and pets was based on hypocrisy. She believed that owners used their pets to fulfill their own needs and denounced a particular type of owner, "the delicate lady who has murdered a half a dozen lap dogs by sheer affection." In *Wuthering Heights*, Emily continues to argue against the prevalent idea in Victorian England that animals are created to be subservient to humans. Instead, she sees animals as an equal part of nature, neither less nor more worthy. In Emily's view, pet keeping is not based on the natural order; rather, it occurs only because humans have more power than animals and can dominate them. In fact, she anticipates the view of the contemporary philosopher Yi-Fu Tuan, who maintains that while dominance with cruelty produces victims, dominance combined with affection produces pets.

Emily herself had experienced being the pet student at Cowan Bridge School, but she never again allowed herself to be dependent on anyone for anything. In *Wuthering Heights*, Heathcliff is also described as a pet. He was found wandering in the Liverpool slums and taken home to Wuthering Heights by Mr. Earnshaw, who "petted him up," meaning the scruffy orphan was indulged and spoiled, to the disgust of the rest of the household, who considered him an interloper. No matter how much he was fussed over, Heathcliff remained wild and independent, alienating everyone except six-year-old Catherine Earnshaw. Within a few months, the two motherless children were inseparable.

Catherine and Heathcliff grew up unsupervised and unrestrained. They spent days together exploring the surrounding hills, and on stormy nights, they would sneak outside to run barefoot across the moors. On one of these adventures, they decided to spy on the Linton children, who lived in the Grange, a stately manor across the valley. Peering in the window, Heathcliff saw Edgar and Isabella Linton fighting over their little spaniel Fanny: "That was their pleasure! To quarrel who should hold a heap of warm hair, and each begin to cry because both, after struggling to get it, refused to take it. We laughed outright at the petted things; we did despise them!"

Heathcliff and Catherine's bond as mutual outsiders does not last because she is quickly won over by Edgar and Isabella Linton's comfortable life. After a long visit at the Grange, Catherine returns with a new sense of herself as a lady, made clear in her treatment of the household dogs: "While her eyes sparkled joyfully when the dogs came bounding up to welcome her, she dare hardly touch them lest they should fawn upon her splendid garments." Realizing that he has lost Catherine, Heathcliff sulks like "a vicious cur that appears to know the kicks it gets are its desert, and yet, hates all the world, as well as the kicker, for what it suffers."

Eventually, Catherine marries Edgar Linton. In revenge, Heathcliff persuades Edgar's sister Isabella to elope with him. The spaniel Fanny tries to accompany her mistress, but Heathcliff recognizes the little dog as the same one he had spied through the Lintons' window. Impulsively, he grabs her, wraps his handkerchief around her neck, and hangs her from a bridle hook stuck in the wall. Here he describes Isabella's reaction: "The first thing she saw me do, on coming out of the Grange, was to hang up her little dog, and when she pleaded for it, the first words I uttered were a wish that I had the hanging of every being belonging to her."

As Fanny struggles to breathe, Isabella, infatuated with Heathcliff, follows him into the carriage, leaving her little dog to strangle. By chance, a servant comes into the garden, spots something white moving in the wind, and discovers the half-dead dog. The horrified servant cuts her down, but Fanny refuses to come back inside. Instead, she runs back and forth, sniffing the ground as she searches for the mistress who has abandoned her.

Heathcliff hangs Fanny in order to intimidate and control Isabella. Emily Brontë was far ahead of her time in recognizing the connection between animal abuse and domestic violence. Some of that knowledge no doubt came from her own mistreatment of Keeper and from observing Branwell's rages. In addition, Emily heard intimate details about village families from Tabby, who also regaled her with frightening Yorkshire tales and legends. Moreover, Emily had absorbed the works of the German Romantic novelists with their unrestrained descriptions of unrestrained characters and erotic passions. And Anne and Charlotte must have related the often-sordid scenes they saw in the wealthy homes where they lived as governesses. These memories were clearly the source of much of Charlotte's *Jane Eyre* and Anne's second novel, *The Tenant of Wildfell Hall.*

Once Isabella marries Heathcliff, his violence toward her escalates; when their son Linton is born, he becomes Heathcliff's next victim. The child enrages Heathcliff by cringing at the sight of his father, "exactly as a spaniel might." So skilled is Emily Brontë in conveying the tense atmosphere inside Wuthering Heights that it sounds uncannily like homes today in which abuse occurs. She is equally adept at depicting the disgust engendered by the victim's loyalty to the abuser. The spaniel Fanny's loyalty to Isabella is uncomfortably similar to Isabella's abject devotion to Heathcliff. He brags that no matter what he does to Isabella, "that pitiful, slavish, mean-minded brach [Yorkshire dialect for *bitch*]" will "still creep shamefully cringing back." Heathcliff is at the center of all activity, coercing, controlling, and intimidating all the inhabitants, animals and humans alike.

Eventually, Linton dies from neglect and abuse. Isabella finally leaves Heathcliff and returns home to the Grange, where Fanny immediately recognizes her and "yelped wild with joy at recovering her mistress." Clearly, Fanny's fidelity is not depicted here as the positive trait customarily assigned to dogs but as an example of fawning subservience.

Emily Brontë attempts to achieve a happy ending by concocting a romance between Catherine's daughter Cathy and Heathcliff's ward Hareton. Nevertheless, it is impossible to accept Hareton as a hero because of Isabella's description of him on the night she fled Wuthering Heights. As she ran through the kitchen, she knocked into Hareton, "who was hanging a litter of puppies from a chair back in the doorway." This casual mention of a boy hanging puppies one at a time, watching each one suffer a terrible death, is not even given a full sentence, and yet it stuns the reader. Another image of a hanged dog—this time puppies—cannot be forgotten, and it leaves the ending steeped in ambiguity.

Throughout *Wuthering Heights*, Emily Brontë turns every familiar image of dogs upside down: Guard dogs do not keep their owners safe, the dog sleeping on the hearth cannot be trusted, and innocent pets are hanged. The novel demonstrates that Emily refused to cloak the human-dog bond in sentimentality, she recognized the powerful emotions it can generate. The hanging of Fanny, so disturbing that it is usually omitted from movie versions of the novel, makes it clear that Emily understood the use of a dog as a scapegoat as well as the seductive nature of violence. What is not clear is how to reconcile Emily's affection for Anne Brontë's dog Flossy (clearly the prototype for Fanny; their names are almost identical) with her portrayal of Fanny as a fawning sycophant.

One reason may have been the attitude toward lapdogs that prevailed in the British countryside. A dog that performed no useful task was despised; furthermore, many of the lapdog breeds were imported from abroad and therefore were not considered to be true English dogs. Some of the outrage engendered by spaniels and other small "foreign" dogs seems due to the fact that the owners were usually wealthy women who allowed their cherished playthings onto their laps and into their beds. Women in royal courts were said to walk about with their lapdogs tucked into the bosoms of their dresses and to place "comfort spaniels" on their stomachs when they were indisposed. Churchmen preached against such excesses, insisting that these pampered women loved their pets more than their husbands or children. There were even hints of sexual contact between women and their dogs; during the French Revolution, lapdogs were burned to death "for a crime that morality prevents us from naming."

When Emily needed to create a dog for the spoiled Linton children, she would have no scruples about using Anne's little Flossy as the model. And the traits she despised in others, namely weakness and servility, she ascribed to the spaniel Fanny and to her owner, Isabella. Her attitude toward the other dogs in the book—guard dogs, hunters, pointers—is essentially the same as she demonstrated toward Keeper: She recognized and respected his instinctive drives for food, sex, and dominance, and, at the same time, she expected him to submit to her because she was more powerful than he.

In chapter after chapter, Emily reveals her belief that the universe treats every species, humans and dogs, with equal indifference. Years earlier, in the essays she had written for M. Heger, Emily had stated bluntly, "Nature is an inexplicable problem, it exists on a principle of destruction; it is necessary that each be the tireless instrument of death to others, or cease to live itself." Beyond the nihilism expressed in *Wuthering Heights*, the world Emily Brontë creates in her novel seems permeated with a longing for death. This is expressed by Catherine just before she dies in childbirth: "I'm tired, tired of being enclosed here. I'm wearying to escape into that glorious world, and to be always there; not seeing it dimly through tears, and yearning for it through the walls of an aching heart; but really with it and in it." The last sentence of the book, in which the narrator stands above the graves of Catherine and Heathcliff, suggests that only in death could either of them achieve peace: "I lingered round them, under that benign sky; watched the moths fluttering among the heath and harebells, listened to the soft wind breathing through the grass, and wondered how anyone could ever imagine unquiet slumbers for the sleepers in that quiet earth."

WHILE SHE WAS writing *Wuthering Heights*, Emily relied on Keeper to be her anchor to reality; she depended on her sisters to act as her audience. As soon as family prayers were finished and Mr. Brontë had gone upstairs, Charlotte, Emily, and Anne walked about in front of the fire, reading aloud from their works and commenting on one another's progress. One wonders what Anne and Charlotte thought as they listened to Emily's pages, filled with coarse language and brutal acts. Years later, in her preface to the second edition of Emily's novel, Charlotte admitted that reading *Wuthering Heights*, with its "storm-heated and electrical atmosphere," made her feel as if she were breathing lightning.

All three of the sisters' novels—*Jane Eyre, Agnes Grey*, and *Wuthering Heights*—were published in 1847 using their noms de plume, Currer, Acton, and Ellis Bell. *Jane Eyre* was an immediate success, hailed as a masterpiece; *Agnes Grey* was mostly overlooked; but *Wuthering Heights* generated a storm of controversy.

For a first novel by an unknown writer, *Wuthering Heights* received an astonishing amount of attention. Some critics admired

The Brontë Sisters, ca. 1834. *Oil by Branwell Brontë, who painted himself out of the portrait.*

the originality of the work; most were shocked by it: "How a human being could have attempted such a book as the present without committing suicide before he had finished a dozen chapters is a mystery. It is a compound of vulgar depravity and unnatural horrors, such as we might suppose a person, inspired by a mixture of brandy and gunpowder might write." Another found the novel "too odiously and abominably pagan to be palatable even to the most vitiated class of English readers." A third recommended the "puzzling" novel but warned that the reviewer had been "shocked, disgusted, almost sickened by details of cruelty, inhumanity, and the most diabolical hate and vengeance."

Charlotte believed Emily was indifferent to the reception of *Wuthering Heights*; in fact, tucked away in Emily's writing desk and discovered only years after her death were a handful of reviews, including one that thanked the author for writing such a powerful book. In the same desk was a letter from a publisher inquiring about the progress of Emily's second novel, suggesting that far from abandoning creative work because of hostile reviews, Emily continued to write.

In August of 1848, Charlotte and Anne decided to go to London to meet their publisher, William Smith Williams, face-to-face. They did not warn him of their visit, and since everyone thought the authors of *Jane Eyre* and *Agnes Grey* were men, no one in the office knew who they were. When Charlotte disclosed their identities to Mr. Williams, he was speechless at first and then ushered them in to meet his partners. Excitement grew as the realization dawned that the two small women in their drab, respectable attire were the authors Currer and Acton Bell. Mr. Williams insisted they come to his mother's home for dinner that evening, and the next night, he escorted them to their first opera. In the ensuing commotion, Charlotte let slip that Emily was Ellis Bell, the author of *Wuthering Heights*.

Back at home, Charlotte confessed her mistake to Emily, who was so angry at this betrayal that she would barely speak to either sister. Trying to placate her, Charlotte wrote a note to Williams:

"Permit me to caution you not to speak of my sisters when you write to me—I mean do not use the word in the plural. 'Ellis Bell' will not endure to be alluded to under any other appellation than the 'nom de plume.' I committed a grand error in betraying ~~her~~ his identity to you."

The upheaval over the pseudonyms was soon forgotten. That September, Branwell, who had been unwell for years, suddenly became much worse and within a few weeks died of consumption complicated by alcoholism. He was thirty-one. Charlotte and Anne's grief was somewhat assuaged by the fact that they had reconciled with him in his final hours, and Mr. Brontë was comforted because his son had repented of his sins. Emily, however, was inconsolable. She attended the funeral, caught a cold, and went to bed.

The family pleaded with Emily to see a doctor, but she refused. The neighbors were convinced she was dying "of a broken heart for love of her brother." How else to explain the hardiest of all the Brontës succumbing so quickly? Her sisters and father tried desperately to keep her alive. Charlotte searched the winter moors for a sprig of heather, certain it would spark her sister's interest, but Emily could no longer recognize her favorite flower. She seemed to have lost the will to live. Charlotte tried to come to terms with what seemed to be Emily's determination to die: "Never in all her life had she lingered over any task before her and she did not linger now."

Emily's cough grew worse. Except for the illnesses that had plagued her whenever she left home, she had always seemed robust and healthy. Now, however, she began to exhibit symptoms of the final stage of tuberculosis: She had a pain in her side, difficulty breathing, and she could no longer keep food down. Charlotte reported that Keeper refused to leave Emily but continually "lay at the side of her dying-bed." As he stayed beside the green sofa in the parlor, he slowed his breathing to match her gasps for air. Even as her strength waned, Emily fought to continue caring for Keeper and Flossy. The night before she died, she insisted on feeding them, but as she staggered into the cold hallway to the kitchen, she slipped and fell on the stone floor.

The next day, December 19, 1848, Emily said the family could call the doctor, but by then, it was too late. According to Charlotte, after "a hard, short conflict," thirty-year-old Emily died, "turning her dying eyes from the pleasant sun."

The accounts of Emily's funeral all mention Keeper. Charlotte wrote, "Emily's large house-dog followed her funeral to the vault, lying in the pew crouched at our feet while the burial service was being read." According to Mrs. Gaskell, "Keeper walked first among the mourners to her funeral; he slept moaning for nights at the door of her empty room, and never, so to speak, rejoiced, dog fashion after her death." Charlotte often spoke about how Keeper, "to the day of its death, slept at her room door, snuffing under it, and whining every morning."

A few months later, on May 28, 1849, Anne died at twenty-nine, also the victim of tuberculosis. Now only Charlotte and her father were left in the parsonage. In their grief and loneliness, they turned to Keeper and Flossy for comfort. The dogs became links to the lost sisters, their very presence a source of support. Mr. Brontë developed a strong attachment to the aging Keeper. One visitor recalled the "superannuated mastiff" that stood by Mr. Brontë's side and vanished when she tried to coax it forward. A journalist, accompanied by his terrier, called on the Brontës and was astonished when the elderly Keeper, still protecting the family home, rolled the younger dog over and bit at it "with his toothless gums." That evening, Keeper presented a gentler demeanor: "The blind old dog curled himself on the hearth at his blind old master's feet." When Mr. Brontë had to undergo cataract surgery, he cried out to Charlotte that if he died, "I shall never feel Keeper's paws on my knees again!"

Charlotte had never been much of a dog lover. She often misspelled Flossy's name, forgot whether the spaniel was male or female, referred to Keeper as "it" or "the house-dog." But after the loss of all her siblings, Charlotte came to appreciate both dogs. She wrote to her friend Ellen after a trip to London, "I got home a little before eight o'clock. . . . Papa and the servants were well. . . . The dogs seemed in strange ecstasy. I am certain they regarded me as the harbinger of others—the dumb creatures thought that as I was returned—those who had been so long absent were not far behind."

Clearly much affected by this sad homecoming, Charlotte wrote about it in even more detail to her publisher, William Smith Williams, who had become her friend: "The ecstasy of these poor animals when I came in was something singular—at former returns from brief absences they always welcomed me warmly—but not in that strange, heart-touching way—I am certain they thought that, as I was returned, my sisters were not far behind—but here my Sisters will come no more. Keeper may visit Emily's little bedroom—as he still does day by day—and Flossy may look wistfully round for Anne—they will never see them again—nor shall I."

In the silence of her empty home, Charlotte often felt close to despair. She kept busy during the day but found the evenings in front of the fire, when she and her sisters had read aloud together, unbearable. Charlotte had always relied on reading and writing to help her endure grief and hardship; now words were no help. She told friends what kept her going was the thought of her father and the presence of the dogs. When she felt overwhelmed by bitterness and desolation, she discovered it was only "some caress from the poor dogs which restores me to softer sentiments and more rational views."

Three years after Emily's death and also in December, Keeper died. By then, Charlotte understood just how important the dog was to both her and her father: "Poor old Keeper died last Monday Morning—after being ill one night—he went gently to sleep—we laid his old faithful head in the garden. Flossy is dull and misses him. There was something very sad in losing the old dog; yet I am glad he met a natural fate—people kept hinting that he ought to be put away which neither Pap nor I liked to think of."

In his last years, Keeper's devotion to Emily had expanded to include Charlotte and Mr. Brontë, but his mournful behavior showed that he never forgot Emily. During her final days, Keeper lay constantly by her side, and when she turned her face away from the sun, Emily would have known that Keeper was nearby.

EMILY BRONTË

1818	July, birth of Emily Brontë.
1820	Brontë family moves to Haworth Parsonage.
1821	September, death of Mrs. Brontë.
1824	Maria, Elizabeth, Charlotte, and Emily sent to Cowan Bridge School.
1825	Deaths of Maria and Elizabeth, ages eleven and ten, from typhoid. Mr. Brontë removes Charlotte and Emily from Cowan Bridge.
1830	[December, birth of Emily Dickinson.]
1835	Emily enrolled in Roe Head School; leaves after three months.
1838	Emily becomes a teacher at Law Hill School; leaves after five months. Mr. Brontë acquires Keeper.
1842	Charlotte and Emily attend Pensionnat Heger in Brussels.

Aunt Branwell dies; they return to Haworth.

1846   *Poems* published.

1847   *Wuthering Heights, Jane Eyre,* and *Agnes Grey* published.

1848   September, death of Branwell.
       December 19, death of Emily Brontë, age thirty. She is buried in the Brontë family vault in Haworth Church.

1849   May, death of Anne.

1851   December, death of Keeper.

1855   March, death of Charlotte.

1861   June, death of Mr. Brontë.
       [June, death of Elizabeth Barrett Browning.]

EMILY DICKINSON
and CARLO

"I talk of all these things with Carlo,
and his eyes grow meaning and his shaggy feet
keep a slower pace."

EMILY DICKINSON

In the winter of 1850, the New England college town of Amherst, Massachusetts, was filled with the sounds of young people home for the holidays, out until all hours at sugaring parties, sleigh rides, charades—party after party. The whirl of activities led twenty-year-old Emily Dickinson to exclaim, "Amherst is alive with fun this winter." Each night, partygoers wrapped in scarves and cloaks strolled from house to house. Their chatter and laughter echoed in the icy air as they gossiped and flirted.

In a warm, welcoming parlor, Austin Dickinson entertained friends and his sisters, Lavinia and Emily, with stories of college life. Then, as the group gathered around the piano to sing, Austin saw Emily slip quietly out the door. From the window, he watched her, lantern in hand, greet her dog, Carlo, who had been outside waiting for her all evening. The giant Newfoundland and the slight young woman walked across the snow-covered common toward home. This image of Emily and her dog stayed with other partygoers as well. One young woman would later reminisce about those evenings: "Rare hours, full of merriment, brilliant wit, and inexhaustible laughter, [Emily] Dickinson with her dog, & Lantern."

In the course of her outwardly quiet life, Emily Dickinson

Emily Dickinson, ca. 1846–47. *The only known likeness of the poet, a daguerreotype taken by an unknown photographer.*

wrote poems of undeniable power and beauty. Today, they enjoy an international reputation, although during her lifetime, fewer than a dozen appeared in print. She gave a few poems to friends and neighbors, tucking them into bouquets from her garden or enclosing them in sympathy notes. Most she kept hidden in a locked chest in her bedroom, where, after her death, her sister, Lavinia, discovered them.

Over time, myths have emerged about the "Belle of Amherst," who dressed only in white: mysterious love affairs, a harsh Victorian father, a confusing array of physical ailments, and various diagnoses of mental illness. Barely visible in the mystery that surrounds Emily Dickinson is the down-to-earth story of her relationship with her dog, Carlo. He appears briefly in her letters and poems, and there is an occasional mention of him by a neighbor or friend. From these bits of information, and following Emily's dictum "Tell all the Truth but tell it slant—," it is possible to piece together the story of Emily Dickinson and Carlo.

Although Emily Dickinson's early years did not contain the trauma and loss of Emily Brontë's childhood, they were nevertheless tinged with sadness. When pregnant with Emily, Mrs. Dickinson—also named Emily—already had a lively baby boy named Austin to care for and was living in the same house with her husband's parents. The young Mrs. Dickinson was terribly homesick for her family, the Norcrosses, who lived on a farm in Monson, Massachusetts, twenty-four miles south of Amherst. Her husband did not approve of his pregnant wife and infant son traveling back and forth to her family, not even during her mother's terminal illness. Unable to go to her dying mother and confined to a house with quarreling in-laws, Mrs. Dickinson suffered bouts of depression in the months before and after Emily's birth. She had no close friends in Amherst. A shy, unfriendly young woman, she rebuffed offers of help from her neighbors, who remembered her as constantly teary and sad.

Two years later, Emily's sister, Lavinia, was born after a delivery that left both mother and infant close to death. So that Mrs.

Dickinson could recuperate, little Emily was sent to the Norcross farm to stay with her aunt, who was already caring for other relatives: a young mother dying of tuberculosis and her frightened children. During the four months Emily spent in that stressful household, her aunt found her unusually quiet and well behaved. Most children would have protested vigorously at being sent away from home or would have clung to the aunt, but Emily appears to have responded by shutting down emotionally.

When she was brought back to Amherst, the Dickinson family was still unsettled. Emily's grandfather was embroiled in a scandal involving the misuse of Amherst College funds; as a consequence, he and Emily's grandmother moved to Ohio and Emily never saw them again. Her father, humiliated by his father's disgrace, worked unremittingly to establish a successful law practice and was rarely home. Mrs. Dickinson was too exhausted from the care of the sickly baby Lavinia and by the demands of four-year-old Austin to pay much attention to Emily. As a young woman, Emily stated categorically, "I never had a mother. I suppose a mother is one to whom you hurry when you are troubled." The pain of an overlooked child is portrayed in one of her poems:

> A loss of something ever felt I -
> The first that I could recollect
> Bereft I was - of what I knew not
> Too young that any should suspect
>
> A Mourner walked among the children. . . .

Mrs. Dickinson was never an active presence in Emily's childhood. For one thing, mother and daughter had very different temperaments and interests. Mrs. Dickinson was immersed in household duties and did not take part in the discussions about nature, literature, or politics that her daughter relished from an early age, leading Emily to conclude, "My mother does not care for thought—." Furthermore, Mrs. Dickinson would periodically withdraw from her family in moods of silent isolation that could last for days, months, or—in one case—several years. Her moods were well known in the Dickinsons' social circle. One woman noted in her diary, "I called on Mrs. E. Dickinson. . . . She was as usual full of plaintive talk." Her recurring illnesses, which today would undoubtedly be diagnosed as depression, frightened her children, who came to see their mother as unreliable and unpredictable, someone they could not count on.

Mrs. Dickinson herself attributed her low spirits to her husband's frequent absences. His career in law and politics required extended trips to Boston and Washington, D.C.; when he was home, he kept up a frenetic round of activities. He was the moderator for Amherst town meetings, served as the treasurer of Amherst College, and became involved in a long, drawn-out campaign to persuade the railway to run a line into the town. Eventually, Emily's father would twice be elected Massachusetts state senator and would serve one term in the United States Congress.

With a depressed mother and an absent father, the Dickinson children developed strong relationships with one another, much as the Brontë siblings had done. Emily and Austin delighted in teasing each other, playing word games, and collaborating in small rebellious acts against their father's rules, which they continued to do even into their twenties. On one occasion, they took turns reading the sentimental bestseller *Reveries of a Bachelor*, hiding it in the piano bench to prevent their father from discovering such a book in the serious Dickinson household. They often came up with excuses for missing services on Sunday, preferring to stay home in the gardens that surrounded the house. When Austin went away to school, Emily missed him terribly: "I think we miss each other more every day that we grow older, for we're . . . unlike most everyone, and are therefore more dependent on each other for delight." Indeed, Emily and Austin never relinquished their ties to each other, even though he eventually married and had children.

Emily was also devoted to her pert, outspoken sister, Lavinia—or Vinnie, as the family called her—even though Emily realized how unlike they were: "It is so weird and so vastly mysterious, she sleeps by my side . . . and the tie is quite vital, yet if we had come up for the first time from two wells . . . her astonishment would not be greater at some things I say." Emily depended on Vinnie and missed her when she was away: "I would like more sisters, that the taking out of one might not leave such stillness. Vinnie has been all, so long, I feel the oddest fright at parting with her for an hour, lest a storm arise, and I go unsheltered."

When Emily was ten, she and Lavinia began classes at Amherst Academy. Both sisters enjoyed school and made friends there. One teacher remembered Emily as "a very bright, but rather delicate and frail looking girl; an excellent scholar . . . somewhat shy, and nervous. Her compositions were strikingly original . . . and always attracted much attention in the school and, I am afraid, excited not a little envy."

In 1847, when she was seventeen, Emily's father enrolled her at Mount Holyoke Female Seminary, now Mount Holyoke College, but at that time an advanced high school. Emily was excited about going to boarding school, as can be seen in this letter to her childhood friend Abiah Root: "I am really at Mt. Holyoke Seminary & this is to be my home for a long year. . . . It has been nearly six weeks since I left home & that is a longer time than I was ever away from home before now. I was very homesick for a few days & it seemed to me I could not live here. But I am now contented & quite happy, if I can be happy when absent from my dear home & friends."

In time, however, Emily grew disenchanted with Mount Holyoke. Her classes were not challenging, and she was disturbed by the school's emphasis on religion. Under the headmistress's direction, assemblies were held in which the girls were encouraged to step forward and declare themselves to be saved. Emily, fiercely private about her religious beliefs, refused to take part in these public displays despite constant pressure from teachers and the other students to do so.

Adding to her unhappiness at Mount Holyoke was the fact that Emily suffered greatly from homesickness, or separation anxiety.

Children who do not experience secure attachment as infants can grow up with either dismissive or anxious attitudes toward others. If they fall into the dismissive category (like Emily Brontë), they are usually indifferent about intimate relationships; if anxious (like Emily Dickinson), they tend to be overly involved in any intimate relationship. Emily's early letters are filled with entreaties to her friends and family pleading for more letters, more attention, and more reassurances that they cared about her. A letter she wrote at this time to Abiah Root shows her escalating anxiety over the state of their friendship: "I mailed a long letter to you the 1st of March, & patiently have I waited a reply, but none has yet cheered me. Slowly, very slowly, I came to the conclusion that you had forgotten me, & I tried hard to forget you, but your image still haunts me, and tantalizes me with fond recollections. . . . If you don't want to be my friend any longer, say so, & I'll try *once* more to blot you from my memory. Tell me very soon, for suspense is intolerable."

Emily did her best to battle homesickness, but her family inadvertently made things worse. Whenever she had so much as a cold, she was brought home. Once she tried to keep a cough secret, but her parents found out and sent her brother to fetch her: "Austin arrived in full sail, with orders from head-quarters to bring me home at all events. At first I had recourse to words, and a desperate battle with those weapons was waged for a few moments. . . . Finding words of no avail, I next resorted to tears. But . . . as you can imagine, Austin was victorious, and poor, defeated I was led off in triumph." When Emily's parents decided she was well enough to return to Mount Holyoke, she found the readjustment painful, particularly because Mr. Dickinson had declared that this would be her last term. As usual, Emily did not question her father's decisions.

When Emily came home from Mount Holyoke in August of 1848, she was confused and uncertain about her future. She loved to write but did not yet see poetry as the vocation it would become for her. She had missed her family terribly when she was away, yet she did not turn to them for support or advice, which was characteristic of the Dickinsons. Although the family appeared to be close, in reality they led quite separate lives. Lavinia, the most out-going, described the family this way: "While contributing to the maintenance of a solid front, each component part remained distinct and independent. . . . [We] all lived like friendly and absolute monarchs, each in his own domain." Lavinia defined the specific role of each family member: "Father was the only one to say 'damn.' Someone in every family ought to say damn of course. As for Emily, she was not withdrawn or exclusive really. . . . She had to think—she was the only of us who had that to do. Father believed; and mother loved; and Austin had Amherst; and I had the family to keep track of."

By the winter of 1849–50, Emily had begun to chafe at being back home. Lavinia was away at school, studying at the Wheaton Seminary in Ipswich. Austin was already following in the footsteps of his father, attending Amherst College. (He would eventually graduate from Harvard Law School.) Emily's father was engrossed in providing a secure future for his family as a lawyer and as a politician. Typical of fathers at that time, Edward Dickinson assumed his daughters would either marry or stay at home and help their mother run the household; thus, after Emily's year at Mount Holyoke, he had no further aspirations for her. As Emily wryly commented, "Father . . . buys me many Books—but begs me not to read them—because he fears they joggle the Mind."

With Vinnie away, Emily resented the extra work that fell to her. Although there were part-time Irish servants to help her and her mother with the household tasks, Emily was responsible for all the baking because her father liked only her bread. She was skilled: Her "Rye & Indian Bread" won second prize at the Amherst Cattle Show, and neighbors often asked for her gingerbread recipe. When Austin came home for a visit, she looked forward to spending time with him, although she dreaded the added work: "Father and Austin still clamor for food, and I, like a martyr am feeding them." She was beginning to realize that if she wanted to write, she would have to fight for the time to do so: "Vinnie away—and my two hands but *two*—not four, or five as they ought to be—and so *many* wants—and me so *very* handy and my time of so *little* account—and my writing so *very* needless."

Emily's letters from this time are filled with questions about her character, wondering if she lacked moral fiber. She wrestled with doubts about God, which she would continue to do for the rest of her life. Emily was strongly steeped in the Christian tradition and well versed in knowledge of the Bible, yet she never joined her family's church. Her spiritual conflicts were of paramount importance to her, and she felt isolated when she could not find answers in organized religion. Moreover, although her young women friends dreamed about falling in love and marrying, Emily had serious reservations about marriage. She had seen how quickly young wives grew burdened, comparing them to flowers burned by the sun: "You have seen flowers at morning, satisfied with the dew, and those same sweet flowers at noon with their heads bowed in anguish before the mighty sun."

Emily could not imagine herself in the conventional roles of wife and mother, but there seemed to be no other possible life for her. Mr. Dickinson would never have allowed his daughters to work as teachers or governesses, as the Brontë sisters had done. And although Emily resented the tedium of housework, she refused to accept the role of an invalid, which had allowed Elizabeth Barrett Browning to avoid household responsibilities. Poised on the threshold of the next stage of her life, Emily longed for the simple world of childhood, writing to Austin, "I wish we were children now. I wish we were always children, how to grow up I don't know."

Faced with an uncertain future, Emily began to experience severe bouts of anxiety and fear that followed a classic vicious cycle: As she felt more distant from friends because she did not share their views about marriage and religion, she became more vulnerable to emotional upheavals, which left her feeling even more isolated. In letters to her friends, Emily sometimes revealed the chaos of emotions she was experiencing, but more often she hid her feelings behind a screen of literary or biblical allusions. She discovered she was less frightened if she kept to familiar surroundings, so she withdrew into the circumscribed space of her home and the immediate neighborhood.

Edward Dickinson recognized his daughter's distress because he also suffered from anxiety. When he had to be away for extended periods of time, he occasionally hired a young student to live with the family as an armed guard. Instead of reassuring Emily, this practice, combined with letters warning his family about a myriad of possible dangers—fire, spoiled food, and falling meteors—reinforced her conviction that the world was a dangerous place. Although he never recognized Emily's genius, Mr. Dickinson was well aware of his daughter's fears. In the same way that Miss Mitford had responded to Elizabeth Barrett Browning's depression with the gift of Flush, Mr. Dickinson decided that Emily needed a dog, a big one that would make her feel safe, a Newfoundland.

If Emily's father wanted a dog to act as a buffer between his daughter and the world that so frightened her, he could not have chosen a better breed. Handsome giants with deep-set, sympathetic eyes, Newfoundlands radiate a sense of peaceful competence. Although the breed comes from Canada, its popularity spread to both England and the United States in the 1800s. No doubt some of its renown was due to the fame of Boatswain, Lord Byron's Newfoundland. When his dog died, the grieving Byron wrote an epitaph: "Near this Spot / are deposited the Remains of one / who possessed Beauty without Vanity, / Strength without Insolence, / Courage without Ferocity / and all the Virtues of Man without his Vices."

The large dogs captured the public's imagination as symbols of courageous protectors. The cover of an American elementary school textbook featured a Newfoundland carrying a little girl's satchel in his mouth as they walked to school together. Even a popular children's song of the time celebrated the breed: "I am the noble Newfoundland / My voice is loud and deep / I keep watch all through the night / While other people sleep."

At some point in 1849, the new puppy arrived in Emily's life. As Flush had done for the Barrett household, Carlo provided welcome relief from the somber mood that had overcome the Dickinsons in Austin and Lavinia's absence: "We don't *have* many jokes tho' *now*, it is pretty much all sobriety, and we do not have much poetry, father having made up his mind that its pretty much all *real life*." On Lavinia's visits home, even the usually optimistic sis-

Newfoundland dog on the cover of an American schoolbook, ca. 1845.

ter agreed with Emily: "Mother has been sick for two days & Father 'is as he is,' so that home has been rather a gloomy place, lately." A clumsy, big-footed Newfoundland puppy, even one confined to the yard as would have been typical then, must have lightened the mood of the Dickinson home.

The first written mention of Carlo appears in a letter twenty-year-old Emily playfully wrote in February of 1850 to a friend of Austin's, George Gould, who was the editor of the Amherst College paper. Emily enclosed a Valentine poem, which Gould published, saying that it stood out from the rest he had received. Her letter accompanying the poem is lively, full of classical allusions and metaphors, including this lofty one: "I am Judith the heroine of the Apocrypha, and you the orator of Ephesus," which was immediately followed by a reference to Carlo, reminiscent of Byron's tribute to Boatswain: "That's what they call a metaphor in our country. Don't be afraid of it, sir, it won't bite. If it was my *Carlo* now! The Dog is the noblest work of Art, sir. I may safely say the noblest—his mistress's rights he doth defend—although it bring him to his end—although to death it doth him send!" Emily showed off her literary skill with a grandiose writing style, somewhat undermined by her idiosyncratic punctuation. She boasted about her dog, and despite the letter's lighthearted tone, it sounds as if Emily truly believed that Carlo would sacrifice his life to save hers.

Carlo grew rapidly: Mature male Newfoundlands range in weight from 110 to 150 pounds and stand between 26 and 28 inches high. By the spring of 1850, the slight young woman with her burly dog was a familiar sight in Amherst. One woman recalled a visit by the poet and her dog: "Miss Dickinson was the first person to call on my mother. . . . She came with her big dog, who usually accompanied her." A neighbor recalled strolling as a child through the village with Emily, "while the huge dog walked solemnly beside them." Another, when asked years later what she recalled of Emily Dickinson, volunteered, "Her companion out of doors was a large Newfoundland dog named Carlo."

In contrast to Carlo, Emily was, as she said, "small, like the Wren"—not much of an exaggeration judging from the size of the white dress that hangs in her room in the Dickinson Homestead Museum. Emily's hair was auburn, her eyes brown: "My Hair is bold, like the Chestnut Bur—and my eyes, like the Sherry in the Glass, that the Guest leaves." Her complexion was so fair that freckles vexed her every summer. In letters to friends, Emily fondly described Carlo as her "dog with ringlets." He became a member of the family, referred to casually in descriptions of everyday life. When a friend was ill, Emily included Carlo in the get-well greeting: "Father and Mother, and Vinnie, and Carlo, send their love to you, and a warm wish for your health."

Emily's parents may have considered Carlo to be a happy addition to the household, but Lavinia merely tolerated him. Instead, she doted on her cats (as an elderly woman, she would be notorious for the number she kept). Emily hated her sister's cats because they killed birds in the garden, and she plotted how to get rid of them: "Vinnie had four Pussies for Christmas Gifts—and two from her Maker, previous, making six, in toto, and finding Assassins for them, is my stealthy Aim." When Carlo chased the cats, Lavinia would lose her famous temper. Emily, in her usual cryptic style, described one such incident: "Evenings get longer with the Autumn—that is nothing new! Vinnie and I are pretty well. Carlo—comfortable—terrifying man and beast, with renewed activity—is cuffed some—hurled from piazza frequently when Miss Lavinia's 'flies'—need her action elsewhere."

Lavinia Dickinson with a cat, 1896.

It is not clear exactly what happened on that particular autumn evening. Did Carlo terrify one of the ubiquitous cats? Did Lavinia, who was known as a strong, spunky woman, hit Carlo? Could she literally "hurl" a full-grown Newfoundland off the porch? What is certain is that sparks could fly between Lavinia and Carlo. Apparently, Emily did not protest Lavinia's treatment of Carlo, but Mrs. Dickinson, who rarely ventured an opinion, believed Lavinia was too harsh with Carlo: "Mother thinks him a model dog, and conjectures what he might have been, had not Vinnie 'demoralized' him."

When she had first come home from Mount Holyoke, Emily had been too anxious and fearful to venture farther than her garden or the immediate neighborhood. Now that she had her dog, she

again spent long afternoons exploring the Pelham Hills that surround Amherst, which she had so enjoyed as a child: "When much
in the Woods as a little Girl, I was told that the Snake would bite
me, that I might pick a poisonous flower, or Goblins kidnap me, but
I went along and met no one but Angels." As a young girl, Emily
had collected enough wildflowers for a sixty-page herbarium, consisting of more than four hundred pressed flowers, each labeled
with its Latin name. The sheer number of flowers and the inclusion
of several exceedingly rare specimens, such as cancerroot and
strawberry blite, testify not only to the extent of Emily's knowledge
of flowers but also to the distance she must have walked to gather
them. Because of Carlo, Emily again felt at home among the familiar hills and woods, but her confidence would prove short-lived.

Even though Carlo was now an important part of Emily's life, she
continued to yearn for more attention from her friends. The letters
she had written from Mount Holyoke suggest an inner emptiness
too deep to be assuaged by any one person: She expected such lev-
els of sustained intimacy that she eventually exhausted anyone who
became close to her. She insisted on a constant flow of letters and
visits but would often refuse to see people when they did come to
call. Some friends resented this inconsistency and lost touch with
Emily; others simply moved away or married. She did not understand why people grew tired of her, and her sense of isolation increased. Then, when she was in her late teens, Emily met Susan
Gilbert.

Susan was a lively, attractive young woman, almost exactly
Emily's age. She was passionate, eager for new experiences, and different from the sheltered girls who had grown up with Emily. As a
child, Susan had lost both her parents and had stayed with various
relatives before settling in Amherst with her oldest sister and her
husband. When Emily and Susan met, they immediately discovered
that they shared a hatred of housework, a love of literature, and an
intense interest in religion. The two women may have been in love;
whether they were or not, they would have a lifelong relationship

marked with jealousy and hurt feelings as well as moments of true understanding and affection.

Emily admired Susan's independent spirit; nevertheless, she was shocked when twenty-one-year-old Susan, tired of relying on her sister's husband to support her, decided to move to Baltimore and take a teaching job. Susan evidently enjoyed the reaction, writing to her brother that she had left her "good friends in Amherst actually staring with aston-ishment." In the year that Susan was away, she and Emily wrote fond letters to each other; at the same time, Austin Dickin-son began to write Susan formal court-ing letters. Soon bro-ther and sister were rivals for the same woman's heart.

At times, Emily tried to accept the situation with humor. When Austin re-turned from visiting Susan in Baltimore,

Susan Gilbert, ca. 1851.

Emily peppered him with questions about her friend and related his nonanswers to Susan: "I asked him how you looked, and what you wore and how your hair was fixed and what you said of me—his an-swers were quite limited—'you looked as you always did—he didn't know what you wore—never did know what people wore.' " Yet there were moments when Emily's despair is clear. Here she describes her reaction when Susan left Amherst after a visit without saying good-bye to her: "I ran to the door, dear Susie—I ran out in the rain, with nothing but my slippers on, I called 'Susie, Susie,' but you didn't look at me; then I ran to the dining room window and rapped with all my might upon the pane, but you rode right on and never heeded me."

In 1853, when Emily was twenty-three, Austin and Susan became engaged. Although Emily felt betrayed by them both, she unleashed her feelings of rejection on Susan: "You need not fear to leave me lest I should be alone, for I often part with things I fancy I have loved,—sometimes to the grave, and sometimes to an oblivion rather bitterer than death." Yet Emily continued to write intimate letters to Susan throughout the couple's three-year engagement. One written in August 1854, with its flat tone and disembodied perspective, suggests that Emily had become very depressed: "I rise, because the sun shines, and sleep has done with me, and I brush my hair, and dress me, and wonder what I am and who has made me so, and then I wash the dishes, and anon, wash them again, and then 'tis afternoon, and Ladies call, and evening, and some members of another sex come in to spend the hour, and then that day is done. And, prithee, what is Life?"

Emily began to withdraw, spending more time with Carlo and less with people. On the rare occasions when she did venture out, she tried to avoid talking to anyone. For example, in the summer of 1853, the entire town gathered to celebrate the new railroad line. Mr. Dickinson had spearheaded the campaign to bring the train to the village and was the chief marshal for the day's events. Emily, no doubt with Carlo at her side, watched from a distance: "Carriages flew like sparks, hither, and thither and yon, and they all said t'was fine. I spose it was—I sat in Prof Tyler's woods and saw the train move off, and then ran home again for fear somebody would see me, or ask me how I did."

That autumn, Emily faced a further ordeal when Mr. Dickinson decided to move the family down the street to the Homestead, the house that had once belonged to Emily's grandfather. In buying it back, Mr. Dickinson believed he was restoring the honor of the family's name. To Emily and her mother, however, the move represented an overwhelming upheaval. Even though the Homestead was less than a mile from her first home, Emily describes the move as if they had followed her grandparents and journeyed out west. She sounds emotionally cut off, almost disassociated, as if she were viewing the experience from far away: "I cannot tell you how we moved. I had rather not remember. I believe my 'effects' were brought in a bandbox, and the 'deathless me,' on foot, not many moments after. . . . It is a kind of *gone-to-Kansas* feeling." Although it seems certain that Carlo would have been at Emily's side as she walked the short distance between the two houses, this time he was not able to calm her anxiety.

Emily's mother became immobilized once she moved back to the home where she had once been so unhappy: "Mother has been an invalid since we came *home.*" Twenty-five-year-old Emily reacted to her mother's depression by regressing to a childlike state of panic: "Mother lies upon the lounge or sits in her easy chair. I don't know what her sickness is, for I am but a simple child, and frightened at myself." In the weeks after the move, Mrs. Dickinson sat silently in her chair while Vinnie set up the new household. Emily tried to help with the unpacking, but she remained agitated. In the evenings, she fled her sister's busyness and her mother's passivity: "I am out with lanterns, looking for myself." This image of Emily is in stark contrast to the younger Emily, happily walking with her lantern and Carlo through the streets of Amherst, seeking the night air out of choice rather than despair.

The move had taken place in November of 1855; by the time winter set in, Emily appreciated the new house. Although close to the center of Amherst, the Homestead was actually a small farm with a barn, vegetable gardens, and an orchard. There were horses, chickens, pigs, and a cow. A meadow across the street was planted with rye. Before they moved in, Mr. Dickinson had had the house substantially remodeled; according to local gossip, he spent nearly five thousand dollars on improvements. Franklin stoves and oil lamps were installed in each bedroom, so that the downstairs hearth was no longer the only source of warmth and light. Instead of sharing a bedroom,

Emily and Vinnie now had their own rooms. These changes would make a considerable difference in Emily's life, although at first she had been too dazed to notice them. What won her heart was the conservatory her father had built for her. A simple glass-walled structure that faced south and east, it became Emily's refuge. Under her care, exotic tropical plants such as oleander, ferns, and camellias flourished throughout the long New England winters. The space was far too small for Carlo, but he could lie on the threshold and savor the scent of the jasmine and hyacinth.

Emily also loved her bedroom, with its own stove and oil lamp. On cold evenings, she could retreat there to write instead of having to stay downstairs with the family. Although the room was small, with only a tiny writing desk and a narrow bed, it was located in the southwest corner of the house, which had the best light and views. From her desk, Emily looked out over the Holyoke Mountains and her family's meadow; from her bed, she could overhear snippets of conversation as townspeople passed by and the chatter of children going back and forth to school. The Homestead was also graced with a cupola, which Emily could reach by a stairway through the attic next to her bedroom. Once there, she could stand unseen and look down on Amherst and across the outlying hills, scenes that would appear often in her poems.

On July 1, 1856, Austin and Susan were married at her aunt's home in Geneva, in upstate New York. None of the Dickinson family attended, which was attributed to Mrs. Dickinson's poor health. Nevertheless, it seems odd that neither of the sisters made the short journey to celebrate the wedding; perhaps Emily was unable to bear witnessing it. Nothing would ever shake her devotion to Austin, and the intensity of her relationship with Susan would ebb and flow for the rest of their lives.

Whatever Emily's feelings about the marriage, she was pleased when the couple decided to stay in Amherst. They moved next door into an imposing home, the Evergreens, which Mr. Dickinson had built for them. Emily and Susan renewed their friendship and began to exchange what they called "letter poems," often sent with the gift of a flower or something they had baked. A stanza from one poem shows Emily's acceptance of Sue as Austin's wife—and her sister-in-law:

> *One Sister have I in our house -*
> *And one, a hedge away.*
> *There's only one recorded,*
> *But both belong to me.*

Three months after Austin and Susan's wedding, Elizabeth Barrett Browning's *Aurora Leigh*, the 350-page epic poem about a woman's struggles to become a serious writer, was published in the United States. Emily mentioned *Aurora Leigh* often in her letters and marked several passages in her copy, including these three:

She had lived / A sort of cage-bird life . . .

The works of women are symbolical. / We sew, sew, prick our fingers, dull our sight, / Producing what?

I may love my art. / You'll grant that even a woman may love art.

She hung Barrett Browning's picture on the wall of her room (where it remains today) and adopted a similar hairstyle. A few years later, Emily described her initial reaction to reading Barrett Browning:

> *I think I was enchanted*
> *When first a sombre Girl -*
> *I read that Foreign Lady -*
> *The Dark - felt beautiful -*

Emily, now twenty-six, focused diligently on her own poetry. In the privacy of her new bedroom, she wrote about familiar subjects: the plants and birds that filled her garden, views of the hills, and stories from the Bible. She never told anyone about her secret cache of poems, which she compiled with painstaking care. Working late at night while her family slept, Emily would select a few poems and recopy them on sheets of good stationery. Then she took her needle and thread and sewed the pages into small manuscript booklets, known as "fascicles." Over time, she created forty fascicles containing about eight hundred poems that appear to be organized by theme.

Even though Mr. Dickinson had by now hired full-time servants, Emily still had to fit her writing in among other responsibilities. She continued to be in charge of the family baking, which called for hours in the kitchen every day except the Sabbath. Determined to write whenever she could steal a moment, Emily had pockets sewn into her dresses so that a pad of paper and pencil were always handy. As she worked in the garden or the kitchen, she often paused to scribble notes on the backs of recipes, on brown bags, and on shopping lists—whatever was handy. When Emily's cousin Louise Norcross visited, she would sit on a footstool in the Dickinsons' apple green and yellow kitchen and watch Emily write poems without a pause in her work: "[She] wrote most emphatic things in the pantry, so cool and quiet, while she skimmed the milk. . . . The blinds were closed, but through the green slats she saw all those fascinating ups and downs going on outside that she wrote about."

Emily preferred to spend her time in the garden, a private, enclosed space, shielded from the outside world by high hedges. Hidden deep in the garden, among transplanted wildflowers, stood a summerhouse surrounded by trellises in which roses and honeysuckle intertwined. Carlo was part of Emily's secret garden world, as indicated by the following poem, in which the two of them watch the dance of a hummingbird as he reels from flower to flower:

> *Till every spice is tasted -*
> *And then his Fairy Gig*
> *Reels in remoter atmospheres -*
> *And I rejoin my Dog. . . .*

The poet is not sure if the bird is real or a figment of her imagination. She believes that her dog shares her confusion.

> *And He and I, perplex us*
> *If positive, 'twere we -*
> *Or bore the Garden in the Brain*
> *This Curiosity -*

She looks to her dog, "the best Logician," for an answer, and he turns her attention to the concrete evidence before her, the vibrating blossoms that prove the bird's existence.

> *But He, the best Logician,*
> *Refers my clumsy eye -*
> *To just vibrating Blossoms!*
> *An Exquisite Reply!*

Some interpret this poem as an example of Emily's serious questioning of the Bible, in this case the story of the Garden of Eden: Is it to be taken as literal truth or as a story invented by mankind? Whatever her intent, the poem presents a delightful image of Emily and Carlo in the garden, exchanging perplexed glances of wonder over the dance of a hummingbird.

In another poem, this one describing a winter night, Carlo appears only as an impression—a quick look, a faint sound:

> *No Squirrel went abroad -*
> *A Dog's belated feet*
> *Like intermittent Plush, he heard*
> *Adown the empty Street -*

The words "intermittent Plush" suggest both the sound a big dog makes padding about as well as the surprising softness of the underside of a dog's paw.

As Emily became ever more absorbed in her writing, Lavinia sheltered her sister from the outside world. She took over dealing with servants and tradespeople, and she put off neighbors who wanted to see Emily. Because of Mr. Dickinson's many activities, the Homestead was a central meeting place in Amherst. The college held numerous teas and dinners there as well as the annual commencement reception. It had been Emily's custom to stand in a corner and pour sherry for the guests, but as she grew more reclusive, she avoided all such occasions completely.

Eventually, few people ever saw Emily face-to-face. She would send a card or flowers downstairs to visitors without appearing herself. Lavinia made light of Emily's removal from social life, saying it was "only a happen," but her explanation does not account for the depth of Emily's anxiety about leaving the safety of the house or garden. Emily refused one invitation by stating, "I don't go from home, unless emergency leads me by the hand." As her anxiety grew more pronounced, Emily depended on Carlo's quiet strength: "He is dumb and brave."

Sometimes, though, not even Carlo could prevent Emily's fears from escalating into a state of irrational terror. This is evident from her description of a few summer nights she spent alone, an event that might have happened only once when Lavinia traveled with their parents. Although the number of robberies in Amherst had increased since the railroad came to town, Emily sounds almost paranoid in this letter to her cousins. She describes her fear as well as her complete inability to soothe herself: "The nights turned hot, when Vinnie had gone and I must keep no window raised for fear of prowling 'booger,' and I must shut my door for fear front door slide open on me at the 'dead of night,' and I must keep 'gas' burning to light the danger up, so I could distinguish it—these gave me a snarl in the brain which don't unravel yet, and that old nail in my breast pricked me."

Beginning sometime in 1856 and continuing into the early 1860s, when Emily was in her late twenties and early thirties, she went through a life-changing crisis. Her letters allude to dreadful inner turmoil, and poems such as this one describe anguish and despair with such stark clarity that they speak to us directly across the generations.

> I felt a Cleaving in my Mind -
> As if my Brain had split -

I tried to match it - Seam by Seam -
But could not make them fit -

The thought behind, I strove to join
Unto the thought before -
But Sequence ravelled out of Sound
Like Balls - upon a Floor.

No one knows exactly what happened. Emily's poems and letters are oblique, disclosing few details, revealing only the underlying emotion. Furthermore, after her death, the family destroyed
and edited much of her correspondence to safeguard her privacy as
well as their own. Dickinson biographers have different theories
about the cause of the crisis but agree there were several possible
reasons for the poet's distraught state during those years.

One source of Emily's emotional pain must have been eye
problems, which began during this period. No doctor's notes have
survived, but Emily's descriptions of her symptoms indicate that
she suffered from rheumatic iritis, a painful disease that renders one
intolerant of light and that can result in total loss of vision. For
someone as dependent on books and writing as Emily, the threat of
blindness would certainly explain her terror.

A case can be made that Emily's distress was caused by an es-
trangement from Susan and Austin. Their son Ned was born on
June 19, 1861, a sickly baby whose inexperienced and frightened
parents were completely absorbed in caring for him. That Emily
felt excluded during this time can be seen in several poems, including this poem/note she sent to Sue: "Could I - then - shut the door - /
Lest my beseeching face - at last - / Rejected - be - of Her?"

The Civil War also affected Emily, although she rarely mentioned it directly in letters or poems. However, the Dickinson family avidly read and discussed newspapers, and the war was a
constant topic of conversation in Amherst, especially after the
Amherst College president's son was killed in action. In a letter to a
friend, Emily defends writing poems during a war by saying that
Robert Browning was continuing to write, even though Elizabeth

Barrett Browning had just died: "I noticed that Robert Browning had made another poem, and was astonished—till I remembered that I, myself, in my smaller way, sang off charnel steps."

The most convincing explanation for Emily's anguish is that she fell in love with someone who was not available.

Samuel Bowles.

Biographers have suggested a minister, Charles Wadsworth, or an Amherst neighbor, William Smith Clark, or Susan Dickinson. Most of the evidence, however, including the thirty-five surviving letters and fifty poems that Emily sent him, points to Samuel Bowles, a married man and the father of five children. A close friend of Austin and Susan, Bowles was the editor of the *Springfield Republican*. He traveled widely and was popular for his urbane manner and witty conversations. He was handsome and comfortable around women, who invariably found him charming and attractive.

On visits to Austin's home, Bowles would flirt with Susan and then slip next door to visit Vinnie and Emily. He shared Emily's love of the poetry of Elizabeth Barrett Browning. When he told Emily he planned to visit the poet's grave in Florence, Emily asked him to touch it for her: "Put one hand on the Head, for me—her unmentioned Mourner." On long summer evenings, Bowles played shuttlecock with Emily. If she refused to see him, Bowles—unlike other visitors, who meekly acquiesced to her wishes—would stand at the foot of the stairs demanding that the "Queen Recluse" come down.

In letters to Bowles, Emily sometimes relied on Carlo as a go-between to convey her feelings. Over the years, she had slipped into this practice, much as Elizabeth Barrett Browning had done with Flush. To her friends, Emily often included Carlo in affectionate closings: "Please have my love, Mother's, and Vinnie's—Carlo sends a brown kiss." When Emily missed her Norcross cousins, she projected her emotions onto Carlo: "Nothing has happened but loneliness, perhaps too daily to relate. Carlo is consistent, has asked for nothing to eat or drink, since you went away." Similarly, when Bowles was traveling in Europe, Emily found it natural to talk about Carlo's reaction rather than her own: "I tell you, Mr. Bowles, it is a Suffering, to have a sea—no care how Blue—between your Soul, and you . . . and the puzzled look—deepens in Carlo's fore-head, as the Days go by, and you never come." Emily's reference to Carlo's puzzled look suggests that Samuel Bowles knew Carlo well enough to understand her allusion to the furrowed brow character-istic of Newfoundlands.

Carlo also appears in the mysterious, passionate letters now known as the Master Letters. Emily never names the recipient, ad-dressing him only as Master. Written in pencil, the three Master Letters may have been drafts that were never sent. They are fervent and impetuous, unlike anything else Emily Dickinson ever wrote. In them, she reveals sexual longing, refers to herself as "Daisy," and begs for a response: "Master. If you saw a bullet hit a Bird—and he told you he wasn't shot—you might weep at his courtesy, but you would certainly doubt his word. One drop more from the gash that stains your Daisy's bosom—then would you *believe*?"

The letters are addressed to someone who is away. Both the probable timing of the letters as well as certain recurring images and expressions strongly support the idea that the Master Letters were intended for Bowles. Especially convincing is Emily's entreaty that the Master spend time alone with her, with only Carlo and the birds as witnesses: "Could you forget me in fight, or flight—or the foreign land? Couldn't Carlo, and you and I walk in the meadows an hour—and nobody care but the Bobolink?"

We do not know if Emily ever sent the Master Letters. A stronger piece of evidence for Bowles as the person Emily was in love with is the following poem, which was discovered by Samuel Bowles's son among family papers. Although Emily always insisted that the "I" in her poetry did not mean her but "a supposed person," it is impossible to read this two-stanza verse as anything but a love poem. Filled with dog imagery, the first stanza compares Emily's feelings to a dog who is desperate for attention:

> *What shall I do - it whimpers so -*
> *This little Hound within the Heart*
> *All day and night with bark and start -*
> *And yet, it will not go -*
> *Would you untie it, were you me -*
> *Would it stop whining - if to Thee -*
> *I sent it - even now?*

In the second stanza, she reassures her lover that her needs will not overpower him, and she pleads with him to use Carlo as a go-between:

> *It should not tease you -*
> *By your chair - Or, on the mat -*
> *Or if it dare - to climb your dizzy knee -*
> *Or - sometimes - at your side to run -*
> *When you were willing -*
> *Shall it come? Tell Carlo -*
> *He'll tell me!*

Because the poet expects rejection, she wants the answer from Carlo. Coming from him, she imagines it will hurt less. Emily believes that Carlo can help her endure the pain she knows is inevitable.

In the midst of this internal crisis, on her twenty-ninth birthday, Emily wrote a letter to a friend. Alone in her room on a frigid

New England winter night, Emily describes her loneliness and her attempts to cope with it: "I cannot walk to the distant friends on nights piercing as these, so I put both hands on the window-pane, and try to think how birds fly, and imitate, and fail. . . . I could make a balloon of a Dandelion, but the fields are gone. . . ." Emily feels trapped and isolated. The image of the poet standing with both hands on the windowpane, looking out at the bleak landscape, recalls a stanza from one of her best-known poems:

> *This is the Hour of Lead -*
> *Remembered, if outlived,*
> *As Freezing persons, recollect the Snow -*
> *First - Chill - then Stupor - then the letting go -*

But, on this night, Emily is not alone, and she turns away from the icy window toward the warm, comforting presence of Carlo. They circle her bedroom, the big dog walking slower and slower until his pace matches Emily's. Her letter continues: "I talk of all these things with Carlo, and his eyes grow meaning, and his shaggy feet keep a slower pace."

Carlo never grew exhausted by Emily's need for constant, attuned attention because it was part of his inbred nature to provide such a response. All dogs naturally look at their owners with a steady gaze, but it can be argued

"Carlo Dreams," 1980. *By Nancy Eckholm Burkert.*

that a Newfoundland's deep-set, dark eyes are the most sympathetic of all. Carlo's silence created an atmosphere that made Emily feel safe and secure; he became a witness to her private thoughts and feelings. As she talked to him, Carlo kept his gaze locked on hers, completely attuned to her. Seeing herself mirrored in her dog's deep eyes, Emily could recognize fragile, vulnerable parts of herself that she never revealed to her parents, siblings, or friends. As Emily watched Carlo's "eyes grow meaning," she felt received and understood. And safe, because whatever she told Carlo would be held in his silence.

By the end of 1862, when Emily was thirty-two, the crisis seems to have come to an end. Her eye problems abated for the time being, there were no more Master Letters, and her letters record only quiet, everyday events. Whatever may have happened between Emily and Samuel Bowles, he remained her close friend for the rest of his life. His understanding of her can be seen in his gift of a jasmine tree, which she awarded center place in her conservatory. In addition to enjoying the plant's beauty, both Bowles and Emily would have understood its symbolic meaning as the poet's plant. Emily's continued esteem for Bowles was shown when she invited him to sit next to her at her father's funeral in 1874.

As for Austin and Susan, their relationships with Emily were once more restored. Austin resumed his regular visits, and Sue wrote an apology for the distance that had grown between her and her sister-in-law: "I have intended to write you Emily to-day but the quiet has not been mine. . . . If you have suffered this past Summer—I am sorry—." Soon the two friends were exchanging daily notes, meeting for morning coffee, and admiring each other's garden. Emily showed Sue drafts of "Safe in their Alabaster Chambers" and accepted her advice about changes. She even allowed Sue to show the poem to Samuel Bowles, who published it on March 1, 1862, in the *Springfield Republican*.

Emily and Carlo now spent long afternoons with Susan and the baby, Ned. In this poem, Emily captures the ability of both dogs and children to find joy in the moment:

A little Dog that wags his tail
And knows no other joy
Of such a little Dog am I
Reminded by a Boy . . .

In one of her letters, which is structured almost like a poem, Emily describes Susan pulling Ned in his wagon, followed by the dignified Carlo and two cats:

The Frogs sing sweet - today - They have such pretty - lazy - times - how nice, to be a Frog! Sue - draws her little Boy - pleasant days - in a Cab - and Carlo - walks behind, accompanied by a Cat - from each establishment.

Emily now turned all her passion into her poetry. She herself connected the outpouring of poems between 1861 and 1864 to the crisis she had endured: "I had a terror . . . I could tell to none—and so I sing, as the Boy does by the Burying Ground—because I am afraid." In 1861, she wrote only 36 poems, but in 1862, she produced 366, an astonishing number that suggests she was writing a poem every day. After that peak year, the numbers declined, although Emily wrote 141 poems in 1863 and 174 poems in 1864.

Such sustained output can prove destructive for the creator. Emily once described how overwhelming her creativity could feel: "When I try to organize—my little Force explodes—and leaves me bare and charred." She responded to poetry at a visceral level: "If I read a book [and] it makes my whole body so cold no fire ever can warm me I know *that* is poetry. If I feel physically as if the top of my head were taken off, I know *that* is poetry." Despite the risks to her emotional stability, Emily continued to write riveting and complex poems, including "Dare you see a Soul at the 'White Heat'?" Like many creative people, she depended on someone else to oversee the balance between having time alone against the need for connection with others to avoid being engulfed by the work. To a large degree, Lavinia played this role as she warded off inquisitive friends and relatives; although Emily appreciated Lavinia's efforts, she rarely shared her poems with her sister. What has never been recognized is the extent to which Emily also relied on Carlo to keep her grounded during the "white heat" of inspiration, in much the same way as Emily Brontë had counted on Keeper.

An image of Carlo in this role pervades the following poem: "I started Early - Took my Dog - / And visited the Sea -." The poem can be read as a metaphor for the way a poet can suddenly fall into uncanny territory. Beginning in a quiet, unruffled tone, the poem's mood abruptly changes; what seemed innocent and benign turns threatening and dangerous. The speaker becomes a helpless Mouse as she confronts staring Mermaids, Frigates that grab at her with "Hempen Hands," and a Sea that tries "to eat me up." Sustained by the Dog's protection, the speaker escapes back to "the Solid Town."

Like the Dog who guided the speaker into the sea and back again to "the Solid Town," Carlo helped keep Emily grounded during her years of peak productivity. During the day, Carlo was with her as she scribbled notes for her poems. At night, he slept at her feet while she revised them. Although it is difficult to imagine a poet working in such isolation for so many years, it helps to picture Carlo with Emily, sleeping as she sewed her fascicles or listening intently as she read a poem to him.

In 1862, Emily submitted four poems to Thomas Higginson, the editor of the *Atlantic Monthly*, in response to an essay he had written encouraging young poets. Higginson would become her friend and almost a literary mentor, even though Emily steadfastly ignored his advice to make her poems follow standard rules of punctuation, rhyming, and spelling. For the rest of her life, Emily would count on his support and friendship, and on two occasions, she told him he had saved her life. She wrote him twenty-one letters, sent him close to a hundred poems, and she even allowed him to visit her twice. When she died, he was one of the few people invited to her funeral service.

Because she trusted Higginson fully, Emily revealed things to him that she kept secret from others, including the extent of her devotion to Carlo. Emily assumed that Higginson would appreciate Carlo as she did: "I think Carlo would please you." In response to one of Higginson's first letters, in which he must have asked for details about her life in Amherst, Emily offered a succinct tribute to Carlo: "You ask of my Companions Hills—Sir and the Sundown—and a Dog—large as myself, that my Father bought me—They are better than Beings—because they know—but do not tell."

Thomas Higginson, ca. 1870.

Emily often told Higginson how much she appreciated Carlo's silence, which she interpreted as evidence that her dog shared her respect for strong emotions: "When I am most grieved I had rather no one speak to me. . . . When I am most sorry, I can say nothing." Furthermore, Emily abhorred careless conversations about death and immortality, which she called Flood subjects. She had spent years pondering these mysteries and had no patience for people's easy opinions about them: "They talk of Hallowed things, aloud—and embarrass my Dog."

In response to something Higginson must have asked about her solitary life, her answer once again included Carlo: "Of 'shunning Men and Women' . . . He [Carlo] and I don't object to them,

if they'll exist their side." By this stage of her life, Emily understood that solitude was imperative for her, and she no longer
wrote letters exhorting her friends to write back to her. She had
chosen to live a cloistered existence: "The Soul selects her own
Society - / Then - shuts the Door -," but she wanted her dog to be
a part of that sheltered space.

Emily told Higginson that Carlo was often the only audience
for her poems. On one occasion when Higginson said that he hesitated to publish her poems because of their odd rhymes and
strange punctuation, Emily insisted that she was more interested
in Carlo's approval than in writing to please the public: "I smile
when you suggest that I delay 'to publish'—that being foreign to
my thought, as Firmament to Fin—If fame belonged to me, I
could not escape her—if she did not, the longest day would pass
me on the chase—and the approbation of my Dog, would forsake
me,—then—."

Perhaps buoyed by Higginson's interest, Emily now proclaimed herself a poet. She dressed entirely in white as a symbol
of her vocation: "A solemn thing - it was - I said - / A Woman -
white - to be -. . . ." The tone of her poems shifted from describing inner states of isolation and terror to ringing acclamations:

> Title divine - is mine!
> The Wife - without the Sign!
> Acute Degree - conferred on me -
> Empress of Calvary!

Then, in February 1863, Higginson went to South Carolina to
take command of a Union regiment composed of ex-slaves. Emily
was surprised by the news, perhaps because her brother, Austin, had
followed local custom and paid someone to take his place in the
army. In an unusually straightforward letter, Emily told Higginson
she was upset by his sudden absence, sorry she had not had a chance
to see him before he left, and hopeful he would be back by summer.
The rest of the letter, as carefully spaced as a poem, tells how Carlo
would take Higginson's place until he returned.

I found you were gone, by accident, as I find Systems are,
or Seasons of the year . . . Carlo - still remained - and I
told him -

> Best Gains - must have the Losses' Test -
>
> To constitute them - Gains -

The letter concludes with Emily's wonderful term of endearment
for Carlo:

> My Shaggy Ally assented -

After the war, Higginson visited Emily at her invitation. Later
he wrote his impressions to his wife: "A step like a pattering child's
& in glided a little plain woman with two smooth bands of reddish
hair & a face . . . with no good features—in a very plain & exquisitely clean white pique & blue net worsted shawl. She came to me
with two day lilies she put in a sort of childlike way into my hand &
said, 'These are my introduction' in a soft frightened breathless
childlike voice—& added under her breath 'Forgive me if I am
frightened; I never see strangers & hardly know what I say'—but
she talked soon & thenceforward continuously . . . saying many
things which you would have thought foolish & I wise,—& some
things you would have liked." As a literary person and political activist, Higginson knew many creative people; he was nevertheless
surprised by the force of Emily's personality: "I never was with anyone who drained my nerve power so much. Without touching her,
she drew from me. I am glad not to live near her."

By the time she was in her midthirties, the period of Emily's intense
creativity had come to an end. Her eyes were much worse. In 1864
and 1865, she spent months at a time in Boston with her cousins,
Louise and Frances Norcross, while she underwent painful treatments. Forbidden by her doctor to read or to write, Emily listened
as her cousins read Shakespeare aloud to her. She missed her dog,
but as she explained to Higginson in one of the few letters she was

allowed to write, she left Carlo home because he could not have borne city life: "Carlo did not come, because that he would die, in Jail, and the Mountains, I could not hold now, so I brought but the Gods—. . . ." She put Carlo's well-being above her own, even though he would have helped her endure the hours of pain and boredom.

In November of 1865, Emily returned home after her second round of eye treatments, grateful to resume her quiet life, including her daily routines with Carlo. By now, he was sixteen, an advanced age for a Newfoundland, and Emily must have realized they had little time left together. Yet when he died late in January of 1866, she was stunned. The only information about his death is the brief note that Emily sent to Higginson. There is no greeting, only the message, a signature, and a question, but the quiet simplicity evokes the depth of her grief:

> Carlo died -
> E. Dickinson
> Would you instruct me now?

Higginson immediately understood the significance of the short communication and acknowledged that Carlo's death was an "event, vast in her small sphere." Along with the note, Emily enclosed a single poem known today by its first line, "Further in Summer," even though Emily, who rarely titled her poems, named it "My Cricket."

> *Further in Summer than the Birds*
> *Pathetic from the Grass*
> *A minor Nation celebrates*
> *Its unobtrusive Mass.*
>
> *No Ordinance be seen*
> *So gradual the Grace*
> *A pensive Custom it becomes*
> *Enlarging Loneliness.*

Antiquest felt at Noon
When August burning low
Arise this spectral Canticle
Repose to typify

Remit as yet no Grace
No Furrow on the Glow,
Yet a Druidic Difference
Enhances Nature now

When Emily uses the word *Druidic*, she may refer to the ancient belief in the wholeness of nature, with no separation between humans and other animals. Could the word *furrow*, which appears in the last stanza, be a reference to Carlo's perpetually furrowed brow? Emily sent copies of the poem to two friends. With one copy was a brief note: "I bring you a chill gift—My Cricket"; with the other, she enclosed a cricket corpse, perhaps to emphasize the poem's focus on death.

Crickets were an important symbol in Emily's writing. In her twenties, she had noted that the sound of crickets was merely background noise during the day, but at night, it became a loud announcement of time passing: "The day went down, long time ago, and still a simple Choir bear the canto on. . . ." Over the years, she observed that in autumn, when the birds grew silent, the crickets' song swelled into a grim announcement of winter's approach. A poem written in 1873, when Emily was forty-three, depicts crickets as reminders of mortality:

'Twas later when the summer went
Than when the Cricket came -
And yet we knew that gentle Clock
Meant nought but Going Home -
'Twas sooner when the Cricket went
Than when the Winter came
Yet that pathetic Pendulum
Keeps Esoteric Time.

Carlo had been like the crickets' song for Emily, a quiet pendulum keeping track of their years together. Like many dog owners, Emily discovered that the death of a beloved dog acts as a sharp notice that a period of life has come to an end. The fact that she sent the poem to Higginson in the same note announcing Carlo's death, together with the poem's tone of pensive loss, suggest that Emily wrote "My Cricket" as an elegy for Carlo.

When Higginson read the poem, he was not sure what it meant and scribbled "insect sounds?" on his copy. He must have asked Emily to explain the meaning, because her next letter began abruptly—and somewhat impatiently: "Whom my Dog understood could not elude others." She also sent a poem that seems to compare Carlo's short life span to her longer one:

> *Except the smaller size*
> *No lives are round -*
> *These - hurry to a sphere*
> *And show and end -*
> *The larger - slower grow*
> *And later hang -*
> *The Summers of Hesperides*
> *Are long.*

Higginson may have found this poem equally baffling with its reference from Greek mythology to the Hesperides, nymphs who live in an enchanted garden where they tend the golden apples of immortality. Although such an existence may seem idyllic, Emily points out that longer lives—unlike those that "hurry to a sphere"—begin to feel slow and heavy. Another copy of this poem was found in Susan's papers. She, or at least her son Ned, apparently did connect it to Carlo because Ned, who was five or six at the time, had sketched a little picture of a dog in the margin.

In the year that followed Carlo's death, Emily wrote almost nothing. Her creativity would never again reach its previous peak; during the next five years, she would write only about seventy poems. Mourning for Carlo permeated the few letters she sent to

Higginson. He understood and respected her loss, saying, "It is hard to understand how you can live so alone with thoughts of such a quality coming up in you & even the companionship of your dog withdrawn."

In response to some question from Higginson, perhaps his oft-repeated urging "You must come down to Boston sometimes? All ladies do," Emily reminded Higginson that she was still mourning her dog: "Thank you, I wish for Carlo." She included a few lines, reminiscent of the poem she had written when Higginson left for war. Like that poem, this, too, deals with loss and seems to defend her continuing grief for her dog:

> *. . . Time is a Test of Trouble -*
> *But not a Remedy -*
> *If such it prove, it prove too*
> *There was no Malady -*

Emily said that when Carlo died, she had lost her childlike connection to creation: "Nature, seems it to myself, plays without a friend." In another short note, she told Higginson, "I explore but little since my mute Confederate," a term of endearment that recalls their early days exploring the Pelham Hills together. In light of the times she lived in, she may also have intended the word *Confederate* to suggest Carlo as a fellow rebel in Emily's stubborn refusal ever to do what was expected of her.

The last twenty years of Emily's life were quiet. Carlo's death was the first in a series of losses, followed as it was by the deaths of her father, mother, and nephew. Perhaps Carlo's death helped to prepare Emily to face the ones that came after. Emily's anxiety, which had once interfered with her ability to connect with others, had diminished. She was able to spend hours with her father as he lay dying and to attend his funeral. When her mother suffered a stroke, Emily nursed her for seven years, during which their relationship was transformed: "We were never intimate Mother and Children while she was our Mother. . . . When she became our Child, the Affection came." She opened her heart to her nephew

Gilbert, born in 1875, and wept with the heartbroken Austin and Susan when he died of typhus eight years later.

Emily never had another dog. Carlo had been her guide and companion throughout the years of her initiation from a troubled young woman to a poet who could state, "There is always one thing to be grateful for—that one is one's self & not somebody else."

On May 15, 1886, Emily died after a two-year illness probably caused by hypertension. She died in her own bed with Austin sitting beside her. Emily's last letter, written to her cousins, contained only the words "Called back," which were later carved on her tombstone. As she had asked of Lavinia, Emily's funeral service was small, with only the family and a few friends in attendance. Thomas Higginson read Emily Brontë's "No Coward Soul," first explaining that Emily had often read it aloud to Lavinia during those last weeks:

> *No coward soul is mine,*
> *No trembler in the world's storm-troubled sphere:*
> *I see Heaven's glories shine,*
> *And Faith shines equal, arming me from Fear.*

Emily had always been curious about the passage between life and death. In an early poem, she had envisioned a dog as the fitting companion for that solitary journey:

> *This Consciousness that is aware*
> *Of Neighbors and the Sun*
> *Will be the one aware of Death*
> *And that itself alone*
>
> *Is traversing the interval*
> *Experience between*
> *And most profound experiment*
> *Appointed unto Men -*
>
> *How adequate unto itself*
> *Its properties shall be*

Itself unto itself and None
Shall make discovery.

Adventure most unto itself
The Soul condemned to be—
Attended by a single Hound
Its own identity.

If Carlo were not there to accompany her as she "traversed the interval," Emily believed he would be waiting on the other side to meet her. Many years earlier, she had said to a young friend, "Gracie, do you know that I believe that the first to come and greet me when I go to heaven will be this dear, faithful, old friend Carlo?"

Chronology

EMILY DICKINSON

1830   December, birth of Emily Dickinson.

1847   Emily enrolls at Mount Holyoke Female Seminary.

1848   [December, death of Emily Brontë.]

1849   Edward Dickinson, Emily's father, acquires Carlo for her.

1850   First written mention of Carlo.

1855   November, the Dickinson family moves to the Homestead.

1856   July, marriage of Austin Dickinson, Emily's brother, to Susan Gilbert.

1856–   Emily begins an emotional crisis of unknown cause.

1861   [June, death of Elizabeth Barrett Browning.]

1862   [January, birth of Edith Wharton.]

        Emily submits four poems to Thomas Higginson.

1864   Emily starts eye treatments.

1866   January, death of Carlo.

1874   Death of Edward Dickinson.

1882   [January, birth of Virginia Woolf.]

        November, death of Emily's mother.

1883   October, death of Gilbert Dickinson, Emily's nephew, age eight.

1886   May 15, death of Emily Dickinson, age fifty-five. She is buried in the Amherst Village Cemetery.

EDITH WHARTON and FOXY, LINKY, and THE DOGS IN BETWEEN

"My little old dog:—
A heart-beat
At my feet."

EDITH WHARTON

On a bright, cold afternoon in the winter of 1865, Edith Jones, nearly four years old, walked with her father down Fifth Avenue in New York City. She was proud of her new pink-and-green plaid velvet bonnet with its grown-up veil of fine white wool, meant to protect her face from the cold, just like the ones her fashionable mother wore. As Edith gazed at the rows of brownstones, the vacant lots where cows were pastured, and the quiet Sunday sidewalks, the familiar landscape was transformed by the gossamer veil into a magical world.

The usually timid child felt safe with her small mittened hand tucked firmly in her father's large warm one. All at once, a carriage stopped, and a friend of Mr. Jones's stepped out and greeted them. Edith never forgot what happened next. As in a dream, the "snowy headed old gentleman with a red face and a spun-sugar moustache and [beard]" placed in Edith's arms a small puppy that "looked as if its coat had been woven out of the donor's luxuriant locks." Edith took in the puppy's fox-like appearance. Typical of a Spitz-type dog, he had pointed ears, a narrow nose, and a backward-curling tail. In the literal, concrete thinking of a child, she immediately decided Foxy was the perfect name.

Edith Newbold Jones, ca. 1881.

In her autobiography, *A Backward Glance*, written when she was in her seventies, Edith Wharton identified this walk with her father as one of her earliest memories. She also said that with the gift of the puppy, "a new life began for me" because, as a well-behaved little girl in a family whose highest value was conventionality, Edith had scant outlet for her strong feelings until Foxy arrived in her life. "How I loved that first 'Foxy' of mine, how I cherished and yearned over and understood him! And how quickly he relegated all dolls and other inanimate toys to the region of my everlasting indifference!" Edith credited Foxy for bringing her passions to life: "The owning of my first dog made me into a conscious sentient person, fiercely possessive, anxiously watchful, and woke in me that long ache of pity for animals, and for all inarticulate beings, which nothing has ever stilled."

By "cherishing" and "yearning over" Foxy, Edith experienced some of the intimate connection lacking in her relationship with her mother. Lucretia Rhinelander Jones came from a family with impeccable social connections but little wealth. As a young woman, she had been humiliated when she had to wear a homemade gown and her mother's too-tight satin slippers to her debutante ball. Once Lucretia married George Frederic Jones, though, her fortunes improved considerably. Her new husband was well-off, and his income from municipal real estate meant that he never had to work. As if to make up for past indignities, Lucretia indulged in such an extravagant lifestyle and became so powerful an arbiter of fashion that the phrase "keeping up with the Joneses" was coined as a wry tribute to her.

In 1862, when Edith was born, Lucretia Jones was thirty-seven and had thought her childbearing days were over. Her two sons were nearly grown, and she was absorbed in her life as a society matron, spending winters on Park Avenue, summers in Newport, and months traveling in Europe. The unplanned-for infant, with her red hair and fiery temperament, was so unlike the rest of the family that rumors began to circulate that the baby was the result of an affair between Lucretia and her sons' tutor. (This unfortunate young man, who did have red hair and was highly intelligent, died with Custer at Little Bighorn.) Biographers still disagree about Edith's biological father, but there is no doubt that George Jones treated her as his own child.

Edith grew up with a mother who seemed to resent her very existence. As an adult, Edith remarked that she had always tried to please God and her implacable mother and that God had been a much easier judge. Edith's father loved her, but he was on the boards of several charities and rarely spent time at home. With her older brothers, Frederic and Harry, usually away at school, Edith was, in effect, an only child. She was surrounded by servants and lovingly cared for by nursemaid Hannah Doyle, or "Doyley," as Edith called her. Then again, a child as sensitive as Edith knows the difference between her family and paid employees. Foxy partly made up for the emptiness in Edith's emotional life because, with him, she could be demanding, possessive, clinging, or angry—moods that upset Doyley and that Lucretia Jones would never have tolerated.

While writing *A Backward Glance*, Edith realized that her memories of the people who had once seemed so important—her "tall splendid father," her mother "in beautiful clothes," and her much-older brothers—had all faded into the background. In the foreground remained Foxy, Doyley, and the "warm cocoon" they created for her, a place where she felt sheltered and safe. Edith never found anything else—not friends, lover, husband, success as a writer, or beautiful homes—that made her feel as protected. And so she made certain that no matter where she lived or traveled, she created an intimate space made up of devoted women servants, dogs, and books.

When the Civil War drew to a close, Edith's father, like others who depended on income from their real estate holdings, decided to rent out his properties and live abroad until the American economy stabilized. Thus, in the early summer of 1866, the Jones family—

except Frederic, who remained in New York—sailed for Europe, where they would live for six years. Harry, at sixteen, was enrolled at Trinity Hall college in Cambridge, while four-year-old Edith and her parents moved on to Rome. With one exception, Edith embraced life in Europe: "For almost everything that constituted my world was still about me: my handsome father, my beautifully dressed mother, and the warmth and sunshine that were Doyley. My childish world, though so well filled, lacked completeness, for my dog Foxy had not come to Europe with us."

Rome delighted Edith. She responded immediately to its beauty, she had other children to play with, and for the first time, she had her mother's attention. Lucretia, free from the rigid routines expected of her in New York, took Edith shopping, sightseeing, and to collect mosaic fragments among the Roman ruins. Lucretia Jones even gave her little girl a nickname, "Pussy," an attempt at motherly affection that Edith seemed to appreciate. Even though she was not fond of cats, she objected neither to the nickname nor to its continued use by her husband and childhood friends when she was an adult.

Eventually, the family settled in Paris, where they leased a large apartment on the Champs-Élysées, considered at the time to be the city's most fashionable street. Among the spacious rooms was an impressive library, where Edith first discovered the joy of books. Even though she could not yet read, she fell in love with the way the leather-bound volumes looked and felt. When Mr. Jones found his daughter trying to sound out the words of *The Alhambra* by Washington Irving, he decided to teach her to read. Both enjoyed the quiet hours they spent together on this task.

Edith also became entranced with what she called "making up stories" and would stop whatever she was doing when she felt the creative urge. In vain, Lucretia would invite suitable little girls to play with her daughter. At first, Edith joined their games. Inevitably, overcome with the impulse to "make up" stories, she would lead the bewildered girls into her mother's sitting room and ask Lucretia to entertain them. Then Edith would disappear into the library, where, although she could not yet print letters, she imagined stories while paging through her father's books.

In the summer of 1870, the Joneses left the Paris apartment for what they thought would be a few weeks' stay at Bad Wildbad, a small village in the Black Forest. Lucretia wanted to take a cure in the mineral springs, so common a practice for wealthy Americans that the Black Forest was said to be another Newport. While her mother visited the springs and her father went hunting, Edith roamed the forest with Doyley and a German tutor, who began teaching Edith to speak the language by naming wildflowers, shrubs, and birds. (As an adult, Edith spoke German, French, and Italian fluently.)

Before long, though, rumors of deteriorating diplomatic relations between Prussia and France made even the pleasure-seeking Americans uneasy. Then, on July 19, 1870, France declared war on Prussia. As the Jones family prepared to flee Bad Wildbad, Edith was stricken by a sudden illness, which began with agonizing pain followed by weeks of fever and confusion.

Edith's parents were consumed with worry. The doctors in Bad Wildbad had all been mobilized into the army except one elderly physician, who was baffled by Edith's symptoms. He sent telegrams to his son—a doctor already with the troops—for advice on how to treat the gravely ill child. The confusion of war prevented an immediate reply, and Edith rapidly grew worse. Her frantic parents, learning that the Czar's physician was visiting the spa for a day, implored him to see their daughter. After examining her, he diagnosed typhoid fever and said the only recourse was to plunge the feverish child into ice water. Then he departed for the front, leaving the Joneses to oversee the treatment themselves. Mrs. Jones and Doyley undertook Edith's regimen, plunging her into freezing baths, pulling her out, and wrapping her in cold, wet sheets. The ordeal must have been as terrifying for them as it was for the child, yet it saved her life. The experience profoundly affected Edith, who later recalled, "This illness formed the dividing line between my little-childhood, and the next stage."

The "next stage" of Edith's life was characterized by irrational terrors. She was frightened of crossing thresholds and of large furry animals, including dogs if they were big ones. In addition, Edith, who would one day publish two collections of ghost stories, was at this point so terrified of such tales that she insisted she could not sleep in a room if the bookshelves contained a single one. She recalled existing in a state of constant dread, haunted day and night by "a dark indefinable menace, forever dogging my steps, lurking, and threatening." Edith's distress bewildered her and upset her family, although, in retrospect, it was a predictable reaction for a sensitive child who had come so close to death amid the threat of imminent war. Edith had not only witnessed her parents' panic but also undergone a terrifying cure at the hands of her trusted nurse and her mother.

Typhoid fever left Edith weak, fearful, and run-down. Because the Prussian and German armies were marching on Paris, the Joneses could not return to their lovely apartment. Instead, they went to Florence, where the only housing available was a large, dark, sparsely furnished hotel suite. Edith wandered forlornly in the cavernous rooms and complained constantly about missing Foxy: "His absence left such a void."

Moved by her pleas for her dog and worried by her continuing lethargy, Edith's parents, or more likely a servant, searched the city for a dog that looked like Foxy. Someone discovered an Italian version of a spitz, called the Volpino Italiano, and bought one for Edith, who promptly named it Florentine Foxy: "My parents finally gave me a Florentine lupetto, as white as Foxy, but much smaller." Once more, Edith had "a joyous companion," who raced with her down the long hallways until she felt strong enough to venture outside. Then Edith, Doyley, and Florentine Foxy would spend hours searching for violets in the Cascine gardens beside the Arno River, where Robert Browning had strolled with Flush twenty-five years earlier.

Thus began Edith's habit of turning to dogs for comfort in times of illness, loneliness, and transition. With Florentine Foxy, she also began her pattern of replacing a lost dog with one that looked as much as possible like the previous one and giving the new dog a name very like its predecessor's. As a result, the little dogs that passed through Edith's early life sometimes seem to blend together. To her parents, who had left the original Foxy in America and would leave Florentine Foxy behind in Italy, the dogs no doubt seemed interchangeable. To Edith, however, each Foxy was an individual, and she mourned the loss of each one.

In 1872, the war in Europe and the improved American economy convinced Mr. Jones that it was time to return to New York. When Edith later described sailing into New York Harbor, she insisted that even though she was only ten, "the glories of Rome and the architectural majesty of Paris" were so fresh in her mind that she was profoundly shocked at the "shameless squalor" of the city docks. Edith's longing for the beauty and culture of Europe became an enduring legacy of her childhood. As an adult, she would try to put down roots in America, but she eventually moved to Europe permanently.

Edith's dislike of New York can be blamed in part on the fact that she was given no opportunity for a formal education such as her brothers had enjoyed. Even though Edith was eager to learn and there were schools for girls in New York, the Joneses never seem to have considered sending her to one. Instead, Edith studied at home with her governess, Anna Bahlmann, who would stay on later as Edith's secretary. In *A Backward Glance*, Edith said that if it had not been for Anna and her father's library, "my mind would have starved at the age when the mental muscles are most in need of feeding."

Although Edith eventually adjusted to life in New York, she was still prey to the fears that had plagued her since her illness. The terrors persisted despite the reassuring company of Doyley, Anna, and the original Foxy, who had somewhat assuaged Edith's sorrow over leaving Florentine Foxy behind. Still, Edith regularly froze on the doorstep of the family's town house, afraid to cross the threshold, until Anna stepped forward to guide the child into her own home. Being unable to cross a threshold can be a symptom of an underlying fear of crossing over to the next stage of life, and Edith herself seemed to make this connection: "I was a 'young lady' with long skirts and my hair up before my heart ceased to beat with fear if I had to stand for half a minute on a door-step!"

One place Edith's fears never intruded was her father's library, where George Jones, delighted by his daughter's passion for reading, allowed her and Foxy free run. Lucretia, on the other hand, was not pleased by her daughter's prodigious reading. One of her maternal duties was to supervise what her daughter read to ensure that Edith remained innocent and therefore marriageable. According to Edith, her mother was far too indolent to take on such a strenuous task and simply forbade Edith to read any novels until she was married. Edith outwardly complied but had no qualms about reading the erotic poems and plays in her father's library because, strictly speaking, they were not forbidden.

When Edith was eleven, she decided that if she could not read other authors' novels, she would write her own. Lucretia would not provide her with writing paper, so Edith begged the servants for the brown wrapping from parcels delivered to the house. She spread the unwieldy sheets across the floor and wrote while crawling on her hands and knees. Still trying to earn her mother's approval, Edith proudly showed Lucretia her completed novel. She read aloud the opening lines: " 'Oh, how do you do, Mrs. Brown?' said Mrs. Tompkins. 'If only I had known you were going to call I should have tidied up the drawing-room.' " Lucretia interrupted her daughter with the icy comment "Drawing rooms are always tidy." Edith found her mother's response so "crushing" that, for several years, she abandoned novels for poetry.

During the summer, the family went to Pencraig, their home on Narragansett Bay outside Newport. Edith found life there easier than in New York, and her terrors receded. She could be a tomboy and play with the neighbor boys, swim in the bay, and ride her pony. And although her inner life of reading and making up stories still absorbed her, she learned to love the outdoors as well. Dogs were an essential part of her tomboy life: "The objective world could never lose its charm to me while it contained puppy-dogs & little boys. . . . Games in which dogs & little boys took part were the chief joy of what I may call my external life."

Until the summer she was eleven, Edith had not been close to either of her brothers, hurt by their constant teasing about her red hair and big feet and hands. In Newport, Edith had the opportunity to spend time with her next older brother, Harry, who was on vacation from his boarding school. (The oldest brother, Frederic, had married while the family was abroad and now lived in New York with his new wife.) Harry encouraged his sister's tomboy side by nicknaming her "John," and Edith reveled in his warm attention. She discovered that she and Harry both loved dogs. When one of the numerous Pencraig dogs had a litter, Harry joined Edith in romping on the lawn with the puppies. Together, they invented a contest that involved the weekly measuring of each puppy's nose to see which was longest.

In an early draft of her autobiography, which expressed her feelings with an intensity missing from the final published version, Edith looked back on this period of her life and focused on the dogs: "*Everybody* had dogs! Dogs of all ages, sizes & characters swarmed through my early years—& how I loved them." And yet Edith recognized that her response to animals was different from other children's: "I always had a deep, instinctive understanding of animals, a yearning to hold them in my arms, a fierce desire to protect them against pain & cruelty." Edith came to believe that her intense connection to animals helped her overcome the fears that had formerly paralyzed her, although she admitted that sometimes her worries about animals immobilized her almost as much as the fears had done: "I passed out of the phase of physical fear that I have just described only to be possessed by a haunting consciousness of the sufferings of animals. The feeling grew in intensity until it became a morbid preoccupation."

The statement suggests that Edith became frightened whenever she experienced intense emotion. Most children learn about feelings from their mothers. When a child has a temper tantrum or a storm of grief, the mother's calmness tells the child that such outbursts are natural and will run their course. Without the presence of a caring adult, children find strong emotions so terrifying that they try to avoid them. This helps explain why the adolescent Edith was simultaneously grateful for the feelings animals stirred in her and yet so disturbed by them that she feared for her sanity: "This lasted for years, & was the last stage of imaginative misery that I passed through before reaching a completely normal & balanced state of mind."

What helped fifteen-year-old Edith overcome her preoccupation with animals and achieve "a completely normal & balanced state of mind" was writing. She took up novel writing again with *Fast and Loose*, the romantic adventures of a debutante, but she allowed only one friend to read it. In 1878, Lucretia, without asking her daughter's permission, arranged to have a selection of Edith's poems privately published in a small volume titled *Verses*. Lucretia's motives are unclear; perhaps she hoped a private publication would satisfy Edith's literary ambitions and thereby put a stop to them. In any case, Edith was furious about the invasion of her privacy and embarrassed by *Verses*, labeling it a "folly." A year later, however, she was thrilled when "Eadgyth," a poem she herself had submitted to the *New York World*, appeared in print. Then a friend of her brother Harry showed Edith's poems to Henry Wadsworth Longfellow, and, at his recommendation, three were published in the *Atlantic Monthly* in 1880. Edith's elation over being a published poet was fleeting, because she was suddenly forced to turn her attention to becoming a debutante.

When Lucretia announced that Edith would make her debut a year earlier than usual, Edith attributed the decision to her bookishness: "When I was seventeen my parents decided that I spent too much time in reading and that I was to come out a year before the accepted age." Lucretia's decision is surprising, especially for a woman whose life was dedicated to following every nuance of the rules of etiquette. She may have thought Edith needed an extra year as a debutante because she was shy, had few friends her own age, and although a handsome girl, was not considered a beauty. More likely, Edith's parents were protecting her from knowing the more serious reason for her early debut: George Jones had begun to experience poor health and worried that he would be too ill to attend his daughter's debut if it were put off another year.

Although Edith had dreaded her debut, to her surprise she enjoyed the evening. Lucretia insisted that the ball be held in a friend's home, which had a stately ballroom, instead of one of the grand restaurants favored by the nouveaux riches, whom Lucretia despised. Edith's initial "agony of shyness" was overcome by her brother Harry and his friends, all older, self-assured, and skilled at ensuring a debutante's success. Dressed in a green brocade gown that brought out the gold highlights in her auburn hair, Edith danced every dance and was swept up in a pleasant "pink blur of emotion." That night, she learned that despite her mother's misgivings, she was capable of carrying out her role in society and could even experience pleasure in doing so. "Oh how I loved it all—my pretty frock, the flowers, the music, the sense that everybody 'liked' me, & wanted to talk to me & dance with me."

As Edith prepared for her second debutante season, her father took a turn for the worse. George Jones was losing weight, had no energy, and looked far older than his fifty-nine years. His doctor advised against another winter in New York, so the family sailed for Europe. Although Edith was worried about her father, she was pleased to be back in Europe and relieved to escape life in New York, which she described as "complete intellectual isolation—so complete that it accustomed me never to be lonely except in company." Even Edith's happiness in Newport had diminished as she grew older: "I was contented enough with swimming and riding, with my dogs, and my reading and dreaming, but I longed to travel and see new places."

The Jones family returned to Paris, where they had lived before the Franco-Prussian War. In a spontaneous gesture that showed how well he understood his daughter, George Jones bought Edith a dog, a French poodle, no doubt in honor of the country they both loved. Edith, following the same childlike logic that had led to Foxy's name, christened the white poodle Mouton, the French word for "sheep." When the weather in Paris cooled, the family moved to Cannes, which pleased Edith: "My keenest pleasure in Cannes came from my joy in the scenery & the flowers, & in the wonderful white poodle, 'Mouton,' whom my father had bought for me in Paris."

Edith adored her father, who represented to her the world of literature, and she blamed her mother for smothering whatever creative spark he once had: "I imagine there was a time when his rather rudimentary love of verse might have been developed had he had any one with whom to share it. But my mother's matter-of-factness must have shriveled up any such buds of fancy. . . . I have wondered since what stifled cravings had once germinated in him, and what manner of man he was really meant to be. That he was a lonely one, haunted by something always unexpressed and unattained, I am sure."

For a time, Mr. Jones's health seemed to improve, so the family traveled to Italy. There, her father gave Edith copies of his favorite travel writing, John Ruskin's *Stones of Venice* and *Mornings in Florence*. Together they retraced Ruskin's steps through those lovely cities. Although Edith noticed how little energy her father had on these excursions, she tried to convince herself that it was due to his age rather than illness.

During the winter of 1881, the family returned to Cannes, where Mr. Jones suffered a stroke. Even Edith could see that he was dying. Years later, she recalled the hours she spent with her father as he lay paralyzed, unable to speak: "I am still haunted by the look in his clear blue eyes, which had followed me so tenderly for nineteen years, and now tried to convey the goodbye messages he could not speak." George Jones, age sixty-one, died on March 15, 1882, and was buried in Cannes. Edith, her brother Harry, and their mother returned to America. This time, Edith's dog was not left behind: As one of her last gifts from her father, Mouton had become a living reminder of Mr. Jones's love.

After the required months of mourning, which were as carefully regulated as every other aspect of her life, Edith resumed the endless rounds of "small dinners, informal Sunday lunches and after-theatre suppers" that made up the coming-out process. As she would later describe in her novel *The House of Mirth*, the pressure to marry was considerable. Each year, another flock of debutantes entered the competition for the relatively few men who had enough wealth and social status to be considered eligible. Even the most popular debutante could quickly become an old maid.

Thus, Edith must have been relieved when Harry Stevens, whom she had met at her debutante ball and again in Cannes, proposed to her in August of 1882. By all reports a likable young man, Stevens unfortunately had a domineering mother who did not approve of her son's engagement to Edith. An imposing widow, Mrs. Stevens was considered to be nouveau riche, and she believed that Edith's mother had once snubbed her. Also, Mrs. Stevens wanted to keep control of her son's sizable inheritance, which he would receive when he married. She pressured Harry to break off the engagement, which he did in October, two months later. The local Newport paper blamed Edith: "The only reason for the breaking of the engagement hitherto existing between Harry Stevens and Miss Edith Jones is an alleged preponderance of intellectuality on the part of the intended bride. Miss Jones is an ambitious authoress, and it is said that, in the eyes of Mr. Stevens, ambition is a grievous fault." Even though the item appeared in the local, gossipy *Town Topics*, it suggests the extent of society's disdain for intellectual and ambitious women. Edith had published fewer than five poems, yet this was so unusual for a woman of her class that she was labeled an "ambitious authoress."

Edith was embarrassed and humiliated by the broken engagement, so instead of returning to Newport the next summer, she and her mother went to Bar Harbor, Maine. There, Edith met Walter

Berry, who was beginning what would prove to be a distinguished career as an international lawyer. A tall, courtly man with dark eyes and fair hair, Walter shared Edith's love of literature and encouraged her desire to be a writer. They were immediately drawn to each other; in fact, Edith may have been in love with him, although he did not propose to her (nor to anyone else, choosing to remain a bachelor). And so, four years after her debut, Edith was perilously close to becoming an old maid and spending her life with her mother.

This was Edith's rather desperate situation when Edward Wharton appeared on the Newport scene the following summer. Known as Teddy, he was a friend of her brother Harry and twelve years older than Edith. Like Edith's father, Teddy had inherited enough money so that he never had to earn a living, although he was never truly wealthy. He loved to socialize and enjoyed sports, especially hunting and fishing, and he was always ready for a game of tennis or a

Teddy Wharton with his dog Jules, ca. 1855.

sail on the bay. As a young man, Teddy was known for his sunny nature and easygoing temperament.

Edith and Teddy enjoyed the summer together in Newport. Lucretia, clearly pleased, arranged an elaborate dinner party in Teddy's honor. The courtship lasted two years, until 1885, when the confirmed bachelor finally asked Lucretia for permission to marry her daughter. Lucretia happily agreed to the proposal, and Edith seemed contented. She was comfortable with Teddy, whose affability reminded her of her brother Harry.

Edith looked forward to marriage and to being in charge of her own household. Even so, as the wedding drew closer, she became fearful, overcome "with dread of the whole dark mystery." As she later described in her more honest, unpublished autobiography, Edith went to her mother for reassurance about her wedding night: "I'm afraid, mamma—I want to know what will happen to me!" Lucretia was shocked, reminding Edith of all the statues and paintings of nudes she had seen in museums. Surely, she asked her daughter, you must have noticed "that men are—made differently from women?" When Edith continued to question her, Lucretia snapped, "For heaven's sake don't ask me any more silly questions. You can't be as stupid as you pretend!"

Edith and Teddy were married on April 29, 1885, at Trinity Chapel, New York City. Edith was twenty-three, Teddy thirty-five. The wedding was small, and Edith had no bridesmaids, a sign of her isolation considering the social set she traveled in and her numerous cousins. The wedding invitation reveals a startling oversight, which was as conspicuous in 1885 as it is today:

MRS. GEORGE FREDERIC JONES
REQUESTS THE HONOUR OF YOUR PRESENCE
AT THE MARRIAGE OF HER DAUGHTER TO
MR. EDWARD R. WHARTON
AT TRINITY CHAPEL
ON WEDNESDAY, APRIL TWENTY-NINTH
AT TWELVE O'CLOCK

Lucretia failed to include Edith's name. Such a flagrant omission demonstrates how easy it was for Lucretia Jones to overlook her daughter.

Edith's anxiety about the sexual aspect of marriage proved justified. She and Teddy did not consummate their marriage for weeks, and within a few years, they had apparently settled into a sexless marriage. Furthermore, while they seemed to have much in common because of their similar family backgrounds, Edith soon realized they were seriously mismatched intellectually. Her interests in literature, art, and architecture bored Teddy, and he felt ill at ease among her clever friends.

In the early years of her marriage, however, Edith was able to ignore these problems as she and Teddy stepped into the roles expected of them as a young married couple in Newport society. Teddy resumed his life of parties and sports and Edith the tedious rounds of calls that took up most of a married woman's day. Until they could afford their own home, the newlyweds lived on the grounds of Lucretia's estate, in a small but charming cottage. Edith set up housekeeping under the direction of Catherine Gross, who had formerly been Edith's personal maid and who had taken the place of Doyley, long since retired. As Edith's housekeeper, the indispensable Gross, as Edith called her, firmly guided the young wife in setting up a smoothly ordered household. Gross would continue this task until her death nearly fifty years later.

One of the Whartons' few shared interests was dogs; right from the start, Edith and Teddy's cottage was full of them. One photograph shows Teddy sitting on horseback holding his dog Jules in front of him. Poor Jules, a tough-looking, shaggy black terrier, had to accept the dominance of the poodle Mouton and tolerate the antics of Edith's two new dogs, long-haired Chihuahuas named Mimi and Miza. Chihuahuas, the smallest dogs in the world, were quite rare in America at that time; they caused a sensation when they first appeared at a dog show in New York in 1884, just a year before the Whartons' wedding. Edith was proud of them, dressing them in jeweled collars and even having a set of studio portraits taken with

Edith with Mimi and Miza, her Chihuahuas, 1890.

them. In one, Miza and Mimi perch on Edith's shoulders and peer around her elaborate hat to glare at the photographer.

In 1888, the Whartons shocked both their families by using their entire income for a year to take a four-month cruise on the Mediterranean and Aegean. When their yacht, the *Vanadis*, docked in Athens, they collected their mail. Teddy was amused to see that Edith had a stronger reaction to learning about the death of one of her dogs than to news she had been named as an heir of a distant relative. Edith's account does not specify which dog had died, only a "little dog we left in America," but it might well have been Mouton, who disappears from Edith's letters and from family photographs about this time. Because Mouton was forever linked to Edith's father, news of the dog's death would have reawakened grief for him, overshadowing the announcement of an unexpected inheritance.

The legacy, which was substantial, came to Edith from her father's second cousin, a recluse whom she never knew. The money enabled the Whartons to rent a small house on Madison Avenue in New York City and to buy a rambling home in Newport called Land's End, which was perched on a bluff above the Atlantic Ocean and as far from Lucretia as possible while still remaining in New-port. The young couple had begun the financial pattern that would characterize their marriage: Edith provided most of the money and decided how it would be spent; Teddy helped her carry out her plans. He was said to have always carried one thousand dollars in case "Puss wanted anything."

Teddy loved Newport's social whirl, but Edith often stayed be-hind at their house in New York. There, spending hours with only Catherine Gross and the two Chihuahuas, she began to write again. She submitted poems to three magazines (enclosing her calling card, just as Emily Dickinson had with the first poems she sent to Thomas Higginson) and waited anxiously for a response: "As long as I live I shall never forget my sensations when I opened the first of the three letters and learned that I was to appear in print. I can still see the narrow hall, the letter-box out of which I fished the let-ters." When she read that all three poems had been accepted for publication, Edith was so excited that she ran up and down the flight of stairs over and over again with Mimi and Miza barking in-cessantly at her heels.

Buoyed by the recognition of her poems, Edith energetically began her next project, remodeling Land's End, replacing its dark, cluttered rooms with light, airy ones that emphasized the views of the sea. Edith, who was already a self-educated expert on European art and architecture, was eager to put her ideas about interior de-sign to work. She hired Ogden Codman, an up-and-coming New-port architect, to draw up the plans and oversee the project. They worked so well together that they decided to collaborate on a book, *The Decoration of Houses.* As Edith struggled to condense pages of research, drawings, and blueprints into a smooth narrative, she turned for advice to her friend Walter Berry, who was visiting that summer. According to Edith, he guided her into making a "lump into a book." The "lump" became a surprise bestseller in 1897 and launched Edith's reputation as a serious writer.

While working on *The Decoration of Houses,* Edith developed the writing ritual she followed until her last days. She began first thing in the morning, after Gross brought her a cup of tea. Then, sitting up in bed with Mimi and Miza tucked in beside her, Edith worked for several hours on an improvised writing board. Wearing an elegant dressing gown sometimes draped with a shawl, Edith was free of the constraining stays and layers of elaborate clothing she would wear for the rest of the day. She wrote rapidly, using her best stationery, and she scattered the finished pages on the floor for Gross to pick up later. Houseguests were warned by a gracious note that their hostess would not be available until noon.

The image of Edith writing alone in her bedroom brings to mind her often-quoted comparison of a woman to a house, which appears in "The Fullness of Life," one of her first stories: "I have sometimes thought that a woman's nature is like a great house full of rooms: there is the hall, through which everyone passes in going in and out; the drawing room, where one receives formal visits; the sitting room, where the members of the family come and go . . . but beyond that, far beyond, are other rooms, the handles of whose doors perhaps are never turned; no one knows the way to them, no one knows whither they lead; and in the innermost room, the holy of holies, the soul sits alone and waits for a footstep that never comes." Edith apparently felt she had revealed too much about herself and her marriage in "The Fullness of Life." She later derided it as "one long shriek" and refused to include it in any collection of her short stories. She was as zealous about guarding her own "innermost room" of emotions as she was about keeping her early morning writing hours sacred.

Throughout the 1890s, when Edith was in her thirties, she endured months of ill health, apparently brought on by unhappiness with her marriage and insecurity about writing fiction. She found Teddy's intellectual limitations difficult to bear; also, as her unpublished memoir reveals, she felt the lack of a sexual relationship. She appears wan and thin in photographs; her letters are filled with accounts of breathing difficulties, loss of appetite, and constant fatigue. As she struggled to emerge from her illness, Edith found solace in the poetry of Walt Whitman. He understood, as she did,

the comfort offered by animals. In her notebook, she copied out
this verse from Whitman's "Song of Myself":

> *I think I could turn and live with animals, they are so placid*
> *and self-contained,*
> *I stand and look at them long and long.*

Some biographers believe Edith suffered a nervous breakdown
and underwent a rest cure in Philadelphia. Others think her illness
was a result of creative intensity, since she subsequently reported
similar symptoms whenever she finished a book. Edith's own account of her illness can be found in a 1908 letter to her childhood
friend Sally Norton, to whom Edith sometimes revealed emotional
turmoil that she hid from others. Edith describes her experience of
"neurasthenia," which today would be considered a type of psycho-
somatic illness: "For *twelve* years I seldom knew what it was to be,
for more than an hour or two of the twenty four, without an intense
feeling of nausea, & such unutterable fatigue that when I got up I
was always more tired than when I lay down. This form of neurasthenia consumed the best years of my youth, & left, in some sort, an
irreparable shade on my life. Mais quoi! I worked through it, &
came out on the other side."

Edith worked through her illness by traveling, writing, and creating a home; for Wharton, these would always be reliable defenses
against depression. She immersed herself in her first novel, *The Valley of Decision*, drawing upon her childhood memories of Italy, the
trips she and Teddy had taken there, and the research she had done
for *The Decoration of Houses*. Set in eighteenth-century Italy, the
novel seems far removed from Edith's own life and was thus less
painful for her to write than her short stories, which are filled with
unhappy marriages.

Published in 1902, when Edith was forty, *The Valley of Decision*
was successful and well reviewed, primarily for its lavish historical
background rather than its stilted characters. Henry James, the
renowned American writer who made his home in England, wrote
to congratulate her and to admonish her about her next novel:

"Don't pass it by—the immediate, the real, the only. . . . *Do New York!*" The letter marked the beginning of a deep and abiding friendship and planted the seed for *The House of Mirth*, in which Edith would give an insider's view of Old New York. Thus, Henry James joined Walter Berry in the group of clever, intellectual men whom Edith called her inner circle. Eventually, the circle would include, among others, writer Percy Lubbock, Oxford don Gaillard Lapsley, and art critic Bernard Berenson. Edith came to count on these men for advice and support to the degree that, over time, they acted almost as a composite husband for her.

Edith had decided it was time to leave Newport, with its damp climate and constant social demands. In 1901, after searching for just the right property, she and Teddy bought 113 acres in Lenox, Massachusetts, in the Berkshires, where his family had often summered. There, Edith designed an elegant house, which she named The Mount in honor of her great-grandfather's former estate on Long Island. Ebenezer Stevens had been a hero of the Revolutionary War and later made a fortune as an East India merchant. Although General Stevens's Mount was gone before Edith's time, she had learned some of its details from her mother and incorporated several ideas for her own Mount, including colorful tiled mantels from Italy and tubs of orange trees on the terrace.

Soon after the purchase, Edith received word that her mother had died in Paris, where she had gone to live with her son Frederic after his divorce. Even though the Whartons traveled in Europe for months every year, they had rarely visited Lucretia. Edith wore mourning for her mother but seemed unaffected by her death. Teddy, who was already in Europe when Lucretia died, attended her funeral; Edith, however, remained in Lenox overseeing construction of The Mount.

Edith might not have grieved for her mother, but she was reduced to helpless tears when Mimi, one of the Chihuahuas, died seven months later. Edith was surprised by the intense grief she felt for her dog. She wrote to Sally Norton, also a dog lover, "Poor little Mimi died, our dear little dog, who had given us eight years of rich unflagging gaiety & affection & we've all been crying ever since. You will understand." Mimi's body was taken to The Mount, where she was buried in a small cemetery that still stands on a hillside covered with periwinkle and sheltered by shade trees. The Pet Cemetery, as it is now known, was carefully located on a hill west of the garden, where it could be seen from both Edith's library and her sitting room. Four gravestones remain, including the first: "Died in January 1902—Mimi."

After Mimi's death, Edith took consolation in her work, turning her attention to *The House of Mirth*. She also kept a worried eye on Miza, the surviving Chihuahua, and on Teddy's Jules, still able to outrun little Miza but definitely slowing down: "Miza looks younger than ever but old Jules is very rheumatic." Edith never waited long after one of her dogs died to find a successor. This time, the new addition was a saucy white Papillon with a black patch over one eye and black ears. He was named Mitou, supposedly Edith's French version of "Me, too!" the cry she imagined she heard him bark if Jules and Miza were fed first. If one Papillon was a good idea, Edith must have thought two would be even better. So Nicette, who had almost exactly the same markings as Mitou, joined the other dogs.

Edith may have chosen Papillons because, with their curled tails and pointed noses, they resembled a Spitz, calling to mind her two Foxys. It is possible that Edith discovered the breed during her extensive research on Italian art for *The Valley of Decision*, since Papillons, once known as Italian Toy Spaniels, often appear in early Italian frescoes. They are also found in the Venetian artist Titian's works. The endearing red-and-white puppy sleeping at the feet of the *Venus of Urbino* is an especially popular example.

At The Mount, Edith and Teddy came as close as they ever would to a conventional family life, with dogs taking the place of children. There was a silk pillow for their pets under the table in the formal dining room and dog beds in front of many of the fireplaces. When the Whartons went to lunch at Sagamore Hill, the country home of Theodore Roosevelt, Edith noted that President

Roosevelt also considered "family [to be] a term which, as in my own house, always included two or three busy and extremely interested dogs." Edith's houseguests learned straightaway that dogs were an integral part of life at The Mount. As visitors made their way up the winding drive, they saw Edith waiting to greet them, holding a Papillon or Chihuahua in her arms. Walter Berry, a regular guest, treated the dogs in a cavalier manner, once holding a nervous Mitou high in the air to pose for a picture. Walter, who liked his independence, never objected to the affection Edith showered on her dogs, perhaps in relief that it was not directed at him.

During his rare visits to America, Henry James would arrange to stay at The Mount. Edith loved to listen to him tell stories or read poetry aloud as they sat on the terrace overlooking her gardens. One warm summer night, James recited "Remembrance," his favorite poem by Emily Brontë. James's deep voice echoed across the Berkshire Hills as he chanted over and over the haunting opening line: "Cold in the earth—and the deep snow piled above thee." Edith carefully copied the poem, then folded it and put it among her private papers, where she kept it for the rest of her life.

During the day, James would complain about the New England heat and Edith's relentless schedule of activities, but never about her dogs. He appreciated their place in Edith's life, especially their ability to calm what he called her "deranging and desolating, ravaging, burning and destroying energy." Henry James himself was so fond an owner of Dachshunds that he understood perfectly Edith's love for her little companions. Like her, Henry James expected his guests to appreciate his dogs as much as he did. In a letter to a friend, he describes Max, one of a succession of his Dachshunds, as "the best & gentlest & most reasonable & well-mannered as well as most beautiful small animal of his kind to be easily come across—so that I think you will speedily find yourselves loving him for his own sweet sake."

Besides maintaining an amused affection for Edith's dogs, Henry James appreciated what he considered her European style of hospitality. On the other hand, some guests found Edith's lifestyle too exacting, especially the way she carefully planned every drive, picnic, and dinner. One guest described the weary hours spent searching for the perfect picnic site: "There must be a view, shelter from the wind, shade if required, a 'back' to lean against, a flat place for a basket." One of the Norton sisters, who lived nearby and often visited The Mount, said the house was "perfect but cold; perfection of a kind [that] leaves coldness—there was never the sound of young and ardent feet, of romping dogs (though dogs she always had and *loved* but they were Papillons or Pekingese)."

Many of Edith's other friends also thought her toy breeds were inferior to big "romping dogs," although no one ever said so to her face. The small dogs, always affectionate, easy to carry and cuddle, clearly took the place of the children Edith would never have. She always kept private her feelings about not having children, but she expressed her sadness indirectly in a letter of congratulations to her niece who was about to be married: "And if you have a boy or girl, to prolong the joy so much the better. Be sure it's worthwhile. *And times come when one would give anything in the world for a reason like that for living on.*" Only in her final years did Edith openly admit to a few close friends her "great grief" over her childlessness.

An inveterate traveler, Edith crisscrossed the Atlantic sixty or seventy times, inspiring Henry James to call her "the pendulum woman." Ostensibly to research her well-received travel books— *Italian Villas and Their Gardens* and *Italian Backgrounds*—and to expand her circle of literary friends, Edith also used travel as a way to avoid being alone with Teddy. Nevertheless, she found the upheaval of these frequent voyages upsetting. Every time she prepared to go abroad, she experienced a mix of anticipation at returning to Europe and anguish over leaving her dogs behind, even though she made careful arrangements for them, once even renting a separate brownstone for the dogs and their caretakers: "The little dogs are settled in Park Ave with Bahlmann [her secretary] and the cook, & seem very happy, but I am not going to see them again before sailing because it would only make them unsettled."

In 1903, Edith decided she would take Mitou with her to Europe, which proved to be a great success. The perky Papillon appears in numerous photographs of the Whartons and their friends as they motored through Italy. In one photo, he sits on the chauffeur's lap; in another, he's in the back with Edith, peeking out of her fur muff. In yet another snapshot, he poses on an Italianate terrace with his tail held high. Edith added messages from Mitou on postcards she sent from Florence: "Mitou sends you his best love." Edith was so devoted to her little dog that she refused to have him quarantined. At that time, England, in an effort to control rabies, required all dogs (and almost all animals) to spend six months in quarantine at a government pound before they would be allowed to enter the country. Edith's outrage over this law is clear in a letter she wrote to Alfred Austin, poet laureate of England, whom she and Teddy had planned to visit: "We hope to be in London by the end of April if I can find any lawful or unlawful way of taking into your cruel country a very small & dear dog whom I cannot possibly leave to himself on the continent, since he has never yet deserted me in a difficulty! When is that barbarous law to be repealed?"

No matter how extensive her travel and entertaining, Edith continued to write every morning. In the spring of 1905, *The House of Mirth* was published to immediate success. The story of Lily Bart, a beautiful young woman unable to break free of the limitations imposed by Old New York, was clearly based on aspects of Edith's life. Her protagonist even displayed Edith's old fear of crossing thresholds, here clearly symbolizing an inability to become an adult. *The House of Mirth* sold one hundred thousand copies in two months and was reviewed as a groundbreaking American novel. Emily Dickinson's former mentor Thomas Higginson, now eighty-two, announced that *The House of Mirth* seemed "to stand at the head of all American fiction, save Hawthorne alone." Edith gloried in her success, keeping careful track of sales figures and demanding higher royalties for her next books.

Even though she enjoyed her new status as a celebrity, Edith was soon overcome by the exhaustion and breathing problems that always followed the publication of a book. She decided to recuperate at a spa in Italy, so the Whartons set sail for Europe. This time, they took the younger Papillon, Nicette, with them. On the passage over, Edith noticed a dark spot on Nicette's thigh and called for the ship's doctor, who was surely not accustomed to treating dogs. The doctor, in Edith's opinion "a stupid creature," dismissed Nicette's injury, which became worse. When they reached Paris, Edith found a veterinarian who diagnosed Nicette's wound as a burn caused by an electric wire or by some contact with acid. All travel plans, including her treatments at the spa, were canceled as Edith nursed Nicette "like a baby, for the poor little creature has been quite helpless, & is only now able to walk." Nicette recovered, but Edith admitted the ordeal left her unnerved, explaining, "The slightest interruption in the household routine completely de-rails me."

Once Nicette recovered, the Whartons wanted to visit Henry James in England, but Edith would never put a dog in quarantine, much less one who had suffered as Nicette had. When her brother Harry offered to keep Nicette in his Paris town house, Edith was surprised and pleased. She had not seen Harry in years, so the dog offered a way for them to reconnect, just as measuring puppies' noses had once done in those long-ago Newport summers. Edith was relieved Nicette would be with a family member, but she still missed her "beyond words!"

After Edith's distraught response to Nicette's injury, she began to travel with two dogs, maybe to assure herself that no matter what, she would always have at least one with her. For their subsequent European travels, the Wharton entourage included everything and everybody Edith could possibly need to feel at home. Neither she nor Teddy seemed to care about the expense, as Teddy casually reported: "Our experiment of taking . . . six servants, two dogs, our motor [car] & chauffeur, cook, has worked out perfectly."

Returning to America was as difficult for the adult Edith as it had been for the child. She was still repelled by the ugliness of American cities when compared with the beauty she saw in Europe: "My first few weeks in America are always miserable, because the tastes I am cursed with are all of a kind that cannot be gratified here." Once back at The Mount, though, "restored by the dear dogs and horses and our own woods," Edith felt at home, as much as she ever could in her native country. As frequent travel continued to characterize the Whartons' existence, their dogs added emotional intensity to the constant round of homecomings and departures: "Teddy arrived on Wednesday evening. . . . Jules' first ecstasy was worked off at the Pittsfield station, so I didn't see it, but Mitou turned somersaults for joy when he saw his master."

As Edith became well known as a writer, Teddy came to resent her success even as he depended on her earnings. Eventually, he felt more and more like an outsider in his own home. Edith loved fast-paced, amusing conversation sprinkled with literary allusions, and she regularly jumped up to take books off the shelf to check quotations. Teddy was keenly aware that he could not keep up: "I am no good on Puss's high plane of thought." He felt excluded by Edith's guests, who recalled the awkward silences that fell when he walked into a room.

Far more disturbing than his intellectual limitations, however, were the signs of Teddy's mental deterioration, which began around 1900 with symptoms of what today would be called a bipolar disorder. His formerly agreeable temperament gave way to fits of rage over minor problems such as small household bills or troubles with the cars. As his outbursts became more virulent, neither Teddy's family nor Edith herself seemed able to face the fact that he was suffering from the same mental illness as his father, who had been institutionalized for years and had committed suicide in 1891. Other people, though, including the decorator Ogden Codman, recognized how seriously ill Teddy was before Edith did. Codman wrote to his mother, "Teddy Wharton seems to be losing his mind which makes it very hard for his wife." Edith found Teddy's behavior exhausting, but she was determined to help him, to find activities that would interest him.

An attempt to engage Teddy's interests might explain Edith's uncharacteristic decision to become involved in the politics of the New York SPCA. Whatever the reason, during the winter of 1906, both

Whartons joined a group of SPCA members who were demanding the resignation of the director. The group charged that dogs in the New York shelter were being euthanized because killing them was less expensive than finding them homes. Edith's speech, mentioned in *The New York Times*, could have been an emotional appeal based on the plight of the dogs. Instead, it was a straightforward account of the troubled financial state of the SPCA: Her businesslike approach to the fate of the euthanized dogs is a good example of the way Edith coped with any painful circumstances over which she had no control, including Teddy's mental illness and, later, the chaos of wartime France.

At the same time as Edith was speaking publicly against euthanasia, she had to decide what to do about her little Chihuahua Miza, who was suffering terribly from a tumor. Even though Edith had passionately defended the shelter dogs' "natural right to a natural death," she believed just as strongly that compassion sometimes required ending a dog's life. Edith wrote in her diary, "Little Miza's tumor became so bad that we had her chloroformed.—She was with us 13 years, & always a joy to us." Writing the sad news to Sally Norton, "We had to snuff out our little Miza," Edith described Mitou's farewell to his companion: "Mitou kissed her prettily." On the following day, Edith's diary entry said simply: "Beautiful day—All very sad about Miza." Soon another gravestone was placed in the Pet Cemetery at The Mount: "Died January 12, 1906—Miza."

After Miza's death, Edith and Teddy focused on the aging Jules. In February of 1907, Teddy wrote to a friend, "My old dog Jules, at 16 yrs. old is wonderfully well at—The Moment." Nine months after Teddy wrote that note, however, Jules died. Both Whartons appreciated Henry James's letter of condolence, written with his customary sprinkling of French phrases and his usual tongue-in-cheek style. James expressed his sorrow about Jules's death as well as affectionate concern for the surviving dogs, Mitou and Nicette: "Yet forgive me so freely breaking into a house of mourning. I received the faire-part of ces messieurs & ces dames on the subject of the late venerable & lamented Jules only a day or two after I had—& at some length—

written you—whereby I rather hung back from a fresh effusion. But won't you kindly represent me *aupres de ces dames* especially. Nicette's sense of bereavement must lend her deportment an imitable shade, but for Mitou I fear the morbid—the morbid being so his danger. Combat it by every art that your psychological *maitrise* may suggest. But ce cher grand Jules—I'm sure he passed away in the grand style."

A year later, Edith was still reliving "my poor Jules' last hours & farewell looks." He was the last Wharton dog buried at The Mount and the last dog to belong to both husband and wife. Unlike the other gravestones in the Pet Cemetery, which simply give the pet's name and date of death, Jules's stone reads, "Our Friend Jules 1891–1907," a tribute to the love both Edith and Teddy felt for him.

As the Wharton's marriage disintegrated, *The House of Mirth* continued to be a bestseller. Edith's literary earnings now far surpassed those of her mentor, Henry James, and would eventually exceed even her inherited wealth. Translated into French, *The House of Mirth* enjoyed a success abroad that ensured Edith would be accepted in Parisian literary circles, where Teddy, who spoke no French, was utterly out of place. Although any hopes she might have had for a happy marriage had died, Edith had created a rich intellectual life with her friends, especially Henry James, Walter Berry, and Bernard Berenson. But in spite of her success as a writer and her many close friendships, Edith believed that at her core, she was numb, "a self that never believed in its chance of having any warm personal life, like other, luckier people."

In Paris in the winter of 1907, Edith met Morton Fullerton, the Paris correspondent for the London *Times*. He was "a dashing well-tailored man with large Victorian moustaches and languid eyes, a bright flower in his button-hole." Edith found him "mysterious," responding to his sexual charisma, which attracted both men and women, and to his intelligence and wit. Morton Fullerton was a fascinating, urbane conversationalist, and Edith felt he understood her as no one ever had before. In one of her first letters to him, she quoted a phrase from Emerson: "The moment my eyes fell on him I was content."

Morton Fullerton's original home was in Lenox, near The Mount, where he visited Edith the following October. As they motored through the Berk-shires, a sudden snow-storm forced them to pull over so that the chauffeur could put chains on the tires. While Edith and Ful-lerton smoked ciga-rettes and waited, they discovered witch hazel—a common New England shrub that does not set out its yellow flowers until its leaves have fallen— blooming through the snow. A week later, Morton enclosed a sprig of the plant in his thank-you note.

Morton Fullerton in Paris, ca. 1908.

Edith, recognizing the flower as "the old woman's flower—the flower that blooms in autumn," realized that finally, "after so long!" she had met a man who understood her. In her journal, Edith made this entry: "You sent the wych—hazel—& sent it without a word— thus telling me (as I choose to think!) that you knew what was in my mind when I found it blooming on that wet bank in the woods."

Edith, who was forty-five when the romance began, had never known sexual passion. Morton Fullerton, at forty-two, had a com-plicated sexual life, the extent of which Edith never fully learned.

Besides numerous dalliances with women, he had had several homosexual relationships, including an erotic—albeit celibate—liaison with Henry James. While involved with Edith, he was married to a French singer, although they had separated. The same week he gave Edith the witch hazel, he became engaged to a cousin who had been raised as his sister, and all the while he was being blackmailed by a former lover. Edith worried that she lacked Morton Fullerton's sexual experience, but she refused to allow that to stand between them: "The way you've spent your emotional life, while I've . . . hoarded mine, is what puts the great gulf between us. . . . And I'm so afraid that the treasures I long to unpack for you, that have come to me in magic ships from enchanted islands, are only, to you the familiar red calico & beads of the clever trader, who has had dealings in every latitude, & knows just what to carry . . . to please the simple native."

Edith's relationship with Morton Fullerton continued intermittently from the spring of 1908 until the summer of 1910, with moments of intimacy and sexual pleasure, followed by days and sometimes months spent waiting for him to write or visit. Her appointment diary is filled with references to him written in German, in order to keep them hidden from Teddy and the servants. She writes of unforgettable hours walking in the woods, taking carriage rides, or just talking. Once he stole into her box at the theater: "He was there . . . for one act—Oh god—god." Other entries seem to refer to sexual encounters: "We were together. *The sweetest hours of my life.*" Edith had finally experienced sexual passion, and she never regretted it: "I have drunk of the wine of life at last, I have known the thing best worth knowing, I have been warmed through & through, never to grow quite cold again till the end."

After the affair ended, Edith, like most of Morton Fullerton's lovers, continued to think well of him, and she wrote to him for the rest of her life. After her death, he said of Edith, "She was not only a great lady, but also a great woman. . . . In love she had the courage of [a] savage. She was fearless, reckless even." Perhaps even more important to Edith than her sexual awakening was her belief that

Morton had truly understood her most private self. He had entered "the innermost room, the holy of holies, where the soul sits alone and waits for a footstep that never comes."

While Edith's attention had been focused on Fullerton, Teddy had been embezzling money from her trust fund. He spent recklessly on cars, an apartment in Boston for his mistress, and solid gold garters for his stockings. Eventually, he would make full restitution from his own inheritance; however, when Edith learned about the embezzlement, she declared she could no longer trust him to manage their finances. Nor could she endure any longer Teddy's indifference to the world of ideas that she had been able to share with Fullerton. This became painfully clear to Edith through an innocuous incident that took place one afternoon as the Whartons were driving to The Mount. She pointed out an interesting passage in a book she was reading, and Teddy replied, "Does that sort of thing really amuse you?" His comment enraged Edith. Later she wrote in her journal that as she listened to her husband, "I heard the key turn in my prison-lock. . . . Oh, gods of derision! And you've given me over twenty years of it!"

By 1910, Teddy was completely unstable. Edith consulted neurologists, she arranged for Teddy to be treated at sanitariums in both America and Europe, but he did not recover. No medication was available at that time for his type of mental illness. Edith tried everything she could think of to keep him occupied. She arranged hunting and sightseeing trips for him, hiring companions if she could not persuade friends to accompany him. But Teddy did not want to leave Edith's side. His moods cycled between bouts of depression, when he stayed in bed, and manic episodes, such as the night he arrived unannounced at the home of friends: "He was dressed like a roaring blade of 20; he talked incessantly about himself, his health, his clothes, and his purchases, and is as mad as a March hare." Although Edith never admitted being afraid of Teddy, her friends, especially Henry James and Walter Berry, worried about his potential for violence and warned her never to be alone with him.

Teddy's doctors believed his moods would stabilize if he and Edith spent more time at The Mount, but after her stimulating life in Paris, Edith now felt suffocated there. Her novel *Ethan Frome*, written during the collapse of her marriage, is permeated with a mood of hopeless entrapment that suggests her inner despair. Being with Morton had ruined Edith's tolerance for life with Teddy: "I had created a world of my own, in which I loved without heeding what went on outside. But since I have known what it was to have some one enter into that world & live there with me, the mortal solitude I came back to has become terrible."

The end of the Whartons' marriage came during the hot, humid summer of 1911. Edith and Teddy had dreadful arguments about selling The Mount, followed by painful scenes in which Teddy begged "Puss" to let him manage the household funds again. Although Edith wrote desperate letters to Morton, who was staying with his family in Lenox, he made excuses and never came to see her. Henry James did visit The Mount, but he left a few days after witnessing several confrontations between Edith and Teddy. He wrote to Gaillard Lapsley, one of their close friends, "The violent and scenic Teddy is negotiable, in a measure, but the pleading, suffering, clinging, helpless Teddy is of course a very awful and irreducible quantity indeed."

That autumn, as Edith prepared to return to Paris, she and Teddy finally decided to sell The Mount. Teddy agreed not to proceed with the sale while Edith was at sea, and so Edith, accompanied by Gross, Mitou, and Nicette, was able to rest on the voyage as she tried to recover from the long, draining summer. She was therefore stunned on her arrival in Paris to receive a telegram with the news that Teddy had sold The Mount.

That winter of 1911, Mitou suffered a heart attack. Edith turned to Morton Fullerton for comfort, even though their affair was over, because he understood what her dog meant to her. She dashed off a postcard to him with the news: "I know you'll be sorry—objectively—when I tell you that your little old Mitou has had a sudden violent heart attack, which *un*luckily didn't quite snuff him out; but will probably overshadow his few remaining months. The devoted Roussel (Nicette's wonderful surgeon) is here working over him now, & his little field-mouse 'cheep' has driven me into another room, quite unmanned!—He has seen me through so many difficult days, and does love life so!" As expected, Mitou did not survive the heart attack.

Just as Edith had found it easier to mourn the death of a dog than the death of her mother, now her grief for Mitou included her sorrow over the loss of The Mount, her ruined marriage, and the ending of her affair with Fullerton. Once again, as he had at the death of Jules, Henry James wrote Edith a note of sympathy, remembering not only the dog that died but the surviving dog as well: "Poor dear little world-worn Mitou, qui avait vu tant de choses [who had seen so much] with those wise, those so disillusioned old eyes of his—& hadn't a single illusion left—unlike Nicette. . . . What a little past-away Person!—& what a little personal loss. They are intense personal losses."

On April 16, 1913, a French court granted Edith a divorce on the grounds of Teddy's adultery, thus ending her twenty-eight-year marriage. Teddy eventually returned to Boston to live with his sister Nancy, then was cared for by a nurse until he died in 1928, at the age of seventy-nine. When she learned of his death, Edith responded, "It is a happy release, for the real Teddy went years ago."

Although she was a celebrated novelist and accepted in literary circles, Edith would always be considered an outsider in Paris. She spoke fluent French, although it was, as someone noted, the French of Louis XIV. Edith stood stiffly at social gatherings and would visibly "draw herself up" when confronted with rudeness or stupidity. She was said to walk like "a full-rigged ship under sail, with an eye for every detail." Edith's haughty manner had evolved out of her shyness as a young woman and became a fixed trait that was emphasized by her exquisite attire. Her dresses, made in Paris of the most beautiful fabrics, were usually in shades of muted browns and greens, with old-fashioned bodices of eighteenth-century Venetian lace inherited from her mother. She wore hats with veils and feathers, gloves of the softest leather, and in winter, she carried a mink muff, which was replaced in spring by umbrellas made in London according to her strict specifications.

Matilda Gay, another expatriate whom Edith had known as a child in Newport, recalled Edith as "a nervous, rather fussy hostess" who smoked gold-tipped cigarettes from England and ate little. She often encouraged her guests to engage in "intellectual fencing matches," goading them on with jeering laughter. However, when the two of them were alone, Edith was transformed into an interested, warm companion. When Matilda's dog Poilu died, Edith's note to her expressed the emotion she rarely showed in public: "I feel for you with all my dog-like heart, dearest Matilda, and thank you for knowing that I was the friend to turn to the day that Poilu went."

Alone in Paris, Edith worked on *The Reef* and *The Custom of the Country*, both of which depict affairs, betrayals, and divorces. She tried to ignore the stories that were circulating about her divorce, Teddy's escapades, and her rumored romance with Walter Berry. She became the focus of even more unpleasant talk when her brother Harry broke off relations with her because he thought she disapproved of his engagement to a Russian countess. Edith was grateful, therefore, that her affair with Morton remained a secret, although she worried that people would learn of it. (As it turned out, their liaison was not discovered until years after Edith's death.)

To escape the rumors and her lonely apartment, Edith spent the next fifteen months in constant travel. Friends braced themselves for her visits, which always included "a good deal of commotion . . . & the usual trail of hectic telephone and telegraph messages. Dear Edith cannot live without it." She was often accompanied by Walter Berry, who had retired to Paris after serving for many years as an international judge in Cairo. Edith tried to persuade Henry James to join them, but he was reluctant to leave his writing and the quiet of his English country house. The names he came up with for Edith convey the effect that her restlessness had on him, especially as his health deteriorated: "The whirling princess, the golden eagle, the Fire Bird, the Shining One, the angel of desolation . . . the historic ravager." Yet James never lost his admiration for Edith, writing to one of her new acquaintances, "Ah . . . you have made friends with EW. I congratulate you. You may find her difficult, but you will find nothing stupid in her and nothing small."

Edith's friendship with the art critic Bernard Berenson and his wife, Mary, deepened during these months as she often visited I Tatti, their magnificent villa in Florence. At afternoon tea, other guests were distracted by Edith's practice of holding Nicette on her lap and letting the dog sip from her teacup, but the Berensons simply laughed and even came to enjoy Nicette's company. In the summer of 1913, Edith and Bernard toured Germany together. Edith reported back to Mary that Bernard had "learned several useful things that appear to have been omitted from his earlier education," such as asking for directions, going briskly through art museums, and "letting Nicette sit on his lap when she feels like it."

Edith was traveling in Spain with Walter Berry on June 28, 1914, when Archduke Francis Ferdinand, heir to the Austro-Hungarian empire, was assassinated in Sarajevo, thus igniting World War I. Edith and Walter returned immediately to Paris, where they joined in efforts to persuade the United States to enter the war, Edith in her role as a celebrated American author and Walter as president of the American Chamber of Commerce in Paris.

In the midst of wartime's chaos, Edith continued to work on novels and another collection of short stories, now with a decidedly propagandist flavor. She also wrote *Fighting France*, which began with the mobilization of Paris. Many writers would try to convey the mix of fear and excitement that characterized Paris in those weeks, but only Edith would include the Parisian dogs in her description of a crowd of civilians seeing off the first French troops on a night in August 1914: "I remember especially the steady-browed faces of the women; and also the small but significant fact that every one of them had remembered to bring her dog. . . . Every one that was portable was snugly lodged in the bend of an elbow, and from this safe perch scores and scores of small serious muzzles, blunt or sharp, smooth or wooly, brown or grey or white or black or brindled, looked out on the scene with the quiet awareness of the Paris dog. It was certainly a good sign that they had not been forgotten that night."

For the first time in her life, Edith had sufficient outlets for her tremendous energy. Using her organizational skills and calling on support from her wealthy friends in Europe and America, Edith established workrooms for unemployed seamstresses, founded the American Hostels for Refugees, led the Children of Flanders Rescue Committee, and was vice president of the committee for aiding soldiers who had contracted tuberculosis. She persuaded well-known writers and artists—including Joseph Conrad, Thomas Hardy, and Jean Cocteau—to donate essays, articles, and poems for *The Book of the Homeless*, a project she created to raise money for refugees. Despite pressure from her publishers to move on to other subjects, Edith continued to focus on the war in both fiction and nonfiction. She and Walter Berry even went to the front lines so that Edith could write firsthand about the condition of the French army. In recognition of her wartime work, Edith was made a Chevalier of the French Legion of Honor, a great honor for a foreigner and a civilian.

On Armistice Day, November 11, 1918, Edith stood on the balcony of her apartment with all her household, including Nicette and her new Pekingese dogs—"My Chineses"—listening to the joyful bells of Paris: "We had fared so long on the thin diet of hope deferred that for a moment or two our hearts wavered and doubted. Then like the bells, they swelled to bursting, and we knew the war was over."

During the war years, Edith had had little time to rest. Her letters describe moods of "lassitude and incapacity," of "jiggling" nerves, of "long weary white nights & the ditto black days. . . . What color-blind idiot called depression blue?" At one point, tired and discouraged, Edith confided in Elisina Tyler, her partner in setting up war-relief agencies in Paris: "It is so difficult for me to care really for anyone—especially in these last years." The war had left her emotionally depleted and too drained to make any deep or intimate connections.

Exhausted, Edith decided to leave Paris after the war. Longing for quiet and saddened by the death of Henry James, who had been gravely ill for months, Edith searched for a home in the country. She had just reached a hotel in the small village of Hyères on the Mediterranean when she received news that Nicette, her elderly Papillon who had stayed in Paris with Gross, had died. That night, Edith wrote to an old friend in America: "You will be sorry to hear that our poor little Nicette, whom you used to know, died the day after I left Paris. It was a great blow to my poor Gross, but luckily a friend gave me a very pretty little Pekinese dog who was sent to Gross in Paris, and so she has had a companion while I have been away."

With Nicette's passing, Pekes became the only dogs in Edith's life. During the war, she had begun adding them to her household. Photographs show Edith and Gross holding a pair of black Pekes and several small gold ones. Each picture is labeled in Edith's nearly indecipherable scrawl: "Tootie," "Choumai," "Petite Tootie," "Coonie," and finally "Linky"—the Pekingese mentioned most often in Edith's letters and diaries.

The breed suited Edith perfectly. Pekes have Spitzlike qualities reminiscent of Edith's childhood Foxys. Their arresting appearance, with big eyes and luxurious coats, would fit Edith's sense of elegance, while their romantic history would appeal to her love of drama. Legend says the breed, known in China as "the butterfly lions," descended from the mating of a butterfly with a lioness. In imperial China, only empresses and high-ranking nobles were allowed to own them. Indeed, the Pekingese was unknown outside China until the Opium War, when British soldiers invaded the Imperial Palace in Peking and discovered the body of a princess who had committed suicide rather than fall into enemy hands. Guarding her body were five exotic dogs that looked like small lions. Several officers took the dogs back to England, and in 1861, they presented the most beautiful of the five to Queen Victoria. This little Peke, appropriately named Looty, so pleased the queen that she had Looty's portrait painted by Sir Edwin Landseer, the preeminent Victorian painter.

The usual temperament of Pekes was much like Edith's. According to the breed standard, the Pekingese is direct and independent with a lionlike image, "implying courage, dignity, boldness and self-esteem rather than daintiness or delicacy," all qualities Edith shared. Until recently, the breed standard actually included the trait of "exasperating stubbornness," which Edith's friends often ascribed to her. Unlike lapdogs that fret if their owners are absent, Pekes are independent: They were equally happy with Edith, her servants and guests, or one another.

A Peke plays a major role in Edith's only writing about dogs, the short story "Kerfol." The unnamed dog is clearly a Pekingese, and Edith's description of him suggests her fascination with the breed: "He was such a remarkably beautiful little dog that for a moment he made me forget the splendid place he was defending. I was not sure of his breed at the time, but have since learned that it was Chinese, and that he was of a rare variety called the 'Sleeve-dog.' He was very small and golden brown, with large brown eyes and a ruffled throat: he looked like a large tawny chrysanthemum." Comparing the little dog to a chrysanthemum refers to the ancient practice of breeding Pekes to match the colors of the empresses' favorite flowers. And *sleeve dog* is another name for a Pekingese because some were bred especially small to fit inside the sleeves of the empresses' robes.

Edith's Pekes soon took Nicette's place as companions on her still-frequent motor-flights. Mary Berenson even began to wonder if Edith traveled simply to divert the dogs: "She was devoted to traveling, but we sometimes thought she traveled more for the sake of giving her favorite dog of the moment a patch of green sward to run on than for anything she wanted to see, for she took in impres-

Edith Wharton and Catherine Gross with Pekes at Ste.-Claire Château, ca. 1924.

sions of works of art with disconcerting swiftness, unless indeed they contained pictures of dogs." One American friend was dismayed by Edith's new dogs and by the way that she babied them: "She liked their haughty imperial ways and was amused by their rather horrid little characters. She did not like children." However, Mary Berenson was more empathetic: "It was evident that the passion of her thwarted motherhood went into her affection for the 3 or 4 little Pekingese dogs she was always surrounded by."

Edith eventually bought two country villas in France: Pavillon Colombe, north of Paris, where she spent summers, and Ste.-Claire Château, outside of the village of Hyères, for the winters. Both homes, including their acres of gardens, needed extensive remodeling, tasks that Edith eagerly took on. After years of living in apartments in Paris, Edith rediscovered how much she enjoyed being outdoors. The writer Percy Lubbock, a frequent visitor, describes her at Pavillon Colombe: "She now stood on the good soil of her garden, with her broad-leafed hat and her basket on her arm, calling and waving to the window where Gross looked out and smiled proudly down at her . . . when she whisked around and made off to do her business among the flowers, with her pair of toy-dogs sputtering and scuffling at her heels."

Happily settled in and finally feeling at home, Edith, now fifty-seven, began writing *The Age of Innocence*. She was finally ready to put the subject of war behind her, so she set her novel in New York society of the 1870s: "I had to get away from the present altogether. . . . I had a momentary escape in going back to my childish memories of a long-vanished America, and wrote 'The Age of Innocence.' " The book, begun in 1919, flowed easily and was published within a year. Throughout the process, Walter Berry helped by reading and offering advice, while Minnie Jones, Edith's former sister-in-law who lived in New York, researched old issues of newspapers and magazines to clarify details of life in 1870. Minnie wrote to Edith in December of 1919, "Your memory is quite amazing; you bring back that time as if it were last week." One reviewer pointed out that the author had described the idiosyncrasies of Old New York "as familiarly as if she loved them and as lucidly as if she hated them."

In 1921, the year after *The Age of Innocence* was published, Edith Wharton was awarded the Pulitzer Prize. In the summer of 1923, at the age of sixty-one, Edith made her final trip to the United States to accept an honorary doctorate from Yale University, the first woman to be so honored. When Edith returned to Europe, she still took short motor trips and a ten-week Mediterranean cruise, but she was more settled and content in the French countryside than she had ever been in her life.

At Pavillon Colombe and Ste.-Claire Château, Edith enjoyed her gardens and took up sketching outdoors, filling her book with drawings of flowers and her sleeping dogs. The little troop

Dozing Peke. *Pencil drawing by Edith Wharton in her unpublished sketchbook.*

of Pekes, led by Linky, who would survive them all, spent the morning with Edith in bed as she wrote. As always, only the dogs; the housekeeper, Gross; and Edith's maid, Elise Duvlenck, were allowed to share these private moments. Elise had become Edith's personal maid in 1914 and proved to be an invaluable traveling companion. Edith learned to appreciate her organizational skills, her strong religious faith, and her unfailing delight in "dog jokes."

Although Edith's friends recognized the importance of "her darlings" Gross and Elise, few understood Edith's attitude toward her dogs. In fact, some visitors resented what they viewed as Edith's excessive regard for the Pekes. Even Mary Berenson sometimes lost patience when Edith interrupted dinner parties to attend to her dogs: "Much as she loved conversation, we all complained bitterly that her frequent endearments to the dogs & expostulations on their behavior ruined all consecutive talk."

The well-educated, wealthy, single men who made up Edith's close circle were accustomed to being the center of attention, and they often complained to one another about the dogs. Edith would have been shocked to learn that her trusted friend Gaillard Lapsley, the Oxford don who became her literary executor, detested the "damned Pekingese." Charles Du Bos, who translated *The House of Mirth* into French, grumbled about "those blessed toy-dogs, always whining and complaining about something, so that Edith has to pounce and chide and console." Percy Lubbock, who would write her first biography, was also irritated by the constant canine presence: "There was always a dog or two about Edith in her home, a small dog of the yapping kind, a still smaller of the fidgeting and whining breed—dogs that had to be called, caressed, rebuked—dogs that had to be let out or carried in or taken for a run."

Signorina Elizabeth Mariano, whom Edith met while visiting Bernard Berenson, was a more perceptive observer of Edith and her dogs. Elizabeth had grown up with large dogs and was at first uncomfortable with Edith's attention to her Pekes, explaining, "The lap-dog and its cult were a new experience for me." Then, while traveling with Edith in Italy, Elizabeth came to see that the bond between Edith and her maid Elise was strengthened by their mutual love for Linky. Elizabeth had hoped to get to know Edith better during the hours spent together in a railroad car; instead, Edith ignored her as she and Elise fussed and joked over Linky. Elizabeth remarked ruefully, "No danger of too much 'tête-à-tête' as long as Linky was about."

When they finally arrived in Rome, Elizabeth was further irritated when Edith hired "the oldest and dirtiest and most ramshackle cab in Rome, with a driver whose black coat had turned greenish with age." Elizabeth interpreted Edith's choice of driver as an insult to her and was astonished when Edith explained that she had hired him because "he looked as if he would be kind to her little dog while we were inside a church." The disreputable-looking driver took excellent care of Linky, and Elizabeth finally understood that the welfare of Edith's dogs would always come first.

Edith had recognized in the driver someone else with an intuitive understanding of dogs. As a child, Edith had believed that she was one of the few who "love and understand the little four-foots . . . [and] have the mysterious animal affinity [to] communicate with [them]"—a belief she never outgrew. She mentioned her ability to communicate with dogs once again, this time in the preface to a book about Africa, written by her friend Vivienne de Watteville. Edith agreed to write the preface because of the passion the two women shared for animals, even though Edith's wilderness was only a garden and her wild animals only "two astute and arrogant Pekingese." Nevertheless, she said that she and Vivienne were part of "the initiated . . . who know how to talk with the animals." That same year, Edith wrote in her autobiography, "I cannot remember when the grasses first spoke to me . . . but on the day when Foxy was given to me, I learned what the animals say to each other, and to us."

Edith's love for her dogs burned even brighter as her close friends began to die. In 1927, Walter Berry suffered a fatal stroke. Edith wrote that in his last days, he "had wanted me so close and held me so fast, that all the old flame and glory came back, in the cold shadow of death and parting." Then Gross became senile. Edith found a convent where "my old Gross" could live out her days, "quite mindless, but gentle & quiet." Finally, Edith's maid Elise, ill from pernicious anemia, retired. Edith paid for both women's care until their deaths only months apart in 1933. Edith felt their absence keenly: "Since Walter's death, I've been incurably lonely *inside*, & these two faithful women kept the hearth-fire going."

Edith relied more and more on Elisina Tyler, who had become a close friend since their war work together. Not only was Elisina a frequent guest, but she also took care of Edith when she was ill. Their friendship included Elisina's son William, who referred to Edith as "Edou," the name he had called her ever since he was a child. Elisina, William, and later his wife, Bettina, and their infant son Royall gradually took the place of Edith's old friends. Edith nicknamed the strapping baby Hercules and often referred to him as Herc. Now, instead of the lofty discussions that had once pre- vailed, her home was filled with the happy sounds of a child. When the young family visited, Edith made sure they had everything they needed for Herc. She even offered to keep her dogs away, but Bet- tina Tyler reassured the housekeeper: "Please tell Mrs. Wharton that . . . it will be quite alright for the Pekingueses to cohabit with the baby, but in that case I must decline all responsibility in the event of the dogs getting bitten."

When the Tylers bought their own Pekingese puppy, Edith wrote, "Linky and I . . . congratulate you and Betsy on the immense privilege of having under your roof a member of the Imperial race. Linky is of course less awe-struck than I, as she is dealing with a peer." She then went on to give them a list of directions about how to care for the puppy. Included in her advice are injunctions to vary the puppy's diet, keep his paws dry, and "never let him go out without his pull-over." Unfortunately, the Tylers' puppy died, as did its successor, prompting a rebuke from Edith: "It takes a good deal of dog-knowledge to bring up little creatures as delicate as that, & it is always a mistake to get a dog less than a year old. Pekes need care enough even then." She ended with the admonition: "I am *so* sorry! But don't try puppies again."

Between houseguests, Edith, now in her seventies, came to appreciate solitude, a condition she had assiduously avoided as a younger woman: "How it clears my soul to be alone, as I have been now for a week. The sediments deposited by others sink to the bottom, & leave me with myself." She continued to write each morning. Now, though, worried about financial security after the collapse of the American stock market, Edith wrote primarily for money to keep her two estates running. After the autobiography, *A Backward Glance*, Edith spent her dwindling energy churning out short stories for American magazines. Critics noted that her English had become stiff and out of date and that she was repeating plots and characters.

Edith's interest shifted to self-reflection, and she began to keep a diary. She had begun several in the past but never kept them up because she had been far too busy. This one she started resolutely: "If I ever have a biographer, it is in these notes that he will find the gist of me." Then she attempted to free-associate: "Let us begin with some stray thoughts—The sub-conscious . . . of the psychologists." The very first thoughts that came up were about dogs: "I am secretly afraid of animals—of *all* animals except dogs, and even of some dogs. I think it is because of the *us*ness in their eyes, with the underlying *not-us*ness which belies it, and is so tragic a reminder of the lost age when we human beings branched off and

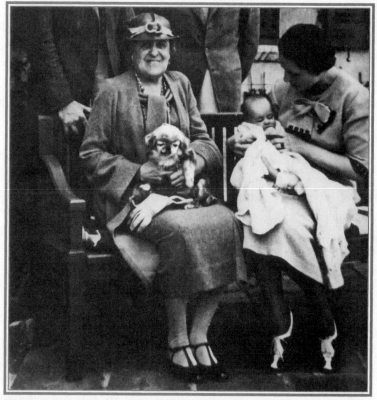

Edith Wharton holding Linky, with Bettina Tyler holding Royall (Herc) Tyler, ca. 1937.

left them: left them to eternal inarticulateness and slavery. *Why?* their eyes seem to ask us." These uncensored words evoke the image of the solitary child Edith had been and call to mind the immediate recognition of kinship she felt when she first held Foxy in her arms. In a later entry, Edith lists in order "the ruling passions" of her life:

Justice and Order
Dogs
Books
Flowers

Architecture

Travel

A good joke—and perhaps that should have come first!

In 1935, Edith suffered a mild stroke, from which she recovered, although she continued to endure bouts of fatigue and weakness. Nevertheless, she could still proclaim: "I'm an incorrigible life-lover, life-wonderer and adventurer." However, Edith's last piece of writing, the somber ghost story "All Souls," suggests she was fearful as she faced the end of her life. The story tells of an elderly woman whose servants mysteriously disappear, leaving her alone and bedridden in a cold and silent house. Edith's publisher found the ending so disturbing that he insisted she add a happy one. Although Edith unwillingly complied, the story is still a bleak portrait of a woman who feels abandoned and who fears she will "lie there alone and untended till she died of cold and of the terror of her solitude."

One by one, Edith's dogs passed away until only Linky remained. For the first time, Edith did not replace the dogs that died but instead grew even fonder of her favorite. The sturdy little Peke's name seems especially fitting for Edith's last dog. Years earlier, she had written about her desire "to keep intact as many links as possible between yesterday and tomorrow." Edith's relationship with her little dog resembled the one she had had with her first Foxy. With Linky, Edith allowed herself to act like a child again. She took pictures of Linky in Herc's pram and wrote silly notes that she attributed to the dog. Her last Christmas card was a photograph of Linky dressed in a pullover.

In April of 1937, Edith began her final diary, which can be read as a testament to her love for Linky. Written on lined notebook paper instead of her usual thick, creamy stationery, the entries are all brief, consisting of only a few sentences written with an obviously shaky hand. It begins with pleasant notes describing what was blooming in Edith's garden and the yellow tulips in a farmer's yard. Then, on April 11 appear the disjointed words "Dear little Linky suddenly taken ill—I feel ~~to~~ ill too."

The next entry begins "Little Linky ill," but Edith continues in a positive vein, noting that the morning had been sunny and that she had an enjoyable tea. The following day Edith was no longer optimistic: "Clouding over. Little Linky still ill. I am still very tired." By April 14, Edith had given up hope of Linky recovering: "I don't remember much of anything, for my Linky is leaving me. Eleven years of much friendship and the last link with the vanished past."

Edith made the decision to have Linky euthanized on April 15. She sent a postcard to William and Bettina Tyler and their son Herc: "He'll be sorry to hear that his little old friend Linky is saying goodbye to life today. A sudden attack of uremia [blood poisoning in the urine] & everything attempted in vain to help her, so we're putting her to sleep—the best & last of her race."

In her diary, Edith describes Linky's death in a mix of present and past tenses: "My little Linky dying. At 4:30 the veterinarian put her gently to sleep. O what a troop of ghosts who used to love her (Walter, Grossie, Elise, and many more) gathered about her, when her little ghost waited for me tonight beside my bed." The day after Linky's death, Edith could write only one line: "Can't remember. Oh my little dog." That afternoon, she told William Tyler, "I wish she could have outlasted me, for I feel for the very first time in my life, quite utterly alone and lonely." The diary entry for April 17 is also brief: "Still can't remember. All the place is haunted for me."

For the next several days, Edith does not mention Linky and focuses instead on visitors, the garden, and the weather. On April 26, she tries to continue in the same vein, but after several sentences, gives up with what sounds like a cry of anguish: "Oh, how shall I ever get used to never seeing Linky anymore?"

The diary remains blank until May 9, when Edith went to lunch and then to see where Linky was buried: "Very shakey and tired. Went to Pierre Lisse to see little Linky's grave." That is the only entry for the entire month. She wrote to William that she was grieving for her dog: "We really communicated with each other—and no one had such wise things to say as Linky. . . . Please

Postcard of Linky at Pavillon Colombe, ca. 1936. Message "Please come & see me soon. Linky" written by Edith Wharton.

let me know if I sent you Linky's photo in Herc's pram. It is too lovely. I meant to—but I really collapsed when she died, and I am only just collecting my wits." In June, Edith picked up the diary again, noting, "Kept no record for May. Too tired and depressed. Gave up Italian trip and stayed here alone. Cannot forget my Linky."

On August 11, four months to the day that Linky became ill, Edith died of a stroke at age seventy-five. Her last days had been peaceful. That summer was unusually beautiful, and friends came to pay short visits while Edith lay on a chaise longue in the garden. As she dozed in the sun, did Edith imagine that Linky was still with her?

> *My little old dog: —*
> *A heart-beat*
> *At my feet.*

Chronology

EDITH WHARTON

1862   January, birth of Edith Wharton.

1865   Foxy given to Edith.

1866   Jones family moves to Europe.

1870   July, Edith contracts typhoid fever in Germany.

1879   Edith makes her social debut at age seventeen.

1882   [January, birth of Virginia Woolf.]
       March, death of George Jones, Edith's father, in Cannes.

1885   April, marriage to Teddy Wharton.

1886   [May, death of Emily Dickinson.]

1897   *The Decoration of Houses* published.

1901   The Whartons start building The Mount.
       Death of Lucretia Jones.

1902   *The Valley of Decision* published.

1905   *The House of Mirth* published.

1907   Edith meets Morton Fullerton.

1911   *Ethan Frome* published.
September, Edith and Teddy separate; Teddy sells The Mount.

1916   February, death of Henry James.
April, Edith made Chevalier of the French Legion of Honor.

1920   *The Age of Innocence* published.

1921   *The Age of Innocence* awarded the Pulitzer Prize.

1923   June, Edith receives an honorary doctorate from Yale.

1927   October, death of Walter Berry.

1928   February, death of Teddy Wharton.

1933   Deaths of Catherine Gross and Elise Duvlenck.

1934   *A Backward Glance* published.

1937   April 18, death of Linky.
August 11, death of Edith Wharton, age seventy-five. She is buried near Walter Berry at the Cimetière des Gonards in Versailles.

VIRGINIA WOOLF
and GURTH, GRIZZLE, and PINKA

"This you'll call sentimental—perhaps—but then
a dog somehow represents—no I can't think of the word—
the private side of life—the play side."

VIRGINIA WOOLF

W HEN SHE WAS called to take the witness stand, nine-year-old Virginia Stephen walked forward bravely. Her voice trembled, but she spoke up and answered each question posed by the magistrate of the London Police Court. She told him that a neighbor's dog, known only as the Big Dog, "had run at her and bitten her cloak besides knocking her up against the wall." Leaning forward in the front row was Julia Stephen, Virginia's mother, listening closely.

The next day, Virginia wrote an account of "The Trial of the Big Dog" for *The Hyde Park Gate News*, a family newspaper produced by the four younger Stephen children. In her report, Virginia admitted that she had been thrilled to be called to court as a witness, but she was a bit worried that the judge might have the dog killed. What she did not mention was that the event had allowed her for once to enjoy her mother's undivided attention. In order to spend an entire afternoon with her daughter, Julia Stephen had excused herself from her numerous obligations. "The Trial of the Big Dog" can be seen as the first time a dog helped Virginia bring someone close to her. For the rest of her life, she would use dogs to attract the attention of, and to express her feelings for, the people she loved.

Virginia Stephen, 1902. *Photograph by George Charles Beresford.*

And yet, Virginia never thought of herself as a dog lover. Unlike Edith Wharton, whose dog Foxy stands in the forefront of her childhood memories, dogs remain in the background of Virginia Woolf's descriptions of her earliest years. But, although they were taken for granted, dogs did provide some sense of stability and consistency in a family that was undergoing chaos, uncertainty, and loss.

Part of the confusion in the Stephens' home was due to the number of people living there. Both Virginia's parents had had previous marriages and children. From her mother's first marriage, Virginia had three half siblings—Stella, George, and Gerald Duckworth—and from her father's previous marriage, a half sister, Laura. After their first spouses died, Virginia's parents married and together had four more children: Vanessa, Thoby, Virginia, and Adrian Stephen. Adding to the strain of caring for eight children, Mrs. Stephen was often called away to nurse ill friends and relatives, which kept her from home for days at a time. She also labored among the poor, distributing food baskets, helping families who had been evicted from their homes, and finding jobs for out-of-work fathers.

At home, Julia Stephen faced constant demands from her husband, Leslie; the baby, Adrian; and her stepdaughter, Laura, who suffered from severe emotional problems, apparently caused by learning disorders or a form of autism. Following the practice of that time, Laura's violent tantrums were managed with strict discipline, which only exacerbated them. It is no wonder, then, that Julia relied on her oldest daughter, Stella Duckworth, to take charge of Vanessa, Thoby, and Virginia. Later, Virginia recalled her mother's unavailability: "Can I remember ever being alone with her for more than a few minutes? Someone was always interrupting."

The happiest moments in Virginia's childhood occurred at St. Ives, a town in Cornwall on England's southwest coast. There, until Virginia was thirteen, the family rented Talland House every summer. In July of 1892, when Virginia was ten, rats were discovered in the house, so Mrs. Stephen asked her son Gerald to purchase a terrier in London and to send it out by train to St. Ives. The four youngest children and their father met every train until at last they spied a gray shaggy puppy tucked into a hamper. The next issue of *The Hyde Park Gate News* was devoted to Shag. The children explained how they chose his name—"He is long-haired and numerous haired"—and gave an assessment of his character: "[He is] very obedient and docile which united with a loveable temper will make him a favourite wherever he goes."

Gerald had paid a large sum for Shag under the impression he was a purebred Irish Terrier, a breed known to be efficient ratters. (Rats may have been the reason Mr. Brontë also chose an Irish Terrier, Grasper, for the first Brontë family dog.) Contrary to expectations, Shag grew up to be odd-looking, not at all like an Irish Terrier. Instead, as described by Virginia, he looked like a collie perched on "terribly Skye-terrier legs." Not only did Shag look like a mongrel, but he also refused to chase rats, so he became the Stephen children's companion and a favorite of the cook, who kept a special spot for him by the kitchen fire.

Shag appears on the periphery of Virginia's memories of Cornwall, including her description of the nightly ritual of moth hunting, which was orchestrated by her brother Thoby. With Shag barking at their heels, the children would steal away from the adults lingering at the candlelit dinner table and run into the wild gardens surrounding the house. There, they coated trees with rum, "sugaring" them to lure white moths. As the moths softly landed on the tree branches, the children tried to snare them with butterfly nets. Shag ran about in frenzied circles, getting in everyone's way. He may have ignored the rats, but he proved to be an indefatigable moth hunter.

One family photograph, taken on the steps of Talland House, shows Shag sitting at the feet of Gerald Duckworth. When Shag failed at catching rats, however, Gerald lost interest in him, so he became Vanessa's dog. Virginia would always associate her older sister with dogs, and even then she imagined Vanessa taking on a motherly role with Shag and the neighbors' assorted canines:

Stephen/Duckworth group at Talland House, 1892. Back row: Horatio Brown, Julia Duckworth Stephen, George Duckworth, and Gerald Duckworth. Front row: Vanessa, Thoby, Virginia, and Adrian Stephen with their dog Shag.

"There then were days of pure enjoyment . . . when . . . [Vanessa] trotted about on various businesses, considering the characters and desires of dogs very gravely." At St. Ives, Virginia's elusive mother, wearing a pale dress and surrounded by children and dogs, would find time to spend quiet moments sitting on the lawn and looking out at the sea.

According to Virginia, all such happiness came to an end when she was thirteen and her mother died. "Her death was the greatest disaster that could happen; it was as though on some brilliant day of spring the racing clouds of a sudden stood still, grew dark, and massed themselves." The doctors had initially diagnosed a mild case of flu, but Julia was too worn down to withstand it. In Virginia's unfinished memoir, "Sketch of the Past," begun in her late fifties, she describes her response to her mother's death: "I remember very clearly how even as I was taken to the bedside I noticed that one nurse was sobbing, and a desire to laugh came over me, and I said to myself as I have often done at moments of crisis since, 'I feel nothing whatever.' Then I stopped and kissed my mother's face." The children sat without expression throughout the required days of mourning, frightened by their father's violent outbursts of grief, the darkened rooms, and the procession of solemn visitors. Virginia never forgot the moment after Julia's funeral when Thoby, preparing to return to school, told his younger siblings not to continue like this: "Sobbing, sitting shrouded he meant. I was shocked at his heartlessness; yet he was right."

Following their brother's advice, Vanessa and Virginia tried to resume their former interests and activities, while Stella ministered to Leslie Stephen. She listened to his ceaseless lamentations and continually reassured him he was not to blame for his wife's death. Virginia described the atmosphere that pervaded the Hyde Park home: "We were all quite naturally unhappy; feeling a definite need, unbearably keen at moments, which was never to be satisfied . . . the sharp pang grew to be almost welcome in the midst of the sultry and opaque life which was not felt, had nothing real in it, and yet swam about us, and choked and blinded us."

Within a few months, Virginia suffered what she later referred to as "my 'first' breakdown." Her memoir contains a straightforward account of her symptoms and hints at their causes: "It was found that I had a pulse that raced. It beat so quick that I could hardly bear it. . . . I was terrified of people—used to turn red if spoken to. Used to sit up in my room raging—at father, at George, and read and read and read. But I never wrote. For two years I never wrote." Virginia raged at her father for his self-centered grief and at George Duckworth for making sexual advances to both her and Vanessa in the turbulent weeks following their mother's death. (Many years later, Virginia would relate that when she was six, Gerald Duckworth had also molested her.) Virginia used images of entrapment to describe her feelings toward her half brother and her father. Of George Duckworth, she wrote, "One felt like an unfortunate minnow shut up in the same tank as an unwieldy and turbulent whale." And of her father, "It was like being shut up in the same cage with a wild beast." The combination of powerlessness, trauma, and loss brought about Virginia's first experience of mental illness.

Virginia was put under the care of the Stephens' family physician, who set up a rigid schedule for her: She must spend four hours outdoors every day, and she must not take any classes. Stella oversaw her half sister's care and dutifully took her on long walks through the parks and to her weekly visits to the doctor. When Virginia was fifteen, she finally felt able to write again and began to keep a diary. With its detailed descriptions of the events of each day, this first diary seemed designed to keep Virginia grounded in reality, much like the "regularity papers" that Emily Brontë depended on when she was writing *Wuthering Heights.*

In addition to watching over Virginia, twenty-six-year-old Stella was also responsible for running the house. Leslie Stephen expected constant attention; Stella and Virginia bore the brunt of his demands because they were the only ones at home during the day. Thoby and Adrian were away at school, Vanessa spent hours at art classes, and Laura had been sent to the asylum where she would spend the rest of her life. As for the Duckworth brothers, Gerald was establishing a publishing house, and George was studying to become a diplomat. Stella, besides running the Hyde Park home, also took over most of her mother's charitable activities. Forced to spend hours alone or with her inconsolable father, Virginia began to rely on Shag and a new puppy, Jerry, for companionship.

Not only did the dogs provide an escape from sorrow, they also acted as a link to Vanessa. Virginia's diary shows that almost every day when Vanessa returned from her classes, the two girls took the reliable Shag and the mischievous Jerry out for a walk. These excursions gave the sisters time alone and allowed them to act like children together. At that time, Britain's dog-muzzling law was strictly enforced to curtail the spread of rabies. Inevitably, Jerry would manage to rub his muzzle off, and then Virginia and Vanessa would be on the lookout for the constable. When they spotted him, they would bundle the unmuzzled puppy deep into Vanessa's coat and smuggle him out of a park. Shag and Jerry often escaped from the house, which resulted in high drama. Servants would be sent to the Queen's Gate of Kensington Gardens to see if they could spot the runaways, while Vanessa pursued them on her bicycle, and Virginia searched on foot. And so dogs became a way for Virginia to entice her sister to spend time with her, in much the same way as the Big Dog had elicited her mother's attention.

The dogs' frequent dashes for freedom helped relieve the gloomy atmosphere of the Hyde Park home, where Mr. Stephen alternated between fits of weeping and harangues at Stella about household expenses. During one of these sessions, Virginia and Vanessa were having tea downstairs in the kitchen, listening to their father berate Stella. Suddenly, the puppy Jerry burst into the kitchen and created an uproar that reverberated throughout the house, giving Stella an excuse to escape their father. Virginia celebrated Jerry's achievement: "[Jerry] caused great confusion—biscuits thrown under the table, where Nessa rescued them in a marvelous way with her feet—Stella came down and carried the little creature off." Both Vanessa and Virginia relied on Stella to protect them from their father's volatile moods and his demands.

Virginia's diary entries from this time occasionally mention her own temper tantrums, often sparked by envy of Vanessa's freedom, but Virginia knew such outbursts were risky. Her half sister Laura's explosions of rage had been the reason she was sent away to an institution. Determined to be quiet, polite, and compliant, Virginia derived vicarious pleasure from Shag's frequent dogfights: "A wicked spotted creature followed us all the way down the street, for the pleasure of fighting Shag on the doorstep—Nessa waved her umbrella wildly and screamed at Shag and the spotted one, till they slunk away in dismay."

One of Virginia and Vanessa's duties was to entertain their father and his friends at afternoon tea. The sisters learned to make the kind of conversation required at such occasions: "It was not an argument, it was not gossip. It was a concoction, a confection; light; ceremonious; and of course unbroken silence was a breach of convention."

They found the teas unbearably drawn out and tedious, made the more so by having to repeat the small talk into Mr. Stephen's hearing trumpet. Virginia was delighted to have the stultifying boredom alleviated when Shag bit an elderly guest who had the audacity to call Shag "by the contemptible lap-dog title of 'Fido.' "

Shortly thereafter, the puppy Jerry disappears from Virginia's diary. An entry in June mentions him on a walk with Vanessa: "Then we lost Jerry & had to walk back in the broiling sun to find him." Apparently they did, but Virginia never mentions Jerry again. Whatever happened to the lively puppy was overshadowed by the tragedy that occurred three weeks later.

On April 10, 1897, Stella, defying Leslie Stephen, finally married her persistent suitor, Jack Hills. The happy couple went off on a honeymoon; on their return, they discovered that Stella was pregnant. Her initial joy and excitement faded as she became ill with an inexplicable infection. At first, it seemed she would recover, but she grew rapidly worse and died during surgery. Virginia's brief diary entries—"One day is so like another that I never write about them. Grey cloudy cold days"—suggest she was numb with shock.

Following Thoby's lead as they had when their mother died, Virginia, Vanessa, and Adrian kept their grief to themselves. They stopped speaking about Stella and tried to avoid even saying her name. As relatives and friends surrounded their weeping father and the distraught Jack Hills, the Stephen siblings sat mute and expressionless. Only as an adult would Virginia acknowledge how seriously Stella's death had affected her: "The blow, the second blow of death, struck on me: tremulous, filmy eyed as I was, with my wings still creased, sitting there on the edge of my broken chrysalis." For the next two years, Virginia struggled to recover from the loss.

At this dark moment, Violet Dickinson, who had been Stella's close friend, took a motherly interest in fifteen-year-old Virginia. Six feet tall and endearingly clumsy, Violet enjoyed unusual freedom because she never married and had inherited wealth and social standing. She often invited Virginia to stay at Burnham Wood, her country home north of London. Virginia later said her first impression of Violet's home was that it was filled with chairs and dogs.

Virginia responded to Violet's friendship with deep gratitude and a mixture of maternal longing and erotic love. The adolescent Virginia was too shy to express herself openly. Instead, she wrote about Violet's dogs as a way to reveal her emotions, a pattern she was to repeat in all her intimate relationships. She playfully asked Violet to imagine her in place of the Chow named Rupert: "So, kiss your dog on its tender snout, and think him me." Virginia even visualized herself merged with Rupert (including an accurate description of a Chow's dark tongue) in this account: "I think with joy of certain exquisite moments when Rupert and I lick your forehead with a red tongue and a purple tongue; and twine your hairs round our noses."

When Virginia was not visiting Violet, she was home at Hyde Park, where life had gradually returned to some kind of normality. Most of Stella's former duties had been delegated to Vanessa, who, however, refused to indulge their father. When Leslie Stephen rebuked her about household accounts, she simply stood silent and then left the house. Determined to become an artist, Vanessa spent as much time as possible away from home, painting and taking classes. Once again, in her loneliness, Virginia turned to a dog for company, a new one, "an attractive young sheep-dog puppy—who, though of authentic breed, was unhappily without a tail."

Named Gurth after a character in *Ivanhoe*, the appealing puppy soon eclipsed Shag. Virginia remembered the formerly dignified Shag making pathetic attempts to perform tricks to attract some attention back to himself: "I can see him now, as in a kind of blundering and shamefaced way he lifted one stiff old paw and gave it to me to shake." Moved to tears, Virginia was reminded of King Lear, but when Shag attacked Gurth, the older dog was immediately sent away to live with one of the servants. Virginia admitted that the decision "was base, unjust, and yet, perhaps, excusable. The old dog has had his day, we said, he must give place to the new generation." Her impersonal response suggests how wary she had become of acknowledging the pain of any loss.

In the spring of 1902, Mr. Stephen was diagnosed with abdominal cancer. Despite intense suffering, he was determined to finish his autobiography. He dictated it to Virginia, which meant she spent hours alone with her dying father. As she sat with him day after day, she came to admire his determination and courage, and her anger at him slowly dissipated. She wrote Violet daily bulletins about Mr. Stephen's condition and her yearning for Violet's maternal protection: "I wish you were a Kangeroo [sic] and a had a pouch for small Kangeroos to creep to." During this time "of great sickness and anxiety," Shag suddenly turned up at the kitchen door, barking to be let in and acting as if he had never been away. His surprising reappearance pleased Virginia, who wrote she would never know "what strange wave of memory or sympathetic instinct" drew Shag back home that night.

On February 22, 1904, Leslie Stephen died. Virginia wrote in her diary, "How to go on without him, I don't know." (Twenty-four years later, on the anniversary of her father's death, she would write a very different diary entry: "His life would have entirely ended mine. What would have happened? No writing, no books—inconceivable.") Immediately after the funeral, the four Stephen children set off on three months' travel in Europe. Thoby, Adrian, and Vanessa were determined to put the years of death and mourning behind them. Virginia, on the other hand, was not so easily distracted. Her letters to Violet from abroad were filled with remorse for not having done more for her father.

Soon after they returned, Virginia suffered a second nervous breakdown, far worse than her first. Under the care of three nurses, she once again stayed at Violet's home. The nurses reported that Virginia heard voices and attempted suicide by jumping out her bedroom window. Years later, rereading letters from this agonizing period of her life, Virginia would write to Violet, "But one thing emerges whole and lucid—how very good you were to me, and how very trying I was—all agog, all aquiver: and so full of storms and rhapsodies."

While still with Violet, Virginia received word from Vanessa that

Shag had wandered out into the street and, too deaf to hear the approach of a hansom cab, had been struck and killed. At Violet's suggestion, Virginia wrote an obituary for him and submitted "On a Faithful Friend" to *The Guardian*, a newspaper for the clergy. The editor, an acquaintance of Violet's, had already published Virginia's first pieces of writing: a book review and an account of her visit to the Brontës' parsonage in Haworth. (Virginia found the Brontë home "unremarkable" except for "the oblong recess beside the staircase into which Emily drove her bulldog during the famous fight, and pinned him while she pummeled him.")

Violet Dickinson with Virginia Stephen, 1902.

For Shag's obituary, Virginia attempted a detached tone: "It was better for him to die thus out among the wheels and the horses than to end in a lethal-chamber or be poisoned in a stable yard," even though she knew Shag had died in pain. A few years earlier, she and Vanessa had witnessed a neighbor's dog endure the same fate: "A cab slowly passed over its middle; we were watching and saw it get up and run about as though it was not hurt. But that night it became unconscious and died." Virginia had naïvely expected the neighbors to give that dog a funeral and had been dismayed when the very next day, they went "off to the Lost Dogs home to buy a new creature." The implicit message was that one did not mourn the death of a dog. Despite Violet's encouragement that she grieve for Shag, Virginia was determined to remain stoic. She knew she was too unsteady to allow any emotions to surface, even regrets or sorrow over the death of an old dog.

By the time Virginia was twenty-two, she had lost both parents and her half sister Stella; she had endured sexual molestation, two nervous breakdowns, and a suicide attempt. Photographs taken at this time show a hollow-cheeked, delicate young woman whose dark eyes suggest the suffering she has experienced. In one, Virginia stands beside Violet, leaning against her as if for support. She looks at the camera with a shy smile, her face on the verge of its adult beauty, already expressing Virginia's boundless curiosity and intelligence.

When she was finally well enough, Virginia joined her siblings in a sunny new house Vanessa had found on Gordon Square in the Bloomsbury section of London, a world away from their somber home in Hyde Park. Virginia was thrilled with Vanessa's choice: "Gordon Square is not one of the most romantic of the Bloomsbury squares. . . . But I can assure you that in October 1904 it was the most beautiful, the most exciting, the most romantic place in the world. . . . The light and the air after the rich red gloom of Hyde Park Square were a revelation." Adding to their sense of release, Virginia and Vanessa were now free of their half brothers, both George and Gerald Duckworth having moved into their own flats.

It was at Gordon Square that the Bloomsbury group had its beginnings. Thoby, who was studying for the bar, missed the intellectual stimulation of his years at university, so he invited some of his fellow Cambridge graduates and their friends for Thursday evening drinks and conversation. They devoted themselves to opposing the previous generation's Victorian customs, sexual constraints, and narrow worldview. The Bloomsbury group, as the intimate circle became known, eventually included, in addition to Thoby, Adrian, Vanessa, and Virginia, an eclectic mix of members: literary figures such as biographer Lytton Strachey and novelist E. M. Forster; artists and art critics Duncan Grant, Clive Bell, and Roger Fry; economist Maynard Keynes; journalists Desmond and Molly MacCarthy; and civil servant Leonard Woolf. Meeting regularly for close to forty years, the Bloomsbury group offered support and encouragement to one another, even though they were often guilty of the elitism they were quick to condemn in others.

Despite Bloomsbury's free and easy lifestyle, with no set times for meals and friends dropping in whenever they pleased, Virginia's life remained regimented. Still under doctor's orders not to attend classes, she began to edit her father's letters for his biographer and to write literary reviews for *The Guardian*. Vanessa, Thoby, and Adrian were gone during the day, studying—respectively—art, law, and psychology. Virginia spent hours alone with Gurth, noting that the appealing puppy had grown into a handsome dog with a coat that was merle-colored, like a "white & grey January day."

Virginia's diary documents her growing attachment to Gurth. She seems eager to take on the responsibility of caring for another being, perhaps as an antidote for the hours she spent as a patient: "I took Gurth out—he is a load on my conscience—for a walk in Regents Park. This is what he most enjoys." Virginia introduced him to what was becoming her favorite pastime, roaming the streets of London—what she would later call street-haunting: "I walked him right along Oxford Street. Streets I do enjoy more than the dreary Regents Park. I like looking at things." As the two of them wandered through the city, Virginia wondered about the nuances of smells Gurth was encountering. Years later, in *Flush: A Biography*, Virginia would imagine a dog's experience of London: "The whole battery of a London street on a hot summer's day assaulted his nostrils. He smelt the swooning smells that corrode iron railings; the fuming, heady smells that rise from basements—smells more complex, corrupt, violently contrasted and compounded than any he had smelt in the fields . . . smells that lay far beyond the range of the human nose."

Virginia followed a British custom that persists to this day, that of taking a dog along wherever one goes. When Violet Dickinson was ill, Virginia took Gurth right into the sickroom, where he lay his head on Violet's bed and let her scratch behind his ears. He accompanied Virginia on her errands, which included research trips to the London Library, and Virginia had no qualms about "wangling" with a driver who protested over Gurth's muddy paws in his cab. She even expected Gurth to sit quietly through a concert and was exasperated when he began howling in the midst of one: "Out after lunch with Gurth to . . . the Joachim concert at the Bechstein Hall, where Gurth accompanied a . . . song with a voluntary bass of his own composition & I had to remove him in haste." In the past, Virginia had never ventured out without Stella or Vanessa to act as a buffer between her and the rest of the world; now, with Gurth, she relished wandering about various London neighborhoods.

Notwithstanding her excursions with Gurth, Virginia was still fettered by her doctor's rules: He decided how many hours she could spend outside and how much she was allowed to write and read. Perhaps she identified those constraints with the London leash laws when she complained that leashes were "so much risk & botheration" and allowed Gurth to run free. Considering the rigid controls that had been placed on Virginia, she must have found it exhilarating to take off Gurth's leash and watch the eager sheepdog streak across a London park.

Virginia was grateful for Gurth's company; nevertheless, she found that looking after him could be a burden. There is an echo of her mother's weary complaint "Oh the torture of never being left alone!" in Virginia's cry "Gurth wears my life out." Bred to herd sheep, Gurth considered Virginia his flock, and his instincts demanded that he keep a vigilant eye on her at all times. With a sheepdog, that means a particularly penetrating stare known as the "eye-stalk." At first, Virginia, already subjected to constant scrutiny by family and doctors, found Gurth's vigilance irritating: "I took that extraordinarily ubiquitous dog for a walk. He never leaves me now, but follows me up stairs & down, sits by my desk as I write."

Over time, however, Virginia found Gurth's attention comforting. His refusal to leave her alone, along with his piercing eye-stalk, may have filled some of Virginia's need for maternal affection. Although she had welcomed Shag during her lonely vigil with her father, she had never formed a close bond with him. Now, spending every day with Gurth, Virginia grew to appreciate his protectiveness. In her longing for a closer connection with Vanessa, Virginia began to refer to her sister as a sheepdog, using the word as a term of endearment. She insisted that even Vanessa's "handwriting has the quality of a great sheep dog's paw—a sheep dog which has been trotting sagaciously through the mud after its lambs all day long." Eventually, Virginia would realize that what she sought from Vanessa was "maternal protection which, for some reason, is what I have always most wished from everyone." And for the rest of her life, Virginia would call the women she loved "sheep dogs," an unacknowledged tribute to Gurth.

In September of 1906, when she was twenty-four, Virginia, Vanessa, and Violet Dickinson set off to meet Thoby and Adrian as they traveled through Greece. Almost as soon as they arrived in Corinth, Vanessa suffered an attack of appendicitis. The group returned to London, where Vanessa recovered, but then both Violet and Thoby were stricken with typhoid fever, which they had contracted abroad. Violet regained her health slowly; Thoby, however, grew worse. He was in great pain and became delirious, so the doctors decided to operate. The surgery proved fruitless, and on November 20, Thoby Stephen died. He was twenty-six. Two days later, Vanessa accepted a proposal from Clive Bell and married him the following March. Virginia tried to be happy for her sister but wrote after the wedding, "That is all over, and I shall never see her alone any more." Within four months, Virginia had, in effect, lost both her brother and her sister.

Gurth, who was actually Vanessa's dog, accompanied the Bells on their honeymoon trip to Wales, and he remained with them in the Gordon Square house when they returned. Virginia and her younger brother, Adrian, moved to a house nearby, but Gurth continued to spend much of his time with Virginia, thus acting as a tangible link between the sisters. Despite Gurth's visits, Virginia and Adrian apparently felt it was important to add a full-time dog to their household. They went to the Battersea Lost Dogs Home (still in existence), where they adopted a Boxer named Hans, who distinguished herself by her male name, her refusal to be housebroken, and her ability to put out matches with her paw. Every time Virginia lit a cigarette, Hans would extinguish the match, a trick Virginia would teach all her dogs. Hans was entertaining, but she must have lacked the qualities Virginia unconsciously sought in a dog. In one letter, Virginia revealed her detached attitude toward Hans, first referring to her as "it" and then as a person: "It is perhaps the most witty, and also cynical person I have ever known. When I talk of the domestic virtues and in particular of tolerance and love it howls."

By the summer of 1908, Virginia had begun to earn a living by writing reviews for *The Guardian*, *The National Review*, and *The Times Literary Supplement*. She had also begun working on her first novel, *The Voyage Out*, the story of a motherless young woman sailing from England to an unknown future. Perhaps to celebrate her hard-won independence, Virginia decided to take a walking tour of Wales on her own. She planned on bringing Hans and then, at the last moment, also borrowed Gurth. In the course of her daylong treks across the fields, sometimes the only words Virginia spoke were reassurances to strangers that her dogs wouldn't bite them. In frequent letters to Vanessa, who was immersed in caring for her newborn son Julian, Virginia extolled the joys of solitude, although she clearly missed her sister. When she returned home, she seemed reluctant to return Gurth to Vanessa: "I will send your dog. I should be glad to keep him, for he is really rather an engaging beast but I suppose he will be better with [you]." Even after their long walks in Wales, Virginia never depended on Hans for companion-

ship as she had with Gurth. Over time, both dogs gradually disappear from her diaries. One can suppose that Gurth lived out his life
with Vanessa and her family, and Hans with Adrian.

In June 1911, thirty-one-year-old Leonard Woolf, who had been a
great admirer and friend of Thoby when they were at Cambridge,
came home on leave from Ceylon (now Sri Lanka), where he had
been serving in the British Foreign Service for more than six years.
On an earlier visit, he had met Vanessa and Virginia and found
them both so beautiful and intelligent that he was determined to
marry one of them. Urged on by their many mutual friends, Virginia and Leonard slowly got to know each other. As a civil admin-
istrator, Leonard had been living a harsh but fascinating life in
Ceylon, which appealed to Virginia: "He is of course very clever &
from living in the wilds seems to me to have got a more interesting
point of view than most of the [Bloomsbury] 'set' who seldom pro-
duce anything very new or original."

Although they had much in common intellectually, Virginia
and Leonard came from dissimilar backgrounds. Leonard's parents
were Jewish, and he was one of nine children. Mr. Woolf, a barris-
ter, died when Leonard was eleven, leaving the family in such dire
economic circumstances that Mrs. Woolf had to sell the family
home. From then on, Leonard depended on scholarships for his
education and hard work for career advances. In contrast, Virginia,
who said once that she was "born not of rich parents, but of well-
to-do parents," took pride in the intellectual and social milieu in
which she was raised. Leonard was acutely aware of the advantages
Virginia's family and her friends enjoyed: "Socially they assumed
things unconsciously which I could never assume either unconsciously or consciously. They lived in a peculiar atmosphere of influence, manners, respectability." How seriously Virginia took
these differences is not clear. When Leonard proposed to her, she
become so upset that she retreated for two weeks to a nursing
home. Eventually, Virginia accepted the proposal. Her ambivalence
toward marrying can be seen in her note to Violet, in which she

misspelled her fiancé's name: "I've got a confession to make. I'm going to marry Leonard Wolf. He's a penniless Jew. I'm more happy than anyone ever said was possible."

What was clear from the beginning of their marriage was that Leonard would take care of Virginia. He knew about her previous breakdowns; in fact, he had met with her doctor before he proposed. Virginia felt safe in Leonard's care: "One's personality seems to echo out across space when he's not there to enclose all one's vibrations." On August 10, 1912, they married at the St. Pancras Register Office in London. Then the newlyweds went on a six-week honeymoon, traveling through France, Spain, and England.

From the outset, Virginia had been honest with Leonard about her lack of passion for him: "As I told you brutally the other day, I feel no physical attraction in you. There are moments—when you kissed me the other day was one—when I feel no more than a rock." When they returned from their honeymoon, the Woolfs confided their sexual problems to Vanessa, who told her husband, "Apparently she still gets no pleasure at all from the act which I think is curious." Within the first year of their marriage, and after consulting several doctors, Leonard decided Virginia was too unstable to risk having children, a decision Virginia would always regret. Fourteen years later, she wrote in her diary, "We might have had a boy of 12, a girl of 10: this always makes me wretched in the early hours."

In spite of their sexual incompatibility, childlessness, and different backgrounds, the marriage of Virginia and Leonard Woolf would survive for thirty years, until Virginia's death. Each at times disappointed the other, sometimes bitterly, yet they also cherished the life they created together. In their private moments, they were often silly and physically affectionate. Virginia came up with animal nicknames for Leonard, calling him "Mandril" or "Marmoset." And right from the beginning, dogs were an essential part of what Virginia called the "private, play side" of their life.

Like Virginia, Leonard had grown up with dogs, and like her, he prided himself on a realistic attitude toward them. In his autobiography, Leonard said that one of the crucial moments of his childhood had been an incident he believed others might find "trivial and sentimental." When the family dog had five puppies, he was told to destroy three of them. The custom then was to drown the unwanted ones in a pail of water when they were a day old. Leonard never forgot what happened after he put the first puppy into the pail: "This blind amorphous thing began to fight desperately for its life, struggling, beating the water with its paws. I suddenly saw that it was an individual, that like me it was an I." Leonard apparently went ahead and drowned the puppy, an example of his ability to combine respect for the powerless with a resolute determination to carry out what he believed was the right thing to do. This approach had characterized his treatment of the natives in Ceylon and would often guide his relationship with Virginia.

Leonard's history with dogs tells something about the no-nonsense side of his character. When he went out to Ceylon, he brought dogs with him, acquired more while he lived there, and often posed with them in photographs; nevertheless, he left them all behind. Virginia's nephew Quentin Bell remembered Leonard as "gruff, abrupt, a systematic disciplinarian" but also as "extremely good at seeing that his dogs were obedient, healthy, and happy." Virginia would always be attracted to dogs who broke rules, while Leonard liked them to be well behaved. Quentin Bell remembered Leonard shouting at his dogs until they "subside[d] into whining passivity." Despite their different expectations, Leonard and Virginia both assumed that dogs would be part of their life together.

In the first year of their marriage, Virginia suffered another breakdown, possibly brought on by the Woolfs' sexual difficulties and by the circumstances surrounding the publication of *The Voyage Out*. Virginia had been working on the novel for more than six years, writing and rewriting it at least ten times. She finally submitted it for publication to Duckworth & Co., the publishing house founded by Gerald. Today, it is difficult to understand why Virginia would hand over her novel, with scenes evoking sexual abuse, to the person who had molested her. Yet, at that time, any sexual transgression was a shameful secret for the victim; neither Vanessa nor

Virginia had yet told anyone what the Duckworth brothers had done. In fact, to all outward appearances, the two men maintained a useful presence in their adult sisters' lives: They had helped with the sale of the Hyde Park house and had arranged for marriage settlements from both Clive Bell and Leonard Woolf. Nevertheless, when the proofs of *The Voyage Out* arrived, Virginia suffered from overwhelming headaches, delusions, and loss of appetite. She spent weeks in a nursing home and, upon being released, attempted suicide by taking an overdose of her medication. For the next two years, as publication of her novel was delayed, Virginia was in and out of nursing homes.

When *The Voyage Out* was finally published in 1915, it received good reviews, with E. M. Forster declaring it had achieved the "unity" of Emily Brontë's *Wuthering Heights*. Indeed, it shares that novel's dark intensity. But sales were weak, and fifteen years later, it had sold only two thousand copies. Leonard's novel about his experiences in Ceylon, *The Village in the Jungle*, came out soon afterward and did fairly well; however, his second, *The Wise Virgins*, did not sell at all. After one last attempt at a collection of short stories, Leonard gave up writing fiction. Later in his life, he would write a five-volume autobiography, but for now, he concentrated on working for the Labour Party, writing reviews for the *New Statesman* and *The Nation*, and writing books on public policy. Leonard had also begun what would be his lifelong task of protecting his wife from her emotions.

As Virginia slowly recovered, Leonard insisted they buy Hogarth House in Richmond, chosen because the quiet London suburb was a far cry from Virginia's sophisticated Bloomsbury life. There he monitored his wife's food, her visitors, her writing, and he even kept track of her menstrual periods. Virginia resumed her reviews for *The Times Literary Supplement* and began working on short stories. At the same time, lighthearted entries began to appear in her diary, such as this description of a walk with a new dog: "I took Max along the River, but we were a good deal impeded, by a bone he stole, by my suspenders coming down, by a dogfight in which his ear was torn & bled horribly. I thought how happy I was, without any of the excitements, which, once, seemed to me to constitute happiness." Virginia was hopeful about the future; her thirty-third birthday was her "happiest ever." Leonard bought her a green handbag, and he took her to see a film and to tea, where they decided to buy a printing press and "a Bull dog, probably called John." Although they never acquired a Bulldog—and Max soon disappears from Virginia's diary—they did buy a small printing press, which they installed in their home. Thus, in 1917, the Hogarth Press was born.

As England prepared for World War I, a neighbor who had been drafted into the army brought his dog Tinker for tea with the Woolfs. Tinker was a purebred Clumber Spaniel, a rare breed and a classic British hunting dog. A favorite of King George III, Clumbers have had a long association with British royalty. Standing almost two feet tall, they resemble miniature draft horses with their solid, muscular bodies; thick coats; and long feathers on their legs. Virginia was immediately drawn to Tinker's appearance, "a stout, active, bold brute, brown & white with large luminous eyes." However, she was daunted by his temperament, noting, "Directly he is loosed, he leaps walls, dashes into open doors & behaves like a spirit in quest of something not to be found." Nevertheless, Leonard and Virginia offered to keep Tinker for the duration of the war.

Tinker intrigued Virginia. Perhaps because she now felt safely contained in her marriage, Virginia did not rely on him for "sheepdog" protectiveness. Instead, she began to pay attention to him with a writer's sensibility. By the end of Tinker's first day with the Woolfs, Virginia wrote that his character was beginning to move in the right direction, since "his spirit is great, but almost under control." Then she tried to walk him. Clumbers weigh around seventy-five pounds and are strong, stubborn dogs: "He fell into the river twice; jumped out again; circled madly with a black poodle, & investigated several garden gates which seem to have a fascination for him." After a few more days, Virginia summed up Tinker's disposition with a statement that is still an apt description of many Clumbers: "He is a human dog, aloof from other dogs."

In an attempt to calm Tinker's "restless mind," Virginia spent an entire evening holding him by a short chain while she tried to write a book review. Perhaps because of her own struggles with restlessness, Virginia was patient with Tinker. As she attempted to write one of her meticulous reviews while constraining a large, fidgeting dog, Virginia noted calmly, "One's right hand becomes quite cramped holding his chain. Let loose he is very random, but on the whole obedient." Toward Tinker, who was neither protective nor a connection to anyone she loved, Virginia displayed what her nephew and biographer Quentin Bell would remember about his aunt's attitude toward dogs: "Her affection was odd and remote. She wanted to know what her dog was feeling but then she wanted to know what everyone was feeling, and perhaps the dogs were no more inscrutable than most humans."

A month after he came to live with the Woolfs, Tinker ran out of their locked garden and into the house next door. From there, he found his way into the neighbor's garden and escaped to freedom. Virginia and Leonard went immediately to the police and reported him lost. "It is melancholy to be asking about lost dogs. . . . I find it hard to be altogether sanguine." They printed and posted notices, and Leonard inquired for Tinker repeatedly at the Lost Dogs Home. Months later, on a foggy January afternoon, Virginia thought for a moment she saw him, but it was only "a vision of Tinker, all but the nose accurate, but each dog has an unmistakable impression." Her careful attention to Tinker had indeed created a clear impression of his appearance and personality. Something about the Clumber had appealed to Virginia. People are often drawn to dogs that resemble them in some way, so perhaps Virginia recognized in Tinker her own aloofness and her own spirit "in quest of something not to be found."

In 1919, the Hogarth Press brought out its first book, *Kew Gardens*, a collection of Virginia's impressionistic stories with a wood-block illustration by Vanessa as its cover. Exhilarated by the success of the book, the Woolfs impulsively bought Monk's House—a cottage in

Rodmell, a village in the Sussex downs south of London—as a second home. Part of its appeal for Virginia was that Monk's House was within a few miles of Charleston, Vanessa's country home.

In October of 1919, Virginia's second novel, *Night and Day*, loosely based on her courtship and marriage, was published by Gerald Duckworth in order to fulfill the terms of her contract with him. This time, the symptoms that had paralyzed her on the publication of *The Voyage Out* did not recur, but Virginia declared, "I don't like writing for my half-brother George" (a notable slip, with the name of one brother replacing the other). From then on, the Woolfs' own Hogarth Press would publish all Virginia's work, giving her "the greatest mercy of being able to do what one likes—no editors, or publishers."

With two well-received novels, a collection of short stories, essays, and literary reviews, Virginia's reputation as a serious writer was growing. She plunged into *Jacob's Room*, in which she imagined what Thoby's life would have been like if he had not died. At the end of the year, she wrote a summary of the achievements and setbacks she and Leonard had experienced thus far in their marriage, ending with the declaration "Yet I daresay we're the happiest couple in England." Shortly thereafter, a cryptic announcement appears in Virginia's diary: "Grizzle now belongs to us." This is the first mention of the mixed-breed terrier who would become an integral part of Virginia and Leonard's private world.

As she had with Tinker, Virginia approached Grizzle with curiosity, eager to discover what was unique about her. With wry humor, she noted Grizzle's idiosyncrasies: "I heard the thunder murmuring as I walked. Grizzle was frightened & ran home—as if God would go out of his way to hurt a mongrel fox terrier walking on the flats at Rodmell! But there's no arguing these things." Virginia simply observed and wondered about Grizzle's behavior. She made no attempt to shape the dog to fit her expectations.

With Grizzle, Virginia's walks over the Sussex downs could take on a heroic dimension. Encountering the familiar sight of a

Grizzle at Monk's House, ca. 1925.

neighbor's herd of cows became a battle with wild stags or an ad-
vancing Greek army. Grizzle let loose with high-pitched terrier
yelps, while Virginia brandished her walking stick at the confused
animals: "How they barked & belled like stags round Grizzle; &
how I waved my stick & stood at bay; & thought of Homer as they
came flourishing & trampling toward me: some mimic battle. Grizzle grew more & more insolent & excited & skirmished about yapping."

   On the evenings Leonard was attending political meetings,
Virginia counted on Grizzle to keep her company. Although she
may have appeared increasingly self-sufficient in her role as a well-
regarded author, her diary reveals she could become anxious when
left by herself. If Leonard was absent, Virginia noted that her terrier acted as a watchdog: "Grizzle pricks an ear; lies flat again." Virginia would interrupt the flow of her thoughts to mention Grizzle:

"Do I hear him? Grizzle says Yes: stands tail wagging—She is right." Virginia craved solitude, yet she was relieved when Leonard finally arrived home: "Thank God here's L. Grizzle knows the way he shuts the door & jumps down & runs out."

Virginia and her dog often walked the few miles over to Charleston, Vanessa's home, which was filled with visitors, art projects, and spontaneous parties. Sometimes Virginia envied her sister's life: her three children, her lovers, her foreign travel, and her involvement in the Postimpressionistic art world. Nevertheless, Virginia realized that her happiness and Leonard's came from their appreciation for everyday life, which included Grizzle: "The immense success of our life, is I think, that our treasure is hid away; or rather in such common things that nothing can touch it. That is, if one enjoys a bus ride to Richmond, sitting on the green smoking . . . combing Grizzle." Virginia valued Grizzle as a companion and watchdog, but even more, as an integral part of the contented life she shared with Leonard.

Virginia knew from the terrifying breakdowns she had experienced that it was important for her to stay connected with "common things," even when she was considering abstract ideas. For instance, the subject of the soul fascinated her, and she often talked about it in her novels, her diaries, and in conversations with friends: "But oh the delicacy & complexity of the soul—for, haven't I begun to tap her & listen to her breathing after all?" Yet she insisted that the soul appears in the most ordinary moments and places, even with her dog: "And the truth is, one can't write directly about the soul. Looked at, it vanishes; but look at the ceiling, at Grizzle . . . & the soul slips in."

In the years following World War I, Hogarth Press flourished, with Leonard and Virginia involved in every detail of its operation: reading manuscripts, setting type, and assembling the printed books. Although they turned down James Joyce's *Ulysses*, they published such writers as Sigmund Freud, T. S. Eliot, Katherine Mansfield, and E. M. Forster. In 1924, Virginia finally convinced Leonard she was well enough to move back to London. They decided to move Hogarth Press as well, keeping its name but relocating it to the basement of the home they leased at 52 Tavistock Square, once again in the Bloomsbury area.

Virginia's excitement at returning to London spills over in the novel she was writing, *Mrs. Dalloway*, with its re-creation of the intensity of city life. "Was everybody dining out, then? Doors were being opened here by a footman to let issue a high-stepping old dame, in buckled shoes, with three purple ostrich feathers in her hair. Doors were being opened for ladies wrapped like mummies in shawls with bright flowers on them. . . . Everbody was going out. What with these doors being opened, and the descent and the start, it seemed as if the whole of London were embarking in little boats moored to the bank, tossing on the waters, as if the whole place were floating off in carnival."

By 1925, Virginia seemed to have come to terms with her hardworking life and a husband who also acted as her nurse and literary adviser. Back in London, she was eager to look up old friends and deepen her connections with a few new acquaintances, including Vita Sackville-West. A few years earlier, in December 1922, Virginia had met the striking aristocrat at a dinner party. Married to diplomat Harold Nicolson and the mother of two sons, Vita was infamous for her many affairs, including a scandalous lesbian affair that had been made much of in the tabloid newspapers. By the time she met Virginia, Vita had already published an astonishing body of work, including bestselling novels, poetry, short stories, and *Knole and the Sackvilles*, the story of her historic family home and flamboyant ancestors.

Virginia's first impression of Vita was not a happy one: "Not much to my severer taste—florid, moustached, parakeet coloured, with all the supple ease of the aristocracy, but not the wit of the artist." What at first put Virginia off—Vita's colorfulness and her unshakable self-confidence—was precisely what she would soon find attractive. The day after the party, Virginia wrote to ask Vita for her poetry and a copy of *Knole and the Sackvilles*. (Knole, now part of England's National Trust, is an impressive example of Elizabethan architecture, with 365 rooms, including the King's Room, where James I is said to have slept.) Virginia suggested to Leonard that they approach Vita about publishing with Hogarth Press, and Vita, flattered and pleased, accepted their offer.

The two women were soon corresponding regularly, mostly literary gossip and concerns about their writing projects: Virginia was immersed in the first drafts of *Mrs. Dalloway* as well as *The Common Reader*, an overview of modern fiction; Vita was composing a long pastoral poem, *The Land*. They began to see each other more often. Vita took Virginia to Knole, where Virginia was impressed by the long gallery of paintings, the tapestries, and "chairs that Shakespeare might have sat on." Vita came to Monk's House and met Leonard. Then Virginia became ill and spent months in bed, unable to work. The letters between the two women grew increasingly intimate.

In December 1925, three years after their first meeting, Virginia invited herself for a few days' visit to Long Barn, Vita's home in Sussex, not far from Monk's House. They wandered about Long Barn, "a sort of covey of noble English life," as Virginia described in her diary, "dogs walloping, children crowding, all very free & stately." She met Vita's sons and her troop of dogs, led by an Elkhound named Canute. That night, Vita wrote to her husband, "Please don't think that a) I shall fall in love with Virginia, b) Virginia will fall in love with me, c) Leonard will fall in love with me, d) I shall fall in love with Leonard because it is not so."

Whatever Vita intended, the notes she and Virginia exchanged following the visit indicate that they did make love that night. In what would become characteristic of their most intimate correspondence, they used dog images to express their feelings. Vita compared herself to a puppy: "The explosion which happened on the sofa in my room here when you behaved so disgracefully and acquired me forever. Acquired me, that's what you did, like buying a puppy in a shop and leading it away on a string." Virginia, not surprisingly, imagined Vita as a sheepdog: "Vita is a dear old rough coated sheep dog: or alternatively, hung with grapes, pink with pearls, lustrous, candle lit."

Virginia was enchanted by Vita: her graceful clothes, her poise, and her casual attitude toward money, so different from Virginia's own despair over what to wear, her dislike of small talk, and the frugal habits she and Leonard practiced. Sometimes Virginia felt cherished by Vita; at other times, she felt drab and unattractive, and then she identified with Grizzle: "If ever a woman was a lighted candlestick, a glow, an illumination which will cross the desert and leave me—it was Vita; and that's the truth of it: and she has nothing, nor will ever have, in common with dog Grizzle who stands before me, raw, greasy, mudstained." When rumors about Vita's socializing with former lovers reached Virginia, she tried to hide her hurt: "Well, my faithless sheep dog,—you'll be turned into a very old collie if you dont look out, blind of one eye, and afflicted with mange on the rump—why dont you come and see me?"

Virginia taught Vita a private language of animal names and nicknames like the ones she shared with Vanessa, Violet, and Leonard. Before long, Virginia and Vita were taking turns assuming the identity of an animal called a potto, actually a kind of lemur, although their Potto is clearly a dog. Here it is Vita's turn to be Potto: "This letter is principally to say that Potto is not very happy; he mopes; and I am not sure he has not got the mange; so he will probably insist on being brought back to Mrs. Woof [sic]." When Vita learned that Virginia was ill, she imagined Virginia as a sick Potto: "Does Potto sit under the sofa . . . Potto has a stary coat and a hot nose. His tail doesn't wag. It just moves, but only just."

Keeping erotic conversations centered on the imaginary Potto helped Virginia avoid her discomfort about falling in love with a woman. Always more attracted to women than to men, Virginia never completely acknowledged that fact about herself; still, she wondered about her sexuality: "If one could be friendly with women, what a pleasure—the relationship so secret & private compared to relations with men."

When Vita left in January 1926 for an extended visit to Persia, where her husband, Harold, was posted with the British Foreign Service, Virginia's letters grew increasingly erotic. Along with Potto, Grizzle now became the symbol of Virginia's passion for Vita: "Remember your dog Grizzle and your Virginia, waiting for you; both rather mangy; but what of that? These shabby mongrels are always the most loving, warmhearted creatures. Grizzle and Virginia will rush down to meet you—they will lick you all over." In May, as Vita began the long trip back from Persia, she imagined her reunion with Virginia by focusing on Grizzle: "And this will be my last letter. The next thing you know of me, will be that I walk in and fondle Grizzle."

Leonard Woolf tried to accept his wife's relationship with Vita, especially in the company of their Bloomsbury friends who prided themselves on their sexual freedom. Nevertheless, he was worried about the effect of the affair on Virginia's emotional state: When she was ill, he often forbade visits from Vita. Unbeknownst to him, Vita was perfectly aware of Virginia's vulnerability, as evidenced in this letter to her husband: "I am scared to death of arousing physical feelings in her, because of the madness. I don't know what effect it would have, you see; and that is a fire with which I have no wish to play." Still, with her typical bravado, Vita went on to boast to Harold that she had already made love twice with Virginia.

Even though Leonard seemingly tolerated the affair with Vita, he resented her upper-class background. In his autobiography, he remarked that while he and Virginia had shared a working-class heritage—he descended from "ghetto Jews," she from "Scottish serfs"—Vita was different from them: "Although she was in many ways an extremely unassuming and modest person, below the surface, and not so very far below, she had the instinctive arrogance of the aristocrat of the ancient regime."

Thus, Leonard was of two minds when Vita presented both Woolfs with a purebred black puppy from a litter born to Pippin, Vita's Cocker Spaniel. Leonard appreciated the spaniel's breeding; still, he was unhappy about accepting such a valuable gift from Vita. His thank-you note praised the puppy while at the same time questioning the expensive gesture: "The puppy . . . is absolutely charming. She is beautiful, full of spirits, has a will of her own and is intelligent. She refuses to sleep anywhere except in my room and usually insists upon a game in the middle of the night. Grizzle unfortunately is extremely jealous. I don't know how to thank you enough for her, but I wish you would let me pay what you would get for her in the market. Will you?" That Grizzle was jealous was undoubtedly true; even so, Leonard may have recognized in Grizzle's reaction to the puppy his own jealousy of Vita.

Virginia immediately associated the puppy with Vita's privileged background, wondering "Can I live up to a Sackville Hound?" She was more comfortable with mixed breeds such as Grizzle, and yet she valued the dog as a token of Vita's love. Named "Pinka" or "Pinker," the little spaniel was an exuberant creature that embarked on the usual destructive path all puppies travel. Virginia kept Vita informed of Pinka's progress in winning over Leonard: "Your puppy has destroyed, by eating holes, my

Leonard Woolf and Pinka, Monk's House, 1931.

skirt, ate L's proofs, and done such damage as could be done to the carpet—But she is an angel of light. Leonard says seriously she makes him believe in God—and this after she has wetted his floor 8 times in one day."

When the Woolfs traveled, Vita cared for both Grizzle and Pinka at Long Barn. As she strode through the halls of her estate followed by her packs of Elkhounds, the Woolfs' two mismatched dogs joined in. Vita was a confirmed dog lover who was unself-consciously physical with her dogs: touching them, letting them climb over her, and working at her desk with at least one sitting on her lap. Her unfailing cure for insomnia was to collect as many dogs as she could find and take them to bed with her. When Pinka visited, she was usually the dog chosen to sleep with Vita: "Pinker and I try to console one another. She sleeps on my bed, and clings to me as the one comparatively familiar thing in a strange and probably hostile world."

On December 4, 1926, a year after she had first stayed with Vita at Long Barn, Virginia was preparing for another weekend visit. She was relieved and happy because Leonard had just finished the final draft of *To the Lighthouse*, with its vivid memories of her parents and childhood summers at St. Ives, and he had declared it a masterpiece. Virginia dashed off a short note to Vita with a joke about Grizzle's eczema: "No—I can't come. I have caught eczema from Grizzle. My hair comes out in tufts. I scratch incessantly. It wouldn't be safe for you, or, what matters more, the puppies. I shall think of you: let that console us. . . . That joke being done with—yes, I'll come at 5.22. It's true I'm incredibly dirty; have washed my head—hair is down—skirt spotted, shoes in holes." In the diary entry just before she left for the weekend, Virginia paused to consider her relationship with Vita: "So we go on—a spirited, creditable affair, I think, innocent (spiritually) & all again, I think; rather a bore for Leonard, but not enough to worry him."

Perhaps she had misjudged her husband. Under Virginia's entry, Anne Olivier Bell, the editor of Virginia's diary, added this footnote: "On 4 December . . . LW, having had Grizzle put down, spent the night with his brother Herbert." In his diary, Leonard himself wrote: "Had Grizzle Destroyed." Surely Virginia would not have joked about Grizzle's eczema if she had known her dog would die that afternoon. Did Leonard have Grizzle put down without telling Virginia to avoid upsetting her? Or was euthanizing Grizzle a retaliatory act? Whatever the reason, it is unexplainable why neither Virginia nor Vita ever mentioned Grizzle's death in subsequent letters. When Shag died, Virginia had written an obituary, and when Vita's dog Pippin died, Virginia wrote a condolence note: "Darling, we are so unhappy about Pippin—we both send our best love—Leonard is very sad." Yet neither Shag nor Pippin had ever been as important as Grizzle was to Virginia. She had even included her in *Mrs. Dalloway*, where a terrier named Grizzle struggles with skin problems and howls throughout Mrs. Dalloway's party. It remains a mystery why Grizzle's death went unrecorded by either woman. Perhaps the loss of the terrier, symbolic of their love for each other, was simply too painful to mention.

With Grizzle gone, Virginia assigned Pinka—despite her aristocratic breeding and appearance—the role of the scruffy mongrel companion. When Vita left for a second journey to Persia in January of 1927, Virginia wrote a farewell letter in which Pinka takes Grizzle's place. "Please Vita dear don't forget your humble creatures—Pinker and Virginia. Here we are sitting by the gas fire alone. Every morning she jumps on to my bed and kisses me, and I say that's Vita."

Virginia Woolf and Pinka, Monk's House, 1931.

When Vita returned from Persia in the spring, she found Virginia absorbed in the favorable reviews and brisk sales of *To the Lighthouse*. On her part, Vita was mourning the death of her father, which meant the family estate of Knole was lost to her as well. Vita had always known that as a woman, she could not inherit Knole, but she was still devastated when it now passed into the hands of her cousin. At the same time, her husband, Harold, had been posted to Berlin, a city she loathed. Restless and bored, she began a risky, very public affair with a woman who was married to a dangerously jealous husband.

As her relationship with Virginia cooled, Vita occasionally expressed her unhappiness through Pinka. Here Vita is responding to Virginia's decision to stay in London rather than visit Long Barn and collect Pinka: "I had to explain [to Pinka] that Mrs. Woolf lived in London, a separate life, a fact which was as unpleasant to me as it could be to any spaniel puppy, so she has adopted me as a substitute." The note continues in a bantering manner until Vita's tone abruptly shifts: "I explained that everybody always betrayed one sooner or later, and usually gave one away to somebody else and that the only thing to do was to make the best of it." Whether the note is a veiled reference to Vita's current affair or an expression of her insecurity about Virginia's feelings toward her, it illustrates how the two women continued to reveal vulnerability within the safety of a conversation supposedly about dogs.

Virginia responded to the growing distance between them by launching into *Orlando*, a fantasy biography of Vita. The novel spans three centuries in which the androgynous Orlando is sometimes a man, accompanied by ten royal Elkhounds, and sometimes a woman, with a sweet spaniel. Whether or not Virginia deliberately intended the novel as a way to draw Vita back, that is what happened. They spent days together taking photographs for *Orlando* while Vita told Virginia stories about all her lovers. *Orlando* was published in October 1928, and it became a top-selling book in both England and America. To celebrate, the two women took a short trip to France, which turned out to be a companionable holiday rather than the romantic escapade they had anticipated. Some

Virginia Woolf and Pinka with Vita Sackville-West and Pippin, 1933.

time later, Virginia wrote, "My friendship with Vita is over. Not with a quarrel, not with a bang, but as ripe fruit falls."

And although Virginia had not registered Grizzle's death, she wrote a vivid description of the death of the imaginary Potto, an even more significant symbol of Virginia and Vita's love for each other. The passage is curious; it sounds as if Virginia is telling a fanciful story to a child, and yet the tone is so exaggerated that it almost seems to be a parody. Carefully hidden is Virginia's sorrow over the end of the relationship. "Potto is dead. For about a month (you have not been for a month and I date his decline from your last visit) I have watched him failing. First his coat lost lustre; then he refused biscuits; finally gravy. When I asked him what ailed him he sighed, but made no answer. The other day coming unexpectedly into the room, I found him wiping away a tear. He still maintained unbroken silence. Last night it was clear that the end was coming. I sat with him holding his paw in mine and felt the pulse grow feebler. At 7:45 he breathed deeply. I leant over him. I just caught and was able to distinguish the following words—'Tell Mrs. Nick that I love her. . . . She has forgotten me. But I forgive her and . . . (here he could hardly speak) die . . . of . . . a . . . broken . . . heart!' He then expired. . . . Oh my God—my Potto."

Even though Vita and Virginia no longer felt sexual passion for each other, they remained friends for the rest of Virginia's life, exchanging copies of their books, occasionally stopping by each other's homes, and writing infrequent letters, in which shaggy sheepdogs and sometimes Potto appeared, shorthand reminders of what they had once shared.

Virginia spent the next year setting down her ideas about the limitations faced by women writers in A Room of One's Own, which was published in the fall of 1929. Although Vita did not like the book's feminist outlook, it so impressed the well-known composer and conductor Dame Ethel Smyth that she arranged to meet Virginia. Ethel, an eccentric woman in her seventies, declared herself madly in love with Virginia and immediately began to flood her with letters. Virginia was often embarrassed by Ethel's outspoken lesbianism and radical feminism, and she could become drained by Ethel's intense, incessant talk. Nevertheless, she trusted and admired Ethel and was glad of her friendship, particularly when it was conducted in letters rather than in person.

Once again, dogs were an important part of her connection

with a woman; in Ethel's case, she actually owned sheepdogs, a succession of them all named Pan, each of which met an untimely
death. Whenever one died, Virginia tried to console Ethel, which
did not, however, prevent Virginia from commenting derisively to
Vita, "Ethel's new dog is dead. The truth is, no dog can stand the
strain of living with Ethel. I went down one day and found it on the
verge of nervous collapse, simply from listening to her conversation." In other moods, Virginia could admire Ethel's tenacity as she
struggled with male-dominated orchestras to have her music
played: "At the dead of last night being sleepless I thought of you
with a clap of admiration, exercising the puppy, writing the book—
thought of you as a little tossing tug boat might think of a majestic
sea going white-spread, fountain-attended dolphin-encircled ship—
forging on and on." In the final years of her life, Virginia would trust
Ethel with uncharacteristically frank letters describing her childhood, her illnesses, and her marriage.

Gradually, Virginia and Leonard bridged whatever distance
had developed between them during Virginia's affair with Vita. The
couple's mutual delight in Pinka helped, even though the little
spaniel would always be a bittersweet reminder of Vita. Pinka, like
her predecessor Grizzle, brought fun into the Woolfs' childless
marriage. In London, they took her on outings to the park and to
work with them at Hogarth Press. An employee remembered
Pinka's frequent visits and described the sight of Leonard, usually
very businesslike, "making an entry in a ledger [while] Pinka calmly
climbed on a chair and licked his nose."

At Monk's House, Pinka took part in the couple's daily routines: She followed Leonard while he gardened and kept up with
Virginia when she walked over to Charleston to visit Vanessa. As
Virginia began the first draft of *The Waves*, which she envisioned as
an elegy for her brother Thoby, Pinka kept her company in the
small writing hut with its window overlooking the fields. On fine
evenings, the couple's cutthroat lawn-bowling games were interrupted when Pinka decided to run after a ball. After supper, she
curled up in her chair in the living room as Virginia and Leonard

read or listened to music. As soon as Leonard announced the word *bed*, Virginia and Pinka had a little ritual: "Pinka jumps down from her chair, and we go in procession through the garden to my room; where I lie, and look through the apple leaves, at the clouds that hide the stars."

Virginia's earnings from *Orlando* allowed the Woolfs to buy a car, and they took Pinka with them on excursions throughout England, delivering Hogarth Press books to booksellers and poking about antique shops. When they went on a vacation to Ireland, they not only brought Pinka, they also brought all her special soaps and combs because, like Grizzle, she had developed skin problems. When visiting a sacred shrine where one could make a wish, Leonard announced that he wished Pinka would not smell so bad. On one rare occasion, Virginia took a short trip without Leonard. He expressed his loneliness through Pinka in a note like the ones Vita and Virginia had once written to each other: "Dearest, it was melancholy to see you fade away in the train, and Pink cannot understand what has happened. She insisted upon going in at once to your room this morning to see whether you were or were not in bed."

Pinka added an amusingly erotic element to Virginia and Leonard's companionable relationship. They enjoyed the spectacle of all the neighbor dogs' coming around whenever Pinka was in heat: "It was a divine day yesterday—O how happy we were!— mildly sauntering down to the river, and protecting Pinka's chastity, now in bloom, from Botten's yellow cur." Virginia gleefully reported Pinka's sexual exploits in letters to friends and family: "Pinka, who has a newspaper under her, as she is violently on heat, yet must be exercised, and if you consider that there are ten fox terriers in the Square, all belonging to old, and mostly maiden, ladies, you can forgive the gusto with which, when I've written this, I must take her out." Somewhat wistfully, Virginia contrasted Pinka's experience of mating in the park to the contemporary stigma against women's making love: "Beauty shines on two dogs doing what two women must not do."

When Pinka gave birth to a litter of puppies in an armchair at Monk's House, Virginia's mixed feelings about motherhood were aroused: "And Pink has five black pups—the sixth she sat on, conveniently, for to tell the truth five black bitches in my room are enough." In her diary, Virginia often mentioned her envy of Vanessa's three children and reminded herself to be honest about her childlessness: "Never pretend that the things you haven't got are not worth having. . . . Never pretend that children, for instance, can be replaced by other things." Yet, based on memories of her own mother and observations of Vanessa, Virginia resented the way motherhood can take over a woman's entire existence. Even though Leonard and Virginia were unabashedly affectionate toward the puppies, calling them "the Poos," Virginia pointed out that Pinka now exhibited all the "maternal vices—absorbed, devoted, zealous, cowish"—that she scorned.

When Pinka was not mating or caring for puppies, she was a calm companion for Virginia: "Pinka is snoring by the fire: there is a thick fog." When illness forced Virginia to stop writing, Pinka helped her endure the empty hours: "Half the horrors of illness cease when one has a book or a dog or a cup of one's own at hand." And just as she had done with Hans and Grizzle, Virginia taught Pinka to put out her matches, a trick the spaniel loved because she was rewarded with treats. Pinka was obedient to Leonard but knew her mistress would never discipline her. Virginia attributed her relaxed attitude to her vocation as a writer: "Why does my spaniel jump onto the chairs when she is dripping from a swim in the river? The answer is that instead of controlling life . . . we writers merely contemplate it." Virginia enjoyed watching dogs be dogs, a theme she would develop later in *Flush: A Biography*.

Long walks with Pinka helped Virginia unwind from writing, and they kept her aware of the changing seasons, even in London: "It is very quiet & very cold. I walked Pinka through the Saturday streets this afternoon & was woken to the fact that it is April by a primrose on the pavement." After hours of grinding work, Virginia needed to walk: "The only cheerful event was walking with Pinker through a field of clouded yellows this afternoon." In town or the country, the two went out no matter the weather, with Virginia dressed in a haphazard assortment of boots, scarves, and hats: "I've just come in from a walk with Pinka across the fields, with 5 mushrooms in my hat. True it drizzles . . . but I don't care."

In 1931, when Virginia was nearly fifty, she completed *The Waves*, an experimental novel that presented the lives of six people with few biographic details and little plot. In *Jacob's Room*, which had been published in 1922, Virginia had tried to imagine Thoby's life if he had lived, but in *The Waves*, she was finally able to write about his death. When she finished the last sentence, she wrote in her diary, "Anyhow it is done and I have been sitting these 15 minutes in a state of glory, and calm, and some tears, thinking of Thoby."

Virginia had learned that after intense creative work, she would fall into a mood of disturbing restlessness, which could lead to another breakdown. Both Emily Dickinson and Emily Brontë had depended on their dogs to keep them grounded during the "white heat" of sustained creative work, and Virginia Woolf found a dog to play a similar role for her. It was not Pinka, as one might expect; instead, she decided to write about another spaniel, Elizabeth Barrett Browning's Flush: "I was so tired after *The Waves*, that I lay in the garden and read the Browning love letters, and the figure of their dog made me laugh so I couldn't resist making him a Life." The Browning letters do contain amusing descriptions of Flush, but they also describe Elizabeth's anguish over her brother's death. Virginia could not have missed the connection to her own grief for Thoby, now reawakened by *The Waves*. Still, she insisted she intended *Flush* as a cheerful book, telling her American editor, "I hope to send you a short and simple little book soon. . . . It is by way of a joke. And then I want to get to work on a longer novel."

Despite her claims that *Flush* was simply a diversion, Virginia approached the book as carefully as she did all her writing projects. Much of her information came from her own spaniel Pinka, whom she used as the model for Flush: "The dog who acted his part here was black—but there can be no doubt that Flush was red." Virginia also studied spaniels in general, learning the history of the breed and the breed standard as set by the British Spaniel Club. After completing her research, Virginia began the first draft. Soon, though, she realized that she faced a dilemma: She could not make up her mind whether or not *Flush* was a serious book, a question that baffles readers to this day. "Four months of work and heaven knows how much reading—not of an exalted kind either—and I can't see how to make anything of it. It is not the right subject for that length: it's too slight and too serious."

Originally, Virginia had thought of *Flush* as a spoof of the serious biographies her friend Lytton Strachey wrote. "I wanted to play a joke on Lytton—it was to parody him." Then Lytton, who had been ill for years, suddenly died, leaving his lover Dora Carrington so devastated that she committed suicide. Disheartened, Virginia put her biographical parody aside but discovered she could not abandon the book: "I nibble at Flush. . . . I feel the point is rather gone, as I meant it for a joke with Lytton, and a skit on him. But I'll see."

Virginia kept putting *Flush* down and coming back to it. She knew it would sell well and predicted it would be popular (it did become a top-selling book, especially in the United States, where it was selected as Book of the Month by the popular book club), but that was not why she was drawn to write it: "I shall very much dislike the popular success of Flush." Virginia knew her friends would disapprove of what they would consider a frivolous subject. In a letter to Ethel Smyth, she admitted, "I write every morning, and I'm enjoying my writing, word by word, hugely. How you'll hate it!" Just as Elizabeth Barrett Browning had enjoyed writing about the real Flush and had dismissed her friends' objections, Virginia Woolf also ignored the criticism she imagined from friends.

Virginia did not think a dog was any less serious a subject than a person. She treated the little spaniel with the same dignity and concern for her subject that she would later show toward her friend the art critic Roger Fry, when she wrote his biography. Her respectful yet lighthearted attitude toward Flush is evident in her reply to one reader: "I am very glad to think that you share my sympathy for Flush. . . . Very little is known about him, and I have had to invent a good deal. I hope however that I have thrown some light upon his character—the more I know him, the more affection I feel for him." In *Flush*, Virginia so vividly imagined the sensual world a dog inhabits that Quentin Bell remarked it was "not so much a book by a dog lover as a book by someone who would love to be a dog."

With charming illustrations by Vanessa and a photograph of Pinka on the cover, *Flush* seems at first merely a pleasant retelling of the story of Elizabeth Barrett Browning's dog. Then, when Flush is stolen by dognappers, the book's ironic humor vanishes. In Elizabeth Barrett Browning's letters, the focus is on her distress over Flush's disappearance and her anger at those who take dogs and hold them for ransom. In Virginia's account, the focus is on Flush. The reader is taken to the dark, dirty cellar in Whitechapel where Flush is held captive and shown his despair as he lies, hungry and desperately thirsty, chained to a stone wall. The reader smells the fear of the terrified pets and hears the shrill barking and quiet whimpering of the dogs, the panicked screeches of stolen birds. It is a nightmare world where dogs lie in their own filth, subject to random kicks and curses, and the air is filled with the sounds of frantic birds trying to escape.

Finally, Flush is ransomed and returned home, his ordeal over, according to Elizabeth Barrett Browning. But Virginia Woolf's version is a more realistic portrayal of the aftereffects of a traumatic event. Her Flush remains hypervigilant, jumping in alarm at any sudden noise, and is listless and indifferent. He suffers from intrusive flashbacks, even though he is safe in Elizabeth's room. "As he lay dazed and exhausted on the sofa . . . the howls of tethered dogs, the screams of birds in terror still sounded in his ears." Flush has lost his innocent view of the world and now sees it as a dangerous place: "This room was no longer the whole world: it was only a shelter . . . in a forest where wild beasts prowled and venomous snakes coiled."

The intensity of the dognapping scenes and their accurate depiction of the inner effects of trauma suggest that writing about Flush's ordeal was a way for Virginia to begin to deal with her own childhood molestation by Gerald Duckworth. Virginia had begun to write about those memories in *Sketch of the Past*, her unfinished memoir, as well as in letters to Ethel Smyth, so it is not surprising to see traces of them in *Flush*. One critic commented that writing *Flush* allowed Virginia to bring "to the surface the repressed emotional narrative of her childhood," and there certainly does seem to be an associative link between the shock of a child molested in her own home by trusted family members and Virginia's description of Flush suddenly snatched from a secure life into a place of shame and fear. "One moment he was in Vere Street, among ribbons and laces; the next he was tumbled head over heels into a bag."

While in captivity, Flush is humiliated by his captors: "A fat woman held him up by his ears and pinched his ribs, and some odious joke was made about him—there was a roar of laughter as she threw him on the floor again." This scene recalls Virginia's memory of an event that occurred when she was about six. Her half brother Gerald, then twenty, had picked her up and placed her on a ledge in front of a mirror in the dining room. He then molested her, while she stood paralyzed watching his face in the mirror. Virginia confided to Ethel, "I still shiver

Pinka posing as Flush on the cover of *Flush: A Biography*.

with shame at the memory of my half brother, standing me on a ledge, aged about 6, and so exploring my private parts. Why should I have felt shame then?"

The layers of meaning beneath the deceptively simple *Flush: A Biography* help to explain why Virginia could not dash off the book as planned; instead, she spent two years on it. Although she was eager to start her next novel (images and ideas that would be transformed into *The Years* were already appearing in her diary), she could not begin until she was satisfied with her current book: "Well, Flush lingers on & I cannot dispatch him. That's the sad truth. I always see something I could press tighter, or enwrap more completely." She grew more and more frustrated "trying to rewrite that abominable dog Flush." Finally, Virginia declared the book completed: "Well Flush is, I swear, dispatched. Nobody can say I don't take trouble with my little stories."

During the years she spent on *Flush*, Virginia was unsettled. She had felt this way while writing other books, but then she had understood the reasons for her feelings: *To the Lighthouse* brought up memories of her mother's death; *Orlando*, her love for Vita; and *The Waves*, Thoby's death. Virginia was apparently unaware of the connection between her childhood molestation and the mood of *Flush*, yet she did realize there was something unexplainable about the book. She wrote to an appreciative reader, "I'm so glad that you liked *Flush*. I think it shows great discrimination in you because it was all a matter of hints and shades, and practically no one has seen what I was after."

In the spring of 1935, Virginia and Leonard, ignoring the threat of war, took a road trip through Holland, Germany, and Italy. Vita was on a cruise, so they left Pinka in the care of Percy, the Woolfs' gardener at Monk's House. On their way back to England, Virginia imagined their homecoming: "This time tomorrow we shall be in Monk's House. Leonard will be talking to Pinka." Instead, as they drove up to the house, they came upon the terrible sight of "poor old Pinka's dead body: She had a fit and died the day before we came, and Percy was burying her in her basket and we were both very unhappy." Later in her diary, Virginia elaborated on the moment they saw Pinka's body and their grief: "Percy was very red, very sad, screwed his eyes up, would not smile at us, & then told us. So that's what's bound to happen we said. A very silent breakfast. I had been saying how she would put out my match & all the usual jokes."

Virginia began to explore her reactions to Pinka's death, then stopped because she was afraid of becoming overwrought: "And the intensity of the sense of death—even for a dog—how odd—our feeling of her character, & the grotesqueness—something pathetic, & the depression, & the I suppose fear of sentimentality & so on." She put the diary aside and went out to her writing hut to work. Too upset and distracted to concentrate, Virginia started a letter to Ethel: "This you'll call sentimental—perhaps—but then a dog somehow represents—no I can't think of the word—the private side of life—the play side." In her diary, Virginia continued to puzzle out why she felt so bereft: "8 years of a dog certainly mean something. I suppose—is it part of our life that's buried in the orchard? That 8 years in London—our walks—something of our play private life, that's gone?"

Even as she contemplated the meaning of Pinka's death, Virginia seemed not to recognize the degree to which she had depended on the dog as an aid to her creative process. While Pinka was alive, Virginia had composed entire sections of books by talking them out loud while she walked with her, in a state of "trance like swimming," as Virginia described it, "flying through the air; the current of sensations & ideas; & the slow, but fresh change of down, of road, of colour." Now, Virginia admitted to being in a "fussing & fidgeting" internal state because she could not write: "I can't get into that stream by standing & wishing it. All sorts of habits, of being unconscious of the surface, attentive to other things have to settle naturally. . . . Habit is the desirable thing in writing." Pinka must have been one of the "unconscious habits" Virginia needed before she could write.

A week later, Virginia wrote a short note to Vita: "And we came back to find Pinka dead. Isn't it a miserable thing—Leonard is so unhappy." Vita immediately offered them a new puppy, which Virginia refused, saying Leonard was still "too melancholy," but she added, "He must have another." She went on to give details indicating that she and Leonard were struggling to understand why their young, healthy dog had suddenly died: "Pinka's death was a mystery. We left her in perfect health with Percy, and she was in the highest spirits for the first fortnight. Suddenly she had three fits; they got the vet, who said he didn't know what it was: but she grew weaker and weaker, wouldn't eat, and died the day before we came."

Exactly one month later, Leonard and Virginia bought Sally, a black-and-white spaniel. Leonard had refused to accept another dog from Vita, so Sally came from a breeder in Ickenham, a London suburb. From the beginning, she was destined to be Leonard's dog: "We've bought a dog who is at once passionately in love with Leonard. Its a curious case of hopeless erotic mania—precisely like a human passion." Virginia reserved judgment on the new dog, appraising the thirteen-month-old spaniel in a detached way. She assessed the dog's appearance with knowledge undoubtedly learned from her research for *Flush:* "She has a fine domed head . . . very globular eyes; a bloodhounds muzzle." She added with a touch of sarcasm that if Sally's nose had been one-eighteenth of an inch longer, she would have been a champion like her sister. Virginia found Sally very affectionate, noting how the puppy would cling to Leonard's breast when they descended the basement steps, which terrified her.

But Virginia never formed an attachment to Sally. For one thing, she was accustomed to adopting dogs or receiving them as gifts and was startled by the puppy's price: "She cost £18—dear me." Nevertheless, she tried to accept what must have been Leonard's arguments for buying an expensive purebred: "Still as we say, its nice to have a good dog. And we shall breed from her." Although Virginia admired Sally's good looks, she believed that the new dog had less substance than Pinka. "She is very distinguished looking. The only question is, has she intelligence? She has already her own rather gentle whimsical manner—fumbles, paws; is lighter, more nervous, perhaps less solid a character than Pinka."

Virginia could not walk Sally because the energetic puppy tugged too hard at the leash, nor did she become involved with Leonard's attempts to mate Sally as she had with Grizzle and Pinka. There are no tales of male dogs chasing them through parks or of battening down the doors against neighborhood strays, only a passing remark that Sally had been "almost surgically mated" by the breeder. When Sally did not conceive, Virginia was unconcerned and wryly placed the blame on Leonard: "Love for him, they say, has turned her barren."

Between the publication of *Flush* in 1933 and Britain's declaration of war on Germany in 1939, Virginia enjoyed a period of sustained productivity. She completed *The Years*, the story of a British family in which Ethel Smyth appears in the character of an outspoken suffragist, and she began *Three Guineas*, a feminist argument against war. Virginia's life changed unalterably, however, once war was declared. The Woolfs' London home and printing press were both bombed; when they saw the wreckage, Virginia was stunned: "The passion of my life, that is the City of London—to see London all blasted, that too raked my heart."

The Woolfs retreated to Monk's House, which was frigid because of coal rationing and crowded with the furniture and boxes of books they had salvaged from London. Because of the war, they had no servants, and Virginia grew exhausted from constant shopping and endless cooking and cleaning: "It's rather a hard lap: the winter lap. So cold often. And so much work to do. And so little fat to cook with. And so much shopping to do. And one has to weigh and measure." German planes began flying over the Downs; when one was shot down, the villagers kicked and battered the bodies of the dead airmen. Virginia and Leonard made a pact to commit suicide if the Germans invaded.

The despair of war intensified Virginia's need for maternal protectiveness from her women friends, and she continued her practice of using dogs to connect with them. When Germany invaded Vienna, Virginia tried to ignore the war news, instead asking Ethel about her new puppy: "And how's he shaping? Dogs and daffodils alone retain their sanity." In one of Virginia's last letters to Vita, written in 1939, Virginia harked back to their love for each other, describing Vita's latest book as "a dose of sanity and sheep dog in this scratching, clawing, and colding universe."

But this time, Virginia could not count on the women in her life for support. Vanessa was immobilized by grief for her son Julian Bell, who had been killed in the Spanish civil war. Violet Dickinson, convalescing with a broken hip, was living in virtual isolation at her country home, while Vita was absorbed in rebuilding Sissinghurst Castle and in volunteering as an ambulance driver. Ethel Smyth did realize Virginia was despondent, and she did her best to stay in close touch, even if only with letters. Virginia admitted to Ethel that she was terribly discouraged by the bad reviews of *Three Guineas* and by Leonard's pessimism about the war. As she had done with Violet and Vita, Virginia imagined herself as Ethel's dog: "Meanwhile, yes, I like laying my furry head on your magnanimous breast . . . in sympathetic reference to Pan." Ethel tried to visit Virginia, but even she could not circumvent wartime travel restrictions.

Nor could Virginia rely on her writing to stave off depression. She could not concentrate on her last novel, *Between the Acts*, which has been described as one long suicide note. Intended as a tribute to the endurance of the English people in wartime, the book is full of foreboding gloom. A bleak diary entry captures Virginia's despair: " 'My books only gave me pain,' Ch. [Charlotte] Brontë said. Today I agree."

With the Hogarth Press closed down, Leonard had few activities outside of volunteer war work in the village, and so he was often home. He worried that they were running out of money, despite their considerable savings, and he pressured Virginia to abandon the novel to write articles. She felt hemmed in by his demands:

"One never is free for more than a dogs chain length." At the same time, she felt that Leonard interrupted her whenever she did try to write: "As I cannot write if anyone is in the room, as L.'s here when we light the fire, this book remains shut." Virginia found no solace in Sally and seemed indifferent to the dog, referring to her as "L.'s old fine trusty crone." As she grew more depressed, Virginia became increasingly hostile to both Leonard and Sally. In January 1941, she tried to begin what would be her last diary, but she felt so exposed by their presence that she could not complete the first entry: "A psychologist would see that the above was written with someone & a dog, in the room."

And although she resented Leonard and Sally's presence, Virginia dreaded solitude: "Very lonely. L. out to lunch. Nessa has Quentin & don't want me. Very useless. No atmosphere round me. No words. Very apprehensive. As if something cold & horrible—a roar of laughter at my expense were about to happen. And I am powerless to ward it off: I have no protection. And this anxiety & nothingness surround me like a vacuum." Leonard was spending hours at Charleston, where Vanessa was painting a portrait of him with Sally, and Virginia suspected they were talking about her behind her back. Indeed, the two were very worried about her. Vanessa wrote what would be her last letter to her sister, a mixture of impatience, concern, and gratitude for how Virginia had helped her after Julian's death: "You must not go and get ill just now. What shall we do when we're invaded if you are a helpless invalid. What should I have done all these last 3 years if you hadn't been able to keep me alive and cheerful. You don't know how much I depend on you." However, not even Vanessa was able to penetrate her sister's despair.

Then Virginia began to hear voices and knew she was going mad again. Her attention was caught by a newspaper report of a woman who drowned herself in the river Ouse. She remembered that she had seen the woman "moon[ing] over the downs with a dog," just as Virginia had done with Pinka. With chilling precision, in view of what she herself was about to do, Virginia noted in her diary the details of the story that particularly struck her: "She had killed her dog. So at last off she goes, on Monday perhaps when the tide was high in the afternoon, & jumps in." It seemed that the nameless woman, who had lost her son in the war, did not feel free to kill herself until she had first killed her dog.

Virginia could not face another breakdown. She made careful plans to take her life, writing a suicide note to Vanessa that ended with the words "If I could I would tell you what you and the children have meant to me. I think you know." To Leonard, she wrote two longer notes, both including the same message: "I don't think two people could have been happier than we have been." She took her walking stick and put stones in the pockets of her fur coat. Disconnected from her friends, feeling estranged from Leonard and Vanessa, unable to write, Virginia no longer had a private, playful side of life into which she could retreat. Pinka could not have prevented her suicide, but perhaps she would have distracted Virginia, offered her comfort, or given her a way to connect with other people. But on March 28, 1941, when Virginia Woolf walked across the fields to drown herself in the river Ouse, she had no dog and so she walked alone.

Chronology

VIRGINIA WOOLF

1882   January, birth of Virginia Woolf.

1886   [May, death of Emily Dickinson.]

1895   May, death of Virginia's mother, Julia Stephen.

1897   July, death of Virginia's half sister, Stella Duckworth.

1904   February, death of Virginia's father, Leslie Stephen.
        Death of Shag.
        October, Virginia and siblings move to the Bloomsbury
        area of London.

1906   November, death of Virginia's brother Thoby Stephen.

1912   August 10, marriage to Leonard Woolf.

1915   Leonard and Virginia buy Hogarth House.
        The Voyage Out published.

1917   Virginia and Leonard start Hogarth Press.

1919   *Kew Gardens* published.
        Virginia and Leonard buy Monk's House.

Night and Day published.
Grizzle arrives.

1922   *Jacob's Room* published.
Virginia meets Vita Sackville-West.

1925   Vita Sackville-West and Virginia start an affair.
Mrs. Dalloway and *The Common Reader* published.

1926   Vita gives Pinka to the Woolfs.
Death of Grizzle.

1927   *To the Lighthouse* published.

1928   The affair with Vita ends.
Orlando published.

1929   *A Room of One's Own* published.

1930   Virginia meets Ethyl Smyth.

1931   October, *The Waves* published.
Virginia starts writing *Flush: A Biography*.

1933   October, *Flush: A Biography* published.

1935   Death of Pinka.

1937   July, death of Vanessa's son Julian Bell, in the Spanish
civil war.
The Years published.
[August, death of Edith Wharton.]

1938   *Three Guineas* published.

1940   Virginia completes a draft of *Between the Acts*.

1941   March 28, death of Virginia Woolf, age fifty-nine. Her
ashes are buried in the garden at Monk's House.

Afterword

THE DOGS

FLUSH, KEEPER, CARLO, Linky, Grizzle, Pinka, and all the other dogs in *Shaggy Muses* were ordinary dogs, not especially heroic, beautiful, or intelligent. Ranging from scruffy mongrel to spoiled lapdog to ferocious guard dog, they simply acted, as Robert Browning said of Flush, "as dogs do."

And yet, just by following their instincts, dogs can be the most responsive companions we will ever know. From their wolf ancestors, whose survival depended on their closely monitoring the dominant wolf, they learned to watch their leader carefully. Our dogs perceive us as their leaders and read us with consummate skill, picking up subtle cues that we are not even aware of giving. During their long history of close contact with humans, dogs have perfected their ability to be attuned to us.

The often celebrated loyalty of dogs arises from their strong need to stay in close proximity to us. Unlike other domesticated animals—such as cows, sheep, or horses—dogs made the first move toward living with people. This occurred when a wolf ancestor, a bit less wary than other wolves, discovered it was easier to survive on food discarded by humans than to hunt. He moved out of the forests and closer to a tribe, where he was gradually joined by other wolves with similar temperaments. When they mated, they produced offspring with increasingly docile dispositions. Inevitably, the moment came when someone adopted an especially appealing puppy, and soon dogs were moving into our homes and hearts.

An ancient myth, found the world over, tells in metaphor the same story as scientific accounts of the dog's domestication: Soon after creation, a deep chasm opened in the earth. As it slowly widened, it began to separate humans from all the other animals. The dog stood on the brink of the chasm, hesitated for a moment, and then leaped across to his place by the side of humans, thus becoming the only animal to live with us by choice.

Elizabeth Barrett Browning, Emily Brontë, Emily Dickinson, Edith Wharton, and Virginia Woolf all recognized these paramount canine traits of responsiveness and loyalty, but they also discovered more to admire in their dogs. They describe their shaggy companions with the same finely honed perceptiveness, fierce intelligence, and uncompromising self-knowledge that they brought to all their writing. And it is abundantly clear how much each woman enjoyed writing about dogs. In fact, Elizabeth Barrett Browning became so intrigued by the subject that she once stated, "If I leave off verse to write in prose, it shall be a dissertation on the Souls of Dogs." She never did abandon poetry to tackle the question of dogs' souls, but neither did she nor the other writers ever underestimate the importance of their canine companions. Reflecting on some of their key passages about dogs can deepen our understanding of what our own dogs mean to us.

"He & I are inseparable companions, and I have vowed him my perpetual society in exchange for his devotion."

Elizabeth Barrett Browning's vow to Flush is the bedrock that underlies every human-dog bond. We take care of our dogs, and, in return, they provide us with a secure, consistent attachment. This dependable link was vitally important to the women in this book because their mothers, for different reasons, were unable to form strong bonds with them. Their fathers, partly as a result of the times in which they lived but also because of their personalities, paid little attention to their gifted daughters. To a certain degree, the women's siblings, servants, and friends helped fill the void left by their parents' emotional absence. Their dogs, though, came closest to providing the kind of secure connection that each woman lacked.

In fact, the dogs in *Shaggy Muses* could be considered attachment figures. Dogs naturally provide the kind of nonverbal, tactile interactions that closely resemble the exquisitely attuned responses found in a healthy mother-infant attachment. Without a caring attachment figure, human infants do not survive. As adults, especially in times of stress, we continue to need attachment figures, whether an actual physical presence or the memory of someone who cared for us. And dogs, in their own quiet, unobtrusive way, can function as attachment figures.

When we are frightened or upset, we desperately want to be near those we consider attachment figures because being in their presence feels like coming into a safe harbor. Edith Wharton counted on her last dog Linky to provide this feeling of warm security. Photographs show the graying Pekingese sitting on Edith's lap and once even in a pram. An elderly woman who dresses her lapdog in sweaters and treats it like a baby can be a target of ridicule, unless one realizes that Edith needed Linky to help endure the pain of losing nearly everyone she loved. This became abundantly clear after Linky's death when Edith, by then terminally ill, wrote, "I feel for the very first time in my life, quite utterly alone and lonely."

Attachment figures also provide a secure base that gives us the courage to venture forth and take risks. As Elizabeth Barrett Browning grew physically stronger and more self-assured, Flush was right beside her as she moved toward autonomy. When he was stolen, she discovered she had the inner strength to face the dognappers and demand his return. The knowledge of her newfound fortitude helped her when she defied her tyrannical father and eloped with Robert Browning.

In addition to providing a safe harbor and a secure base, attachment figures teach us how to tolerate and moderate unsettling emotions. A child's powerful feelings are terrifying if they are experienced alone. In the sheltering presence of a caring adult, a child learns that strong emotions are part of life and not to be feared. A striking example of a dog taking on this role occurred when Emily Brontë flew into a rage and beat Keeper for sleeping on the parsonage beds. He did not retaliate, Emily's anger ran its course, and she ended the outburst by contritely caring for Keeper's wounds. This one incident may have helped her realize that anger was a force she could control, not one that would overpower her, since there are no further reports of Emily abusing her dog. After their relationship settled into one of mutual devotion, Keeper appears to have filled almost all of Emily Brontë's attachment needs. Without him, she would have been truly isolated.

More typically, a dog becomes an attachment figure only during difficult life transitions. Elizabeth Barrett Browning depended on Flush as her "chief consoler" during the years she struggled with grief and depression, but once she fell in love with Robert Browning, she no longer needed Flush for emotional support. Like most dogs, he adjusted easily to this change. In Italy, he ran about with other dogs and did not seem to miss his formerly cloistered life as Elizabeth's sole companion. Dogs do not feel betrayed if they are moved from the center of our emotional lives as long as they are allowed to continue to share our lives, our "perpetual society."

"I talk of all these things with Carlo, and his eyes grow meaning and his shaggy feet keep a slower pace."

Emily Dickinson's description of Carlo serves as a perfect example of a dog in the role of witness, in the ancient sense of one who bears testimony to the truth. Carlo—unlike Emily's friends and family, who often felt drained by her intensity—would wait patiently while she poured out her anxiety and loneliness to him. When he slowed his pace to match hers and gazed at her with dark

Newfoundland eyes, he seemed to be encouraging her to continue talking. Emily then saw Carlo's "eyes grow meaning," and she felt truly seen and witnessed.

Because they belong to a different species, dogs do not perceive, much less judge, changes in our appearance, our social status, or our profession. This is why, according to Sigmund Freud, "One can love an animal . . . with such an extraordinary intensity: affection without ambivalence, the simplicity of a life free from the almost unbearable conflicts of civilization, the beauty of an existence, complete in itself." Dogs respond to aspects of ourselves that others do not notice. To us, this can feel as though they see the truth beneath surface appearances and recognize our true selves. Elizabeth Barrett Browning was comforted by her belief that Flush continued to see her as "Miss Barrett" despite the changes brought about by her marriage, emigration to Italy, and motherhood. When Edith Wharton felt buffeted and isolated after her scandalous divorce, she knew she could rely on her lapdogs to continue greeting her with yelps of affection as they had always done.

Dogs often witness parts of ourselves we have trouble recognizing and accepting. As Emily Brontë tended Keeper, he was a witness to the feminine, nurturing side of her that rarely surfaced. And Emily Dickinson used Carlo to convey her passion to her lover. Her request that he "Tell Carlo and *he'll* tell *me*" reveals her hope that Carlo will cushion the lover's inevitable rejection of her sexual feelings, so well concealed beneath her "woman in white" persona.

A dog can also act as a witness for his owner's creative work. Jungian analyst Maria von Franz discovered a pattern in hundreds of creation myths in which there is "an active creator and a relatively more passive other, who does little but is still absolutely essential." One example is the Native American creation myth, which describes Father Raven creating the world, while a small sparrow acts as a witness. The sparrow's job is to make sure that Father Raven is not swept away by the dangerous forces of the creative process. Like the watchful sparrow, the dogs in this book helped their owners stay connected to the everyday world, no matter how compelling or disturbing their writing became.

"My little old dog:— / A heart-beat / At my feet."

In this short poem, Edith Wharton portrays the solace she found in the sound of Linky's breathing and the feel of that solid little Peke body nestled next to her. The poem evokes the mythic image of a dog sleeping on the hearth, an archetypal symbol of peace and safety, dating back to earliest times when humans knew if the dog lay down, it was safe for them to do so.

Wharton's poem also suggests the concept of limbic resonance, an idea recently identified by scientists who have studied the limbic area of the brain, the part that regulates emotions. Limbic resonance refers to the ability of mammals to soothe one another by regulating their heartbeats and breathing to be in synchrony. The result is a shared sense of well-being and safety. The wordless harmony known as limbic resonance can occur across species, especially between humans and dogs.

Elizabeth Barrett Browning's descriptions of her hours alone with Flush in the dark sickroom sound like experiences of limbic resonance: "Flush's breathing is my loudest sound—& then the watch's ticking—& then my own heart when it beats too turbulently." As the fragile woman and her sturdy spaniel lay quietly in her bed, their bodily rhythms ebbed and flowed in harmony, creating the healing silence that Elizabeth needed to mourn the deaths of her mother and brothers.

When one mammal senses another's agitation, it attempts to quiet the other by keeping close to it. When young Virginia Woolf was recovering from her first suicide attempt, she complained that sheepdog Gurth, "that extraordinarily ubiquitous dog," would never leave her alone. She eventually discovered that his focused attention calmed her, and she began to depend on it. In middle age, Virginia would often fall into a reverie while sitting with her spaniel Pinka. Her nephew remembered how peaceful she was in those moments: "Sometimes, when talking, she would slowly caress Pinka's nose, thoughtfully stroking it in the wrong direction."

Another example of limbic resonance, this time a dog being comforted by his owner, can be seen in Charlotte Bronte's description of Emily and Keeper in front of the fire: "One hand of the mistress generally reposes on the loving serf's rude head, because if she takes it away he groans and is discontented." Dogs can be calmed by the touch of a hand or the voice of someone they know. Keeper had been a suspicious and aggressive dog, but once he and Emily learned to trust each other, the wary mastiff could finally let down his guard.

"A dog somehow represents . . . the private side of life—the play side."

When Virginia Woolf came upon Pinka's paw prints on her blotter the morning after the young spaniel's sudden death, she felt a stab of grief. Pinka was a good-sized Cocker Spaniel, and Virginia's writing table is quite small, so it is not clear how the paw prints got on her blotter. Perhaps the two of them had devised a game in which Pinka jumped onto the desk, distracting Virginia from her intense inward focus, in the same way Flush had when he tumbled down Elizabeth Barrett Browning's shoulders.

Playing silly repetitive games with dogs reconnects us to childhood pleasures, with an added appreciation we did not have as children. We can receive from our dog a love that feels maternal and unconditional, while at the same time, we can love our dog as if he were our child. According to scientist Alan Beck and psychiatrist Aaron Katcher, who have done extensive research on the human-dog bond, this two-edged emotion explains why a pet can bring so much joy: "Life with a pet recreates a childhood that never was."

Pets invite the childlike behavior that we discard as we become adults. Virginia Woolf, the ferociously witty center of the Bloomsbury set, seems far less formidable when we learn that she patiently taught each of her dogs to put out a match with his paw and delighted in this trick whenever she lit a cigarette. Even Emily Brontë reveals a playful side with her sketches of the family dogs, which were obviously undertaken with pleasure. The sketches of Keeper curled up with the family cat and Flossy chasing a goshawk are reminders of the carefree hours Emily spent on the moors with her animals.

Caring for a dog reconnects us to the natural world that we knew so well as children. Beck and Katcher point out that dogs immerse their owners in the "constancy of cyclical time—life in the cycles of days, months, seasons, and lifetimes." Virginia Woolf relied on long walks with Pinka through the streets of London or across the Sussex downs to unwind after hours of writing. Emily Dickinson and Carlo strolled about the garden and marveled at the flight of a hummingbird, all the while staying alert for Lavinia's cats. Edith Wharton spent her later years in two beautiful châteaus in France. There, surrounded by old friends and young families, Edith followed her dogs' example as she relaxed in her gardens and invited children to play. Finally, this restless, driven woman discovered the pleasure of sleeping in the sun.

"Keeper walked first among the mourners to her funeral; he slept moaning for nights at the door of her empty room, and never, so to speak, rejoiced, dog fashion after her death."

Here, Mrs. Gaskell writes movingly of Keeper's behavior after Emily Brontë's death. Of the dogs described in this book, only Keeper outlived his owner. During Emily's final weeks, he never left his place beside her as she lay struggling to breathe. After fifteen years together, they were so attuned to each other that Keeper was able to ease Emily's pain by imperceptible means, such as leaning against her or simply gazing at her. Lying by the sofa and moderating his breathing in rhythm with hers, a finely tuned example of limbic resonance, Keeper kept the two of them in harmony until the very end.

As Emily lay dying, Keeper seemed to take on the role of *psychopomp*, a Greek word meaning one who acts as a guide on the passage between the worlds of the living and the dead. Throughout the world, myth and folktales depict dogs in this role as they help souls find their way between the two worlds. In ancient Mexico, families kept a small red dog as a cherished house pet. If a child died, the red dog was killed and buried with the child so that the familiar dog could lead the frightened child safely to the next world. In Persian mythology, a yellow-eared dog guided the dead over the Rainbow Bridge, while the Iroquois tribe told of a silver dog who led the way across the River of Death.

The other dogs in *Shaggy Muses* acted as psychopomps in symbolic ways, primarily by making their owners face the reality of death. Most dogs live for only ten to fifteen years, so their entire life span fits into a relatively small portion of ours. Edith Wharton agonized each time she had to "snuff out" one of her dogs, as she described it, although she always decided in favor of sparing the dog from suffering. She tried to come to terms with the inevitable loss each would bring: "Staunch & faithful little lovers that they are, they give back a hundred fold every sign of love one ever gives them—& it mitigates the pang of losing them to know how very happy a little affection has made them." Elizabeth Barrett Browning was stunned when Flush died at fourteen. She knew he was ailing, but like many owners of elderly dogs, she was still caught by surprise and wrote to her sister, "It has been quite a shock to me and a sadness." She added an epitaph that speaks to us still: "A dear dog he was." Emily Dickinson imagined Carlo greeting her when she arrived in heaven, and Edith Wharton hoped that the "little ghost" of Linky would be with her as she faced her final days alone. Perhaps such visions would help us all to cope with the death of a beloved dog.

There are dogs we will never forget due to the profound impact of their few years with us. Some fill our lives with intensity, some become an essential part of everyday life, while others happen to be with us during especially joyful or troubled times. Attachment figures, witnesses, playmates, and guides—in all these ways our dogs make our lives less lonely and help us to feel more at home in the world. We rely on them to provide a secure base when we venture into the unknown and to be a safe harbor when we retreat from the world. Alone with our dog, we can cry or shout, laugh or even read aloud a poem we have written. In times of change and upheaval, we look to our dog to keep us on track and to remind us of the inner core of self that always remains the same. No wonder they inspire such deep love in us, here described by Elizabeth Barrett Browning: "I love him—dear little Flushie—as far as dog-love can go—& that is farther than I supposed possible before I had knowledge of him." Like the dogs in this book, our own dogs, in their different ways, become our mute confederates, our own shaggy muses.

Acknowledgments

I owe special thanks to Susanna Porter, my editor, whose close reading and informed suggestions helped transform scholarly articles into *Shaggy Muses*. Deborah Ritchken, my agent, saw the book's potential from the beginning and remained cheerfully optimistic throughout this long process. Ann Honeywell has been indispensable in her roles of editorial assistant, literary inspiration, and dear friend.

Shaggy Muses began as papers presented at conferences on the human-animal bond and as articles in scholarly journals. I give special thanks to Lynette Hart and all who encouraged those early efforts, including David Anderson, Anne Alden, Marion Copeland, Anne Docherty, Penny Bernstein, Anthony Podberscek, Clint Saunders, James Serpell, and Ken Shapiro.

Preliminary chapters of *Shaggy Muses* appeared as these publications: "Emily Brontë & Keeper," *Brontë Studies* 29 (March 2004): 43–52; "Emily Brontë and Dogs: Transformation within the Human-Dog Bond," *Society & Animals* 9, no. 1 (2000): 152–67; "Emily Dickinson Had a Dog: An Interpretation of the Human-Dog Bond," *Anthrozoös* 12, no. 3 (1999): 132–37; "Emily Dickinson's Dog", *Enriching Our Lives: A Celebration of the First 20 Years of SCAS* (May 1999): 29–31.

When I decided to expand the articles into a book, Margaret Forster, author of *Elizabeth Barrett Browning: The Life and Loves of a Poet*; Philip Kelley, editor of *The Brownings' Correspondence*; and Bob Duckett, editor of *Brontë Studies*, generously shared their knowledge. Leah Chamberlain, Erica Donnis, and David Dashill, from The Mount, answered numerous questions about Edith Wharton. Nancy Eckholm Burkert generously provided a photograph of her painting, "Carlo Dreams." Janet Jacobsen, authority on toy breeds, deepened my appreciation for these little dogs and introduced me to several Pekes. While I acknowledge all this assistance and advice, please note that any mistakes are my own.

My husband and I traveled throughout the eastern United States and in England while I researched the book. Retracing Virginia Woolf's walks over the Sussex downs, Emily Brontë's across the moors, and standing on the steps of 50 Wimpole Street were highlights of those trips. Our private tour of The Mount one snowy afternoon and our explorations of Emily Dickinson's home and visit to her grave were equally memorable. Thank you to all the helpful people at the Battersea Lost Dogs Home in London, the Special Collections at the University of Sussex, Monk's House, and the Brontë Parsonage Museum. In the United States, thank you to the staffs of the Berg Collection of the New York Public Library, the Lilly Library at the University of Indiana, the Beinecke Library at Yale University, and the Harry Ransom Center at the University of Texas at Austin.

I appreciate colleagues Sheila Albert, Donna Hardy, Debra Hill, Judith Nelson, and Cynthia O'Connell for helping to clarify the psychological concepts underlying the book. My students at the University of San Francisco enriched my understanding of attachment theory through their unexpected questions and lively discussions. I am indebted to USF librarian Eric Shappy, who hunted down out-of-print books and esoteric journals.

My writing groups, the first led by Kathleen Hill and my present group—Mary Shea, Rose Murphy, Terry McNeely, Lisa Yanover, Janet Constantino, Todd Evans, and Wayne Schake—

have patiently listened to countless revisions. And I offer deepest gratitude to my Jungian analyst, Chauncy Irvine, for helping me recognize parts of myself in each of these stories.

My parents, Richard and Margaret Kelleher Burke, instilled a love of reading and also capitulated to my demands for my first dog. I appreciate their help as well as that of my sisters and brothers— Kathy Gibney, Peggy Fogelman, Pat O'Connor, and Richard and Tim Burke—and all my extended family, especially my nieces Ellen, Colleen, Cheryl, and Leslie.

Above all, my children, Kate and Andrew, are a constant source of loving support, and their spouses, Atif and Christine, are now part of that endeavor. Finally, *Shaggy Muses* would never have happened without my husband Marty's never-flagging enthusiasm and constant support. Heartfelt thanks to all of you—and also to all of the dogs in my life: Nicky, Misty, Brendan, Toby, Cody, Hank, Higgins, and Kipper.

Notes

ELIZABETH BARRETT BROWNING AND FLUSH

I am especially indebted to Margaret Forster, *Elizabeth Barrett Browning: The Life and Loves of a Poet* (New York: St. Martin's Press, 1988); Philip Kelley, ed. *The Brownings' Correspondence*, vols. 1–15 (Waco, Tex: Wedgestone Press, 1984–2005).

BACKGROUND TEXTS

Garrett, Martin, ed. *Elizabeth Barrett Browning and Robert Browning: Interviews and Recollections.* New York: St. Martin's Press, 2000.

Howell, Philip. "Flush and the Banditti: Dog-stealing in Victorian London." In *Animal Spaces, Beastly Places: New Geographies of Human-Animal Relations,* edited by Chris Philo and Chris Wilbert, pp. 35–55. London: Routledge, 2000.

Markus, Julia. *Dared and Done: The Marriage of Elizabeth Barrett and Robert Browning.* New York: Knopf, 1995.

Phelan, Joseph. "Ethnology and Biography: The Case of the Brownings." *Biography* 26 (Spring 2003): pp. 261–278.

WORKS AND LETTERS BY ELIZABETH BARRETT BROWNING

BC Philip Kelley and Ronald Hudson, eds., vols. 5–8; Philip Kelley and Scott Lewis, eds., vols. 9–14. *The Brownings' Correspondence.* Waco, Tex.: Wedgestone Press, 1984–87.

L Scott Lewis, ed. *The Letters of Elizabeth Barrett Browning to Her Sister Arabella.* Vols. 1 and 2. Waco, Tex.: Wedgestone Press, 2002.

LK Frederick G. Kenyon, ed. *The Letters of Elizabeth Barrett.* New York: Macmillan, 1899.

LM Betty Miller, ed. *Elizabeth Barrett to Miss Mitford: The Unpublished Letters of Elizabeth Barrett to Mary Russell Mitford.* London: John Murray, 1954.

P Elizabeth Barrett Browning. *The Complete Poetical Works of Elizabeth Barrett Browning.* Edited by Horace E. Scudder. Cutchogue, N.Y.: Buccaneer Books, 1993.

7 "crowded with": *BC*, vol. 10, p. 300.

7 "pale spiritual": In Garrett, p. 7.

8 "Literature": In Forster, p. 27.

9 "I live": Ibid., p. 71.

10 "We advise": Ibid., p. 76.

10 "Very pretty": Ibid., p. 82.

11 "a genuine": Ibid., p. 89.

11 "such pretty": Ibid., p. 95.

12 "pettish": Ibid., p. 99.

12 "For three": In Markus, p. 23.

13 "It is a wonder": In Forster, p. 100.

13 "bound, more": Ibid.

13 "Why there": *LM*, p. 68.

14 "affectionate feeling": *LM*, p. 70.

14 "But I shall": Ibid.

14 "How I thank": *BC*, vol. 5, p. 10.

14 "Such a quiet": Ibid., p. 20.

14 "He is much": Ibid., p. 104.

14 "He dances": Ibid.

15 "How he makes": Ibid., p. 106.

15 "The first": *LM*, p. 162.

15 "with his silky": *BC*, vol. 7, p. 293.

15 "little bantam": *LM*, p. 183.

16 "In every": *BC*, vol. 5, p. 105.

16 "And when": Ibid., p. 10.

16 "*joyaunce*": Ibid., p. 236.

16 "I have": Ibid., p. 44.

16 "I have a": Ibid., p. 30.

17 "After what": In Markus, p. 83.

17 "He & I": *BC*, vol. 9, p. 157.

17 "When I was": *LM*, p. 139.

17 "His glittering": *LM*, p. 86.

17 "And when": *LM*, p. 87.

18 "I was in despair": Ibid.

18 "Everybody likes": *LM*, p. 72.

19 "Now, I may": In Forster, p. 126.

19 "Poor Flushie": *BC*, vol. 8, p. 315.

19 "Here is": *BC*, vol. 9, p. 79.

19 "It is amusing": *BC*, vol. 8, p. 64.

20 "My brothers": Ibid.

20 "My castle-building": In Forster, p. 109.

20 "where the silence": *BC*, vol. 6, p. 335.

20 "So profound": Ibid., p. 7.

20 "Flush lies": *BC*, vol. 7, p. 270.

20 "two dark": In Forster, p. 151.

21 "[It] shows": *BC*, vol. 8, p. 289.

21 "feeble": In Forster, p. 113.

21 "And yet": *P,* pp. 436–37.

21 "I tell": *P,* p. 99.

21 "*When some*": Ibid.

22 "He can't bear": *BC*, vol. 6, p. 15.

22 "shivering with": *BC*, vol. 12, no. 2,271.

22 "Through the": *BC*, vol. 6, p. 25.

22 "For Flush": *BC*, vol. 12, no. 2,271.

22 "Why what *is*": *BC*, vol. 9, p. 272.

23 "Think of": *BC*, vol. 8, p. 45.

23 "the dreadful": In Markus, p. 33.

24 "A cough": *BC*, vol. 8, p. 112.

24 "in his eternal": *BC*, vol. 5, p. 338.

24 "It is strange": Ibid.

24 "obvious inconvenience": *BC*, vol. 10, no. 1,974.

24 "And although": *LM*, p. 211.

25 "Think of my": *BC*, vol. 6, p. 45.

26 "the prince": *LM*, p. 162.

26 "After an": *LM*, p. 129.

26 "There never": *LM*, p. 162.

26 dog stealing in London: See Howell.

26 "It is not *dogs*": *LM*, p. 200.

27 "My despair": In Forster, p. 118.

27 "It was excusable": *BC*, vol. 7, p. 355.

27 "Did I": Ibid., p. 357.

28 "I am sure": *LM*, p. 336.

28 "Dear Flushie": *BC*, vol. 9, no, 1,791.

28 "drenched with": *BC*, vol. 9, no. 1,743.

28 "low and": Ibid.

28 "I [was]": *BC*, vol. 11, no. 2,080.

28   "Flush came": Ibid.

29   *You see*: *P*, p. 196.

30   *"Leap!"*: *P*, p. 163.

30   "Leave out Flush": *BC*, vol. 8, p. 84.

31   "You asked": Ibid., p. 29.

31   "You have": Ibid., p. 313.

31   "I thought": *BC*, vol. 7, p. 273.

33   "Ba's poet": In Forster, p. 151.

33   "I shall": *BC*, vol. 11, no. 2,061.

33   "Like Flush": *BC*, vol. 12, no. 2,274.

33   "I must": *BC*, vol. 13, no. 2,472.

34   "So, when": *BC*, vol. 12, no. 2,247.

34   "The day": *BC*, vol. 11, no. 2,006.

34   "with Flush's": *BC*, vol. 12, no. 2,228.

34   "I slapped": *BC*, vol. 13, no. 2,474.

34   "Oh, poor": Ibid., no. 2,080.

35   "dogs who are": Ibid., no. 2,502.

35   "transient": Ibid.

35   "Therefore I": Ibid., no. 2,424.

35   "Think of": Ibid., no. 2,552.

35   Mr. Barrett's objections to his children's marrying: See Markus and Phelan.

36   "But you": *BC*, vol. 13, no. 2,554.

36   "fenced": *BC*, vol. 11, no. 2,080.

36   "Here is": *BC*, vol. 13, no. 2,574.

37   "Poor Flush": Ibid., no. 2,575.

37   "You think": Ibid., no. 2,578.

37   "I ought to": Ibid., no. 2,579.

37   "I am": Ibid., no. 2,582.

38   *"A sick"*: *P*, pp. 298–99.

39   "Against you": *LM*, p. 274.

39   "exhausted": In Forster, p. 186.

39   "boiling": *BC*, vol. 14, no. 2,624.

39   "Flush proved": Ibid.

40   "sit through": In Forster, p. 188.

40   "death warrant": Ibid., p. 189.

40   "hard and unsparing": Ibid.

41   "a mere palace": From "The Browning Society: Casa Guidi," http://www.browningsociety.org/casaguidi.shtml (accessed May 20, 2006).

41   "My Flush": *LK*, p. 357.

41   "Flush & I": *BC*, vol. 14, no. 2,680.

41   "I have Flush": Ibid., no. 2,648.

42   "very fond": Ibid., no. 2,703.

42   "to the Casine": *L*, no. 24.

42   "sighing": *BC*, vol. 14, no. 2,701.

42   "quite disgraceful": Ibid.

42   "For a whole": *LK*, p. 402.

43   "The affection": *LM*, p. 287.

43   "I have never": *LM*, pp. 371–72.

43   "I wonder": *L*, no. 41.

44   "He calls me": *BC*, vol. 14, no. 2,678.

44   "an old dog": From "How It Strikes a Contemporary," http://people.a2000.nl/avanarum/Burbank_notes/Contemporary_RB.htm (accessed Nov. 10, 2001).

44   "By the time": In Garrett, p. 63.

44   "a beautiful": Ibid., p. 67.

44   "I recollect": Ibid.

45   "Another thing": *L*, no. 11.

45   "He & I": *BC*, vol. 9, p. 157.

EMILY BRONTË AND KEEPER

I am especially indebted to Juliet Barker, *The Brontës* (New York: St. Martin's Press, 1994), Juliet Barker, *The Brontës: A Life in Letters* (Woodstock, N.Y.: Overlook Press, 1998); Edward Chitham, *A Life of Emily Brontë* (Oxford, U.K.: Blackwell, 1987); Stevie Davies, *Emily Brontë: Heretic* (London: Women's Press, 1994); Elizabeth Gaskell, *The Life of*

Charlotte Brontë (London: Penguin, 1987. First published 1857); Lucasta Miller, *The Brontë Myth* (New York: Knopf, 2003).

BACKGROUND TEXTS

Alexander, Christine, and Jane Sellars. *The Art of the Brontës*. Cambridge, U.K.: Cambridge University Press, 1995.

Ascione, Frank, and Philip Arkow, eds. *Child Abuse, Domestic Violence, and Animal Abuse: Linking the Circles of Compassion for Prevention and Intervention*. West Lafayette, Ind.: Purdue University Press, 1999.

Dale-Green, Patricia. *Dog*. London: Rupert Hart-Davis, 1966.

Evans, R., and Gareth Lloyd. *The Scribner Companion to the Brontës*. New York: Scribner's, 1982.

Gérin, Winifred. *Emily Brontë*. Oxford, U.K.: Oxford University Press, 1978.

Kete, Kathleen. *The Beast in the Boudoir: Pet-keeping in Nineteenth-Century Paris*. Berkeley: University of California Press, 1994.

Nelson, Jane. "Inside Wuthering Heights." In *Country Life* CLXXV, No. 4524 (May 3, 1984): pp. 1,238–1,239.

Ratchford, Fannie. *The Brontës' Web of Childhood*. New York: Columbia University Press, 1941.

Ritvo, Harriet. *The Animal Estate: The English and Other Creatures in the Victorian Age*. Cambridge, Mass.: Harvard University Press, 1987.

———. "The Emergence of Modern Pet-Keeping" In *Animals and People Sharing the World*, edited by Andrew Rowan, 13–31. Hanover N.H.: University Press of New England for Tufts University, 1988.

Serpell, James. "From Paragon to Pariah: Some Reflections on Human Attitudes to Dogs." In *The Domestic Dog: Its Evolution, Behaviour, and Interactions with People*, edited by James Serpell, 245–56. Cambridge, U.K.: Cambridge University Press, 1995.

Shorter, Clement. *Charlotte Brontë and Her Circle*. New York: Dodd, Mead, 1896.

Tuan, Yi-Fu. *Dominance & Affection: The Making of Pets*. New Haven, Conn.: Yale University Press, 1984.

Wise, Thomas. *The Brontës: Their Lives, Friendships and Correspondence*. Vols. 1–4 Philadelphia: Porcupine Press, 1980.

Wyett, Jodi. "The Lap of Luxury: Lapdogs, Literature, and Social Meaning in the 'Long' Eighteenth Century." *Literature Interpretation Theory* 10, no. 4 (2000): pp. 273–301.

LETTERS AND WORKS BY EMILY AND CHARLOTTE BRONTË

BL Juliet Barker. *The Brontës: A Life in Letters*. Woodstock, N.Y.: Overlook Press, 1998.

E Emily Brontë. *Five Essays*. Translated by L. W. Nagel. Folcraft, Pa.: Folcraft Library Editions, 1974.

L Margaret Smith, ed. *The Letters of Charlotte Brontë: With a Selection of Letters by Family and Friends*. Oxford, U.K.: Clarendon Press, 1995.

P C. W. Hatfield, ed. *The Complete Poems of Emily Jane Brontë*. New York: Columbia University Press, 1995. First published 1941.

S Charlotte Brontë. *Shirley*. Oxford, U.K.: Oxford World's Classics, 1998. First published 1849.

WH Emily Brontë. *Wuthering Heights*. London: Penguin, 1995. First published 1847.

54 *"The linnet"*: In Davies, p. 180.
54 "Reads little": In Chitham, p. 37.
55 "a darling": *BL*, p. 9.
55 *"Down, down"*: In Chitham, p. 49.
56 "the eyes": Ibid., p. 26.
56 "She never": In Gaskell, p. 268.
56 "We wove": In Ratchford, title page.
57 *"High waving"*: *P*, p. 31.
58 *"Cold in the"*: *P*, p. 222.
58 "No coward": *P*, p. 243.
58 "Emily Brontë": In Chitham, p. 76.
59 "making them": Ibid., p. 78.
59 "stooped down": Ibid., p. 81.
59 "Grasper—from": In Alexander, pp. 375–76.
59 *"And hungry"*: In Ratchford, p. 94.
61 "Am [I]": In Chitham, p. 88.
61 "Her health": Ibid., p. 89.
61 *"Cold clear"*: In Ratchford, p. 135.
62 "hard labour": In Barker (1994), p. 294.

62 *"For the moors"*: *P*, p. 92.
63 "savage brute": In Evans, p. 115.
64 "Vaste, huge": In Dale-Green, p. 132.
64 "one who": *Oxford English Dictionary* (Oxford, U.K.: Oxford University Press, 1971), p. 665.
64 "A private": *BL*, p. 310.
64 "We . . . all": *BL*, p. 96.
65 "a conglomerate": *L*, p. 332.
65 "a smart battle": *WH*, p. 196.
65 "limping, and": *WH*, p. 195.
66 "till one or": Gaskell, p. 268.
66 "a devouring": *L*, p. 332.
66 "rather large": *S*, pp. 6–7.
66 "[She] must": Gaskell, p. 507.
66 "Keeper and": In Evans, p. 115.
66 "fierce, wild": Gaskell, p. 268.
68 *"Riches I"*: *P*, p. 163.
68 "Sometimes": In Shorter, p. 179.
68 "huge purple": *WH*, p. 49.
69 "Down-stairs came": Gaskell, p. 269.
69 dogs as scapegoats: See Serpell.
70 "She had not": *S*, p. 358.
70 "kneeling on": In Gérin, p. 156.
71 "Poor old": In Shorter, p. 178.
71 "The tawny": *S*, p. 386.
71 "I am": *BL*, p. 95.
73 "Tell me": *BL*, p. 111.
73 "hardly ever": In Barker (1994), p. 393.
73 "I simply": *BL*, p. 106.
73 "worked like": In Barker (1994), p. 384.
73 "She should": In Gaskell, p. 230.
73 "Yesterday": *E*, pp. 164–65.
74 description of notebooks: See Irene Taylor, "Foreword," in *P*.
75 "I have": *BL*, p. 132.
75 "who I": *BL*, p. 131.
75 "I am quite": Ibid.
76 "If you": *L*, p. 37.

76   "I long": In Ratchford, p. 149.

76   "Tabby in": *L*, p. 53.

76   "We were": *BL*, p. 131.

76   "The Gondals are": *BL*, p. 133.

76   "The Gondals still": *BL*, p. 131.

78   "Keeper and": In Shorter, p. 178.

78   sketches and watercolor of Flossy: See Alexander, pp. 388–89.

79   "that infamous little": *L*, p. 374.

79   "Emily was": *L*, p. 432.

79   "for if": Ibid

80   "peculiar music": *WH*, p. xxvii.

80   "an inspiration": In Barker (1994), p. 497.

80   "He comes": *P*, pp. 238–39.

81   "Whether": *WH*, p. xxxvi.

82   "hopeless being": In Chitham, p. 232.

82   *"Well some"*: *P*, p. 132.

83   "regularity paper": In Barker (1994), p. 358.

83   "a huge, liver-coloured": *WH*, p. 5.

83   "She's not": *WH*, p. 6.

84   "the delicate": *E*, p. 10. For the connection between dominance and pets, see Tuan.

84   "petted him up": *WH*, p. 38.

84   "That was": *WH*, p. 48.

85   "While her": *WH*, p. 52.

85   "a vicious cur": *WH*, p. 57.

85   "The first thing": *WH*, p. 149.

85   animal abuse and domestic violence: See Ascione.

86   "exactly as": *WH*, p. 270.

86   "that pitiful": *WH*, p. 149.

86   "yelped wild": *WH*, p. 181.

86   "who was": Ibid.

87   For the image of the hanged dog, see Davies, pp. 117–18.

87   lapdogs in England: See Wyett.

87   "for a crime": Kete, p. 41.

88   "Nature is": In Davies, p. 108.

88   "I'm tired": *WH*, p. 160.

88   "I lingered": *WH*, p. 334.

88–89   "storm-heated": *WH*, p. xxxv.

90   "How a": In Davies, pp. 89–90.

90   "too odiously": In Miller, p. 208.

90   "puzzling": Ibid., p. 209.

90   "Permit me": Ibid., p. 192.

90   "of a broken": In Chitham, p. 231.

90   "Never in all": *WH*, p. xxxi.

91   "lay at the": In Barker (1994), p. 576.

92   "a hard, short": Ibid.

92   "Emily's large": *BL*, p. 240.

92   "Keeper walked": Gaskell, p. 269.

92   "to the day": In Wise, vol. 4, p. 87.

92   "superannuated": Ibid., vol. 3, p. 168.

92   "with his": In Shorter, p. 440.

92   "The blind": Ibid., p. 441.

92   "I shall never": In Wise, vol. 4, p. 91.

92   "I got home": *BL*, p. 239.

93   "The ecstasy": Ibid.

93   "some caress": *BL*, p. 240.

93   "Poor old": *BL*, p. 339.

EMILY DICKINSON AND CARLO

I am especially indebted to Alfred Habegger, *My Wars Are Laid Away in Books: The Life of Emily Dickinson* (New York: Random House, 2001); Richard Sewall, *The Life of Emily Dickinson* (Cambridge, Mass.: Harvard University Press, 1974); and Cynthia Griffin Wolff, *Emily Dickinson* (New York: Knopf, 1986).

BACKGROUND TEXTS

Bauer, Mattias. "The Language of Dogs: Mythos and Logos in Emily Dickinson." *Connotations* 5, nos. 2–3 (1995–96): pp. 208–27.

Brose, Nancy, Juliana Dupre, Wendy Kohler, and Jean Mudge. *Emily Dickinson: Profile of the Poet as Cook.* Amherst, Mass.: Newell Printing, 1976.

Burkert, Nancy, and Jane Langton. *Acts of Light: Emily Dickinson.* Boston: New York Graphic Society, 1980.

Farr, Judith, with Louise Carter. *The Gardens of Emily Dickinson.* Cambridge, Mass.: Harvard University Press, 2004.

Figley, Mary Rhodes " 'Brown Kisses' and 'Shaggy Feet': How Carlo Illuminates Dickinson for Children" *The Emily Dickinson Journal* 14, no. 2 (2005): pp. 120–127.

Fuss, Diana. *The Sense of an Interior: Four Writers and the Rooms That Shaped Them.* New York: Routledge, 2004.

Garber, Marjorie. *Dog Love.* New York: Simon & Schuster, 1996.

Hart, Ellen Louise, and Martha Nell Smith. *Open Me Carefully: Emily Dickinson's Intimate Letters to Susan Huntington Dickinson.* Ashfield, Mass.: Paris Press, 1998.

Hausman, G., and L. Hausman. *The Mythology of Dogs: Canine Legend and Lore Through the Ages.* New York: St. Martin's Press, 1997.

Higginson, Thomas Wentworth. *The Magnificent Activist: The Writings of Thomas Wentworth Higginson.* Edited by Howard N. Meyer. New York: Perseus Press, 2000.

Howey, M. O. *The Cult of the Dog.* Essex, U.K.: C. W. Daniel Co., 1972.

Jones, Ruth Owen. "Neighbor—and friend—and Bridegroom—: William Smith Clark as Emily Dickinson's Master Figure." *The Emily Dickinson Journal* 11, no. 2 (2002): pp. 48–85.

Lerman, Rhoda. *In the Company of Newfies: A Shared Life.* New York: Henry Holt, 1996.

Leyda, Jay. *The Years and Hours of Emily Dickinson.* 2 vols. New Haven, Conn.: Yale University Press, 1960.

Matthews, Pamela. "Talking of Hallowed Things: The Importance of Silence in Emily Dickinson's Poetry." *Dickinson Studies* 47 (1983): pp. 14–21.

Pratt, Freda, and Carol Cooper. *A Friend in Deed.* Cornwall, U.K.: R. Booth Bookbinders, 1993.

Scharnhorst, Gary. "A Glimpse of Dickinson at Work." *American Literature* 57, no. 5 (Oct. 1985): pp. 483–85.

Stetson, J., ed. *This Is the Newfoundland: Official Breed Book of the Newfoundland Club of America.* Orange, Conn.: Practical Science Publishing, 1956.

LETTERS AND POEMS OF EMILY DICKINSON

B   Millicent Todd Bingham. *Emily Dickinson's Home: Letters of Ed-*

ward Dickinson and His Family. New York: Harper & Brothers, 1955.

L Emily Dickinson. *The Letters of Emily Dickinson.* Edited by Thomas H. Johnson and Theodora Ward. 3 vols. Cambridge, Mass.: Belknap Press of Harvard University Press, 1958.

P Emily Dickinson. *The Complete Poems of Emily Dickinson.* Edited by Thomas Johnson. Boston: Back Bay Books, 1960. First published 1890.

99 "Amherst is alive": *L,* no. 29.
99 "Rare hours": In Leyda, vol. 1, p. 367.
101 "Belle of": Title of play by William Luce.
101 "Tell all the Truth": *P,* no. 1,129.
101 "I never had": *L,* no. 342b. For Emily's first three years, see Wolff, pp. 36–65.
102 *"A loss of ": P,* no. 959.
102 "My mother does": *L,* no. 261.
103 "I called": In Wolff, p. 109.
103 Mr. Dickinson's career: See Fuss, p. 53.
103 "I think": *L,* no. 114.
103 "It is so weird": In Sewall, p. 145.
104 "I would like": *L,* p. 404.
104 "a very bright": In Sewall, p. 342.
104 "I am really": *L,* no. 18.
105 "I mailed": *L,* no. 26.
105 "Austin arrived": *L,* no. 23.
106 "While contributing": *B,* p. 413.
106 "Father was": Ibid.
106 "Father . . . buys": *L,* no. 261.
106 "Father and": *L,* no. 36.
106 "Vinnie away": *L,* no. 30.
107 "You have seen": *L,* no. 93.
107 "I wish": *L,* no. 115.

108 Newfoundlands: See Pratt, Stetson.
108 "Near this spot": In Benita Eisler, *Byron: Child of Passion, Fool of Fame* (New York: Vintage Books, 2108), p. 161.
109 "I am the noble": In Hausman, p. 195.
109 "We don't": *L,* no. 65.
109 "Mother has": *B,* p. 238.
109 "I am Judith": *L,* no. 34.
110 "Miss Dickinson": In Leyda, vol. 1, p. 358.
110 "while the huge": Ibid., p. 21.
110 "Her companion": Ibid.
110 "small, like": *L,* no. 268.
110 "My Hair": *L,* no. 271.
110 "dog with ringlets": *L,* no. 218.
110 "Father and": *L,* no. 266.
110–111 "Vinnie had": *L,* no. 685.
111 "Evenings get": *L,* no. 194.
111 "Mother thinks": *L,* no. 285.
112 "When much": *L,* no. 271.
112 herbarium: See Habegger, pp. 154–61.
113 "good friends": In Hart, p. 3.
113 "I asked": Ibid., p. 55.
113 "I ran": Ibid., p. 39.
114 "You need not fear": *L,* no. 173.
114 "I rise": *L,* no. 172.
114 "Carriages flew": *L,* no. 127.
115 "I cannot": *L,* no. 182.
115 "Mother has": Ibid.
115 "Mother lies": Ibid.
115 "I am out": Ibid.
115 remodeling of the Homestead: See Fuss, pp. 9–56.
116 the conservatory: See Farr, pp. 148–51.
116 her bedroom: See Fuss, pp. 56–66.
117 *"One sister": P,* no. 14.
117 "She had": In Leyda, vol. 1, p. 338.

117 "The works": Ibid.
117 "I may": Ibid.
117 "*I think*": *P*, no. 593.
118 "[She] wrote": In Scharnhorst, p. 485.
118 "*Till every*": *P*, no. 500.
119 interpretation: See Bauer, pp. 213–16.
119 "*No squirrel*": *P*, no. 589.
120 "only a happen": In Sewall, p. 153.
120 "I don't go": *L*, no. 166.
120 "He is dumb": *L*, no. 271.
120 increased robberies: Personal communication, Ruth Owen Jones.
120 "The nights turned": *L*, no. 281.
120 "*I felt*": *P*, no. 937.
121 "Could I": *P*, no. 220.
121 "I noticed": In Habegger, p. 400.
122 "Put one hand": In Leyda, vol. 1, p. 62.
123 the "Queen Recluse": In Habegger, p. 447.
123 "Please have": *L*, no. 213.
123 "Nothing has": *L*, no. 285.
123 "I tell you": *L*, no. 272.
123 "Master. If you": *L*, no. 233.
123 "Could you forget": Ibid.
124 "*What shall I do*": *P*, no. 186.
125 "I cannot": *L*, no. 212.
125 "*This is the Hour*": *P*, no. 341.
126 plants and Bowles: Farr, pp. 44–49.
126 "I have": In Hart, p. 101.
127 "*A little*": *P*, no. 1,185.
127 "The Frogs": *L*, no. 262.
127 "I had a terror": *L*, no. 261.
127 number of poems: Habegger, p. 405.
127 "When I try": *L*, no. 271.
127 "If I read a book": In Sewall, p. 566.
127 "Dare you": *P*, no. 365.

128 "I started Early": *P*, no. 520.
129 "I think Carlo": *L*, no. 271.
129 "You ask": *L*, no. 261.
129 "When I am": In Matthews, p. 15.
129 "They talk of": *L*, no. 271.
129 "Of 'shunning' ": Ibid.
130 "The Soul selects": *P*, no. 303.
130 "I smile": *L*, no. 265.
130 "A solemn thing": *P*, no. 271.
130 "*Title divine*": *P*, no. 1,072.
131 "I found": *L*, no. 280.
131 "A step like": *L*, no. 342a.
131 "I never was": In Habegger, p. 524.
132 "Carlo did not": *L*, no. 290.
132 "Carlo died": *L*, no. 314.
132 "event, vast": Higginson, p. 554.
132 "*Further in Summer*": *P*, no. 1,068.
133 *furrow:* Personal communication, Ellen Fogelman.
133 "I bring": In Sewall, p. 582.
133 cricket corpse: Farr, p. 26.
133 "The day": In Habegger, p. 352.
133 " *'Twas later*": *P*, no. 1,276.
134 "insect sounds": In Wolff, p. 309.
134 "Whom my dog": *L*, no. 316.
134 "*Except the*": *P*, no. 1,067.
134 Ned's picture: Hart, p. 142.
135 "It is hard": In Garber, p. 245.
135 "You must": Ibid.
135 "Thank you": *L*, no. 319.
135 "*Time is a Test*": Ibid.
135 "Nature, seems it": Ibid.
135 "I explore": Ibid.
135 "We were": *L*, no. 792.
136 "There is": In Sewall, p. 566.
136 "Called back": *L*, no. 1,046.
136 "*No coward soul*": Emily Brontë, in *The Complete Poems of Emily*

Jane Brontë, edited by C.W. Hatfield (Columbia University Press, 1941, 1995), p. 243.

136 "This Consciousness": *P*, no. 822.

137 "Gracie, do you": In Leyda, vol. 1, p. 21.

EDITH WHARTON AND FOXY, LINKY, AND THE DOGS IN BETWEEN

I am especially indebted to Shari Benstock, *No Gifts from Chance: A Biography of Edith Wharton* (New York: Scribner's, 1994); Gloria C. Erlich, *The Sexual Education of Edith Wharton* (Berkeley: University of California Press, 1992); and Cynthia Griffin Wolff, *A Feast of Words: The Triumph of Edith Wharton* (Reading, Mass.: Addison-Wesley, 1995).

BACKGROUND TEXTS

Auchincloss, Louis. *Edith Wharton: A Woman in Her Time.* New York: Viking Press, 1971.

Bell, Millicent. *Edith Wharton and Henry James: The Story of Their Friendship.* New York: George Braziller, 1965.

Boit, Louise. "Henry James as Landlord." *Atlantic Monthly* 178, no. 2 (Aug. 1946): pp. 118–21.

Dwight, Eleanor. *Edith Wharton: An Extraordinary Life.* New York: Abrams, 1994.

Funston, Judith E. "Macaws and Pekingese: Vivienne de Watteville and Edith Wharton." *Edith Wharton Review* 7, no. 1 (1990): pp. 13–14.

Godden, Rumer. *The Butterfly Lions: The Pekingese in History, Legend and Art.* London: William Clowes & Sons, 1977.

Jacobsen, Janet Allen. "Pekingese Appreciation." Unpublished MS.

Lewis, R. W. B. *Edith Wharton: A Biography.* New York: Harper & Row, 1975.

Lubbock, Percy. *Portrait of Edith Wharton.* London: Jonathan Cape, 1947.

Mainwaring, Marion. *Mysteries of Paris: The Quest for Morton Fullerton.* Hanover, N.H.: University Press of New England, 2001.

Powers, Lyall H., ed. *Henry James and Edith Wharton: Letters, 1900–1915.* New York: Scribner's, 1990.

Price, Alan. *The End of the Age of Innocence: Edith Wharton and the First World War.* New York: St. Martin's Press, 1996.

Price, Kenneth M., and Phyllis McBride. " 'The Life Apart': Text and Contexts of Edith Wharton's Love Diary." *American Literature* 66, no. 4 (Dec. 1994): pp. 663–88.

Ramsden, George. *Edith Wharton's Library.* Yorkshire, U.K: Stone Trough Books, 1999.

Rieder, William. *A Charmed Couple: The Art and Life of Walter and Matilda Gay.* New York: Abrams, 2000.

Tyler, William Royall, "Personal Memories of Edith Wharton," *Massachusetts Historical Society Proceedings* 85 [no number] (1973): pp. 91–104.

Wimhurst, C.G.E. *The Book of Toy Dogs*. London: Frederick Muller, Ltd., 1965.

Wright, Sarah Bird. *Edith Wharton, A to Z*. New York: Facts on File, 1998.

WORKS AND LETTERS BY EDITH WHARTON

BG Edith Wharton. *A Backward Glance: An Autobiography*. New York: Simon & Schuster, Touchstone Edition, 1998. First published 1938.

CSS Edith Wharton. *The Collected Short Stories of Edith Wharton*. Vols. 1 and 2. Edited by R.W.B. Lewis. New York: Scribner's, 1968.

FF Edith Wharton. *Fighting France: From Dunkerque to Belport*. New York: Scribner's, 1919.

L Edith Wharton. *The Letters of Edith Wharton*. Edited by R.W.B. Lewis and Nancy Lewis. London: Simon & Schuster, 1988.

L&I Edith Wharton. "Life and I." In *Edith Wharton: Novellas and Other Writings*, edited by Cynthia Griffin Wolff. New York: Literary Classics of the United States, 1990.

MFF Edith Wharton. *A Motor-Flight through France*. New York: Charles Scribner, 1908.

LITERARY ARCHIVES

BL Beinecke Rare Book and Manuscript Library, Yale University.

LL Lilly Library, William Royall Tyler Collection, University of Indiana.

UT Harry Ransom Humanities Research Center, University of Texas, Austin.

ABBREVIATIONS FOR UNPUBLISHED LETTERS AND REMINISCENCES

ET Elisina Tyler.

EW Emelyn Washburn.

HP Hayford Peirce.

MB Mary Berenson.

MC Margaret Chanler.

MF Morton Fullerton.

RN Robert Norton.

SN Sara Norton.

TW Teddy Wharton.

WT William Tyler.

143 "snowy headed": *BG*, p. 3.
145 "a new life": *BG*, p. 4.
145 "How I": Ibid.
145 "The owning": Ibid.
146 "tall splendid": *BG*, p. 26.
147 "For almost": *BG*, p. 41.
148 "this illness": *L&I*, p. 1,078.
149 "a dark": *L&I*, p. 1,080.
149 "His absence": *BG*, p. 41.
149 "My parents": Ibid.
150 "the glories": *BG*, p. 44.
150 "my mind": *BG*, p. 48.
151 "I was a 'young' ": *L&I*, p. 1,080.
151 "Oh, how": *BG*, p. 73.
152 "The objective world": *L&I*, p. 1,078.
152 "*Everybody* had": *L&I*, p. 1,081.
152 "I always": *L&I*, p. 1,082.
152 "I passed": Ibid.
153 "This lasted": Ibid.
153 "folly": *L&I*, p. 1,090.
153 "When I": *BG*, p. 77.
154 "agony of": *BG*, p. 78.
154 "pink blur": *L&I*, p. 1,093.

154 "Oh how": Ibid.
154 "complete": *BG*, p. 169.
154 "I was": *BG*, p. 77.
155 "My keenest": *L&I*, p. 1,095.
155 "I imagine": *BG*, p. 39.
155 "I am": *BG*, p. 88.
156 "small dinners": *BG*, p. 78.
156 "The only": In Benstock, p. 46.
158 "with dread": *L&I*, p. 1,087.
158 "I'm afraid": Ibid.
158 "Mrs. George": In Auchincloss, p. 46.
159 history of Chihuahuas: See Wimhurst, pp. 64–65.
160 "little dog": *BG*, p. 100.
161 "Puss wanted": In Auchincloss, p. 48.
161 "As long": *BG*, p. 109.
161 "lump into": In Wright, p. 24.
162 "I have": *CSS*, p. 14.
162 "one long": In Benstock, p. 72.
163 "*I think*": In Wolff, p. 86.
163 "For *twelve*": *L*, pp. 139–40.
164 "Don't pass": In Wright, p. 134.
164 "Poor little": EW–SN, Feb. 4, 1902, BL.
165 description of Pet Cemetery: Scott Marshall, unpublished notes, ca. 1988.
165 "Miza looks": EW–SN, June 5, 1903, BL.
165 "Me, too": In Lewis, p. 160.
166 "family [to be]": *BG*, p. 316.
166 "Cold in the": *BG*, p. 185.
166 "deranging and": In Benstock, p. 197.
166 "the best &": In Boit, p. 119.
167 "There must": RN, Wharton Reminiscences, BL, p. 35.
167 "perfect but": In Lubbock, p. 46.
167 "And if": In Benstock, p. 290.
167 "great grief": Ibid., p. 167.
167 "the pendulum": In Dwight, p. 141.

167 "The little": EW–SN, Nov. 29, 1903, BL.
168 "Mitou sends": *L*, p. 81.
168 "We hope": *L*, pp. 76–77.
168 "to stand": In Lewis, p. 152.
169 "a stupid creature": EW–SN, Apr. 28, 1905, BL.
169 "like a baby": Ibid.
169 "The slightest": Ibid.
169 "beyond words": *L*, p. 89.
169 "Our experiment": TW–SN, Feb. 26, 1907, BL.
169 "My first": *L*, p. 85.
170 "restored by": In Lewis, p. 102.
170 "Teddy arrived": EW–SN, Aug. 15, 1902, BL.
170 "I am no": In Wright, p. 93.
170 "Teddy Wharton": In Benstock, p. 133.
171 "natural right": EW–SN, Jan. 10, 1906, BL.
171 "Little Miza's": Diary, Jan. 5, 1906, BL.
171 "We had": EW–SN, Jan. 10, 1906, BL.
171 "Beautiful day": Diary, Jan. 6, 1906, BL.
171 "My old": TW–SN, Feb. 26, 1907, BL.
171 "Yet forgive": In Powers, pp. 73–74.
172 "my poor": *L*, p. 155.
172 "a self": *L*, p. 138.
172 "a dashing": In Erlich, p. 87.
172 "mysterious": In Benstock, p. 170.
173 "The moment": *L*, p. 129.
173 "the old": In K. Price, p. 671.
173 "You sent": Ibid., 670.
174 "The way": *L*, p. 135.
174 "He was": Diary, March 3, 1908, LL.
174 "We were": Ibid., April 18, 1908, LL.

174 "I have": In K. Price, p. 680.

174 "She was": MF–ET, Mar. 30, 1950, LL.

175 "the innermost": *CSS*, p. 14.

175 "Does that": In K. Price, p. 682.

175 "I heard": Ibid.

175 "He was": In Rieder, p. 127.

176 "I had": In Benstock, p. 186.

176 "The violent": In Bell, p. 172.

176 "I know": EW–MF, undated postcard, UT.

177 "Poor dear": In Powers, p. 201.

177 "It is a happy": *L*, p. 514.

177 "draw herself": In A. Price, p. xvi.

177 "a full-rigged": Ibid.

177–78   description of her clothes: In Benstock, p. 123.

178 "a nervous": In Rieder, p. 127.

178 "intellectual fencing matches": Ibid.

178 "I feel": In Rieder, p. 126.

178 "a good": ET–HP, Aug. 7, 1927, LL.

179 "The whirling": In Wolff, pp. 140–41.

179 "Ah . . . you": In Lubbock, p. 59.

179 "learned several": *L*, p. 307.

179 "I remember": *FF*, p. 17.

180 "We had fared": In A. Price, p. 17.

180 "lassitude and": EW–ET, June 6, 1919, LL.

180 "What color": Ibid.

181 "It is so": EW–ET, Aug. 10, 1918, LL.

181 "You will be": EW–EW[ashburn], Mar. 21, 1919, BL.

181 pictures of the Pekes: See LL.

181–82   history of the Pekingese: See Godden.

182 "implying courage": Jacobsen, n.p.

182 "exasperating stubbornness": Ibid.

182 "He was": *CSS*, vol. 2, p. 284.

182 "She was": MB, Wharton Reminiscences, BL.

182 "She liked": MC, Wharton Reminiscences, BL.

182 "It was": MB, Wharton Reminiscences, BL.

184 "She now": Lubbock, p. 132.

184 "I had": BG, p. 369.

184 "Your memory": In Benstock, p. 360.

184 "as familiarly": In Lewis, p. 429.

185 "Much as": MB, Wharton Reminiscences, BL.

185 "damned Pekingese": In Lubbock, p. 133.

185 "those blessed": Ibid.

186 "There was": In Lubbock, p. 133.

186 "the lap-dog": Ibid., p. 210.

186 "No danger": Ibid.

186 "the oldest": Ibid.

186 "he looked": Ibid.

186 "love and": In Rieder, p. 126.

187 "two astute and arrogant": In Funston, p. 13.

187 "I cannot": *BG*, pp. 4–5.

187 "had wanted": *L*, p. 504.

187 "my old": *L*, p. 561.

187 "Since Walter's": Ibid.

187 "Please tell": Bettina Tyler to Madame Friderick, Mar. 11, 1937, LL.

187 "Linky and I": EW–WT, Nov. 13, 1934, LL.

188 "It takes": EW–WT, Jan. 30, 1935, LL.

188 "How it": Diary, July 15, 1927, BL.

188 "If I": Diary, 1924–1934, Inscription inside cover, BL.

189 "the ruling": In Dwight, p. 282.

190 "I'm an": In Lewis, p. 514.

190 "lie there": *CSS*, vol. 2, p. 890.

190 "to keep": *MFF,* p. 169.

190 "Dear little": Diary, April 11, 1937, BL.

191 "Little Linky": Diary, April 12, 1937, BL.

191 "Clouding over": Diary, April 13, 1937, BL.

191 "I don't": Diary, April 14, 1937, BL.

191 "He'll be": EW–WT, April 15, 1937, *LL.*

191 "My little": Diary, April 15, 1937, BL.

191 "Can't remember": Diary, April 19, 1937, BL.

191 "I wish": in Tyler, p. 103.

191 "Still can't": Diary, April 20, 1937, BL.

191 "Oh, how": Diary, April 26, 1937, BL.

191 "Very shakey": Diary, May 9, 1937, BL.

191 "We really": EW–WT May 16, 1937, *LL.*

192 "Kept no": Diary, June 19, 1937 BL.

192 *"My little"*: In George Ramsden, *Edith Wharton's Library* (Yorkshire, U.K: Stone Trough Books, 1999) p. 28.

VIRGINIA WOOLF AND GURTH, GRIZZLE, AND PINKA

I am especially indebted to Quentin Bell, *Virginia Woolf: A Biography* (New York: Harcourt Brace Jovanovich, 1972); Katherine Dalsimer, *Virginia Woolf: Becoming a Writer* (New Haven, Conn.: Yale University Press, 2001); Louise DeSalvo, *Virginia Woolf: The Impact of Childhood Sexual Abuse on Her Life and Work*

(New York: Ballantine, 1989); Jane Dunn, *A Very Close Conspiracy: Vanessa Bell and Virginia Woolf* (Boston: Little, Brown, 1990); and Hermione Lee, *Virginia Woolf* (New York: Knopf, 1997).

BACKGROUND TEXTS

Bell, Quentin. *Virginia Woolf: A Biography.* New York: Harcourt Brace Jovanovich, 1972.

Caws, Mary Ann. *Virginia Woolf.* Woodstock, N.Y.: Overlook Press, 2001.

Coppinger, Raymond and Lorna Coppinger, *Dogs: A Startling New Understanding of Canine Origin, Behavior & Evolution* (New York: Scribner, 2001).

Cottesloe, Gloria. *Lost, Stolen or Strayed: The Story of the Battersea Dogs' Home.* London: Arthur Barker, Ltd., 1971.

Curtis, Vanessa. *Virginia Woolf's Women.* Madison: University of Wisconsin Press, 2002.

Eberly, David. "Housebroken: The Domesticated Relations of *Flush.*" In *Virginia Woolf: Texts and Contexts,* edited by Beth Rigel and Eileen Barrett Daugherty, pp. 21–29. New York: Pace University Press, 1995.

Glendinning, Victoria. *Vita: A Biography of Vita Sackville-West.* New York: Quill, 1983.

Hill-Miller, Katherine C. *From the Lighthouse to Monk's House: A Guide to Virginia Woolf's Literary Landscapes.* London: Gerald Duckworth & Co., 2001.

Humm, Maggie. *Snapshots of Blooms-bury: The Private Lives of Virginia Woolf and Vanessa Bell.* New Brunswick, N.J.: Rutgers University Press, 2006.

Sackville-West, Vita. *The Letters of Vita Sackville-West to Virginia Woolf.* Edited by Louise DeSalvo and Mitchell Leaska. New York: Morrow, 1985.

Spalding, Frances. *Vanessa Bell.* New Haven, Conn.: Ticknor & Fields, 1983.

Spater, George, and Ian Parsons. *A Marriage of True Minds: An Intimate Portrait of Leonard and Virginia Woolf.* New York: Harcourt Brace Jovanovich, 1977.

Szladits, Lola L. "The Life, Character and Opinions of Flush the Spaniel." *Bulletin of the New York Public Library* 74 (1970): pp. 211–18.

Woolf, Leonard. *The Journey Not the Arrival Matters.* New York: Harcourt Brace & World, 1969.

———. *Letters of Leonard Woolf.* Edited by Frederic Spotts. New York: Harcourt Brace Jovanovich, 1989.

WORKS, DIARIES, AND LETTERS BY VIRGINIA WOOLF

D   Anne Oliver Bell, ed. *The Diaries of Virginia Woolf.* Vols. 1–5. New York: Harcourt Brace Jovanovich, 1977–84.

E   Andrew McNeillie, ed. *The Essays of Virginia Woolf.* San Diego: Harcourt Brace Jovanovich, 1986.

F   Virginia Woolf. *Flush: A Biography.* Introduction by Margaret Forster. London: Vintage, 2002. First published 1933.

L   Nigel Nicolson and Joanne Trautmann, eds. *The Letters of Virginia Woolf.* Vols. 1–6. New York: Harcourt Brace Jovanovich, 1975–80.

M   Jeanne Schulkind, ed. *Moments of Being.* New York: Harcourt Brace Jovanovich, 1976.

PA   Mitchell A. Leaska, ed. *Passionate Apprentice: The Early Journals of Virginia Woolf.* New York: Harcourt Brace Jovanovich, 1990.

197 "had run": In Dalsimer, p. 30.
199 "Can I remember": Ibid., p. 4.
200 "He is long-haired": Ibid., p. 33.
200 "terribly Skye-terrier": *E*, p. 13.
201 "Then there were": *M*, p. 31.
201 "Her death": *M*, p. 40.
201 "I remember": *M*, p. 93.
202 "Sobbing, sitting": *M*, p. 95.
202 "We were all": *M*, p. 45.
202 "my 'first' breakdown": In Lee, p. 174.
202 "One felt": In Dunn, p. 38.
202 "It was like": *M*, p. 116.
204 "[Jerry] caused": *PA*, p. 26.
204 "A wicked spotted": *PA*, p. 31.
204 "It was not": *M*, p. 149.
205 "by the contemptible": *E*, p. 13.
205 "Then we lost": *PA*, p. 108.
205 "One day": In Dalsimer, p. 55.
205 "The blow": *M*, p. 124.
206 "So, kiss your dog": *L*, no. 381.
206 "I think with joy": *L*, no. 424.
206 "an attractive": *E*, p. 13.
206 "I can see": *E*, p. 14.
206 "was base": Ibid.

207 "I wish you": In Dalsimer, p. 71.
207 "of great sickness": *E*, p. 14.
207 "what strange wave": *E*, p. 15.
207 "How to go": In Dunn, p. 80.
207 "His life would have": *D*, vol. 3, p. 208.
207 "But one thing": *L*, no. 3,197.
208 "unremarkable" except: *E*, p. 8.
208 "It was better": *E*, p. 15.
208 "A cab": *L*, no. 10.
209 "Gordon Square": In Hill-Miller, p. 68.
210 "white & grey": *PA*, p. 218.
210 "I took Gurth": *PA*, p. 238.
210 "I walked": *PA*, p. 243.
210 "The whole battery": *F*, p. 28.
211 "Out after lunch": *PA*, p. 27.
211 "so much risk": *PA*, p. 234.
211 "Oh the torture": In Lee, p. 111.
211 "Gurth wears": *PA*, p. 245.
211 "eye-stalk": See Coppinger, pp. 100–215.
211 "I took that": *PA*, p. 243.
212 "handwriting has": *L*, no. 990.
212 "maternal protection": *D*, vol. 3, p. 52.
212 "That is all": In Lee, p. 228.
213 Battersea Lost Dogs Home: See Cottesloe.
213 "It is perhaps": *L*, no. 294.
213 "I will send": *L*, no. 434.
214 "He is": In Dunn, p. 176.
214 "born not of rich": In Lee, p. 51.
214 "Socially": In Spalding, p. 65.
215 "I've got": In Dunn, p. 182.
215 "One's personality": *D*, vol. 1, p. 70.
215 "As I told": In Dunn, p. 177.
215 "Apparently": In Spalding, p. 62.
215 "We might": In Dunn, p. 192.
215 "private, play": *L*, no. 3,025.
216 "trivial and sentimental": L. Woolf (1969), p. 21.
216 "this blind": Ibid.

216 "gruff, abrupt": Bell, p. 175.
217 "unity": In Spater, p. 68.
217 "I took Max": *D*, vol. 1, p. 20.
218 "A Bull dog": Ibid., p. 28.
218 "a stout, active": Ibid., p. 59.
218 "Directly he is": Ibid., p. 60.
218 "his spirit": Ibid.
218 "He fell": Ibid.
218 "He is a human": Ibid.
218 "restless mind": Ibid., p. 62.
219 "One's right hand": Ibid.
219 "Her affection": Bell, p. 175.
219 "It is melancholy": *D*, vol. 1, p. 72.
219 "a vision": Ibid., p. 105.
220 "I don't like": In Lee, p. 368.
220 "the greatest": Ibid., p. 369.
220 "Yet I daresay": *D*, vol. 1, p. 318.
220 "Grizzle now": *D*, vol. 2, p. 182.
220 "I heard": Ibid., p. 205.
221 "How they": Ibid., p. 311.
221 "Grizzle pricks": Ibid., p. 313.
221 "Do I": *D*, vol. 3, p. 87.
222 "Thank God": *D*, vol. 2, p. 295.
222 "The immense success": *D*, vol. 3, p. 31.
222 "But oh the": *D*, vol. 2, p. 308.
222 "And the truth" *D*, vol. 3, p. 62.
223 "Was everybody dining": In Lee, p. 466.
223 "Not much": In Glendinning, p. 128.
224 "chairs that": In Lee, p. 489.
224 "a sort of covey": *D*, vol. 3, p. 125.
224 "Please don't": In Glendinning, p. 149.
224 "The explosion": Sackville-West, pp. 238–39.
224 "Vita is a dear": *L*, no. 160.
225 "If ever": *L*, no. 1,607.
225 "Well, my": *L*, no. 2,660.
225 "This letter": Sackville-West, p. 286.

225 "Does Potto": Sackville-West, p. 313.

225 "If one": In Lee, p. 485.

226 "Remember your": *L*, no. 1,628.

226 "And this will": Sackville-West, p. 122.

226 "I am scared": In Lee, p. 497.

226 "ghetto Jews": L. Woolf (1969), p. 57.

226 "The puppy": L. Woolf (1989), p. 299.

227 "Can I": *L*, no. 1,533.

227 "Your puppy": *L*, no. 1,660.

228 "Pinker and I": Sackville-West, p. 152.

228 "No—I can't": *L*, no. 1,690.

228 "So we go on": *D*, vol. 3, p. 117.

228 "On 4 December": Editor's note in *D*, vol. 3, p. 118.

228 "Had Grizzle": L. Woolf. Diary, Dec. 4, 1926. Special Collections, University of Sussex, Brighton, U.K.

229 "Darling, we are": *L*, no. 2,048.

229 "Please Vita": *L*, no. 1,717.

230 "I had to explain": Sackville-West, p. 152.

231 "My friendship": *D*, vol. 4, p. 287.

232 "Potto is dead": *L*, no. 2,411.

232 "Ethel's new": *L*, no. 3,206.

232 "At the dead": *L*, no. 3,223.

233 "making an entry": In Trekkie Ritchie, introduction, *Flush: A Biography*, by Virginia Woolf (New York: Harcourt Brace, 1933), p. viii.

234 "Pinka jumps": *L*, no. 2,915.

234 "Dearest it was": L. Woolf (1989), p. 233.

234 "It was a divine": *L*, no. 2,346.

234 "Pinka, who has": *L*, no. 2,025.

234 "Beauty shines": *L*, no. 2,012.

235 "And Pink": *L*, no. 2,189.

235 "Never pretend": In Dunn, 225.

235 "maternal vices": *L*, no. 1,922.

235 "Pinka is snoring": *L*, no. 2,858.

235 "Half the": *L*, no. 1,688.

235 "Why does": *L*, no. 1,794.

235 "It is very": *D*, vol. 3, p. 220.

235 "The only": *L*, no. 1,805.

236 "I've just": *L*, no. 2,217.

236 "Anyhow it is": In Szladits, p. 216.

236 "I was so": *L*, no. 2,628.

236 "I hope to send": *L*, no. 2,700.

236 "The dog": *L*, no. 2,715.

237 "Four months": In Ritchie, p. xiii.

237 "I wanted": *L*, no. 2,707.

237 "I nibble": *L*, no. 2,615.

237 "I shall": *D*, vol. 4, p. 181.

237 "I write": *L*, no. 2,640.

237 "I am very": *L*, no. 2,715.

238 "not so much": Bell, p. 175.

238 "As he lay": *F*, p. 96.

239 "to the surface": Eberly, p. 80.

239 "One moment": Ibid., p. 77.

239 "A fat woman": *F*, p. 81.

239 "I still": *L*, no. 3,678.

240 "Well, Flush lingers": *D*, vol. 4, p. 144.

240 "trying to re-write": Ibid., p. 139.

240 "Well Flush is": Ibid., p. 144.

240 "I'm so glad": *L*, no. 2,808.

240 "This time": *D*, vol. 5, p. 100.

240 "poor old": *L*, no. 3,025.

241 "Percy was": *D*, vol. 5, p. 317.

241 "And the intensity": Ibid.

241 "This you'll": *L*, no. 3,025.

241 "8 years": *D*, vol. 5, p. 318.

241 "trance like": *D*, vol. 4, p. 246.

241 "fussing & fidgeting": *D*, vol. 5, p. 318.

242 "And we": *L*, no. 3,026.

242 "too melancholy": *L*, no. 3,029.

242 "We've bought": *L*, no. 3,039.

242 "She has": *D*, vol. 4, p. 328.

242 "She cost £18": Ibid.

243 "almost surgically": *D*, vol. 5. p. 80.

243 "Love for him": *L*, no. 3,358.

243 "The passion": In Dunn, p. 293.

243 "It's rather": *D*, vol. 5, p. 343.

244 "And how's": *L*, no. 3,373.

244 "a dose of": *L*, no. 3,571.

244 "Meanwhile, yes": no. 3,441.

244 " 'My books' ": *D*, vol. 5, p. 310.

245 "One never": Ibid.

245 "As I cannot": Ibid., p. 343.

245 "L's old fine": Ibid., p. 334.

245 "A psychologist": Ibid., p. 351.

245 "Very lonely": Ibid., p. 63.

245 "You must not": In Dunn, p. 299.

245 "moon[ing] over": *D*, vol. 5, p. 161.

246 "She had killed": Ibid.

246 "If I could": In Dunn, p. 300.

246 "I don't think": Ibid.

AFTERWORD

BACKGROUND TEXTS

Beck, Alan, and Aaron Katcher. *Between Pets and People: The Importance of Animal Companionship.* West Lafayette, Ind.: Purdue University Press, 1996.

Coppinger, Raymond, and Lorna Coppinger. *Dogs: A Startling New Understanding of Canine Origin, Behavior & Evolution.* New York: Scribner's, 2001.

Dale-Green, Patricia. *Dog.* London: Rupert Hart-Davis, 1966.

Leach, Maria. *God Had a Dog: Folklore of the Dog.* New Brunswick, N.J.: Rutgers University Press, 1961.

Lewis, Thomas, Fari Amini, and Richard Lannon. *A General Theory of Love.* New York: Vintage Books, 2001.

Menache, Sophia. "Dogs and Human Beings." *Society & Animals* 6, no. 1 (1998): pp. 67–86.

Serpell, James, ed. *The Domestic Dog: Its Evolution, Behaviour, and Interactions with People.* Cambridge, U.K.: Cambridge University Press, 1995.

Von Franz, Marie-Louise, *Creation Myths.* Boston: Shambhala Publications, 1988.

Woloy, Eleanora. *The Symbol of the Dog in the Human Psyche.* Wilmette, Ill.: Chiron, 1990.

249 "as dogs": Philip Kelley and Scott Lewis, eds., *The Brownings' Correspondence*, vol. 13 (Winfield, Kans.: Wedgestone Press, 1987), no. 2,502.

251 "*He & I*": Ibid., p. 157.

251 "I feel": Tyler, William Royall, "Personal Memories of Edith Wharton," *Massachusetts Historical Society Proceedings* 85 (1973): p. 103.

252 "*I talk of* ": Emily Dickinson, *The Letters of Emily Dickinson*, vol. 1, edited by Thomas H. Johnson and Theodora Ward (Cambridge, Mass.: Belknap Press of Harvard University Press, 1958), no. 212.

253 "One can love": In Beck, p. 127.

253 "Tell Carlo": Emily Dickinson, *The Complete Poems of Emily Dickinson*, edited by Thomas Johnson (Boston: Back Bay

Books, 1960), no. 186. First published 1890.

253 "an active creator": Marie-Louise von Franz, *Creation Myths* (Boston: Shambhala Publications, 1988), pp. 34–35.

254 "*My little*": in George Ramsden, *Edith Wharton's Library* (Yorkshire, U.K.: Stone Trough Books, 1999), p. 28.

254 limbic resonance: See Lewis, pp. 63–65

254 "Flush's breathing": Philip Kelley and Ronald Hudson, *Brownings' Correspondence*, vol. 6 (1984–87), p. 335.

254 "that extraordinarily": Mitchell A. Leaska, ed. *Passionate Apprentice: The Early Journals of Virginia Woolf* (New York: Harcourt Brace Jovanovich, 1990), p. 243.

255 "Sometimes, when": Quentin Bell, *Virginia Woolf: A Biography* (New York: Harcourt Brace Jovanovich, 1972), p. 175.

255 "One hand": Charlotte Bronte, *Shirley* (Oxford, U.K.: Oxford

World's Classics, 1998), p. 386. First published 1849.

255 "*A dog somehow*": In Nigel Nicolson and Joanne Trautmann, eds., *The Letters of Virginia Woolf*, vol. 5 (New York: Harcourt Brace Jovanovich, 1975–80), no. 3,025.

255 "Life with": Beck, p. 73.

256 "constancy of": Ibid., p. 27.

256 "*Keeper walked*": Elizabeth Gaskell, *The Life of Charlotte Brontë* (London: Penguin, 1987), p. 269. First published 1857.

257 "Staunch & faithful": Edith Wharton, *The Letters of Edith Wharton*, edited by R.W.B. Lewis and Nancy Lewis (London: Simon & Schuster, 1988), p. 155.

257 "It has been": Scott Lewis, ed., *The Letters of Elizabeth Barrett Browning to Her Sister Arabella*, vol. 1 (Waco, Tex.: Wedgestone Press, 2002), no. 11, p. 13.

258 "I love him": Kelley and Lewis, *Brownings' Correspondence*, vol. 5 (1987), p. 338.

Illustration and Text Credits

ILLUSTRATION CREDITS

PAGE

6 Courtesy of the National Portrait Gallery, London.

25 Courtesy of the Provost and Fellows of Eton College.

28 Courtesy of the Henry W. and Albert A. Berg Collection of English and American Literature, New York Public Library; Astor, Lenox and Tilden Foundations.

31 Courtesy of The Robert Browning Settlement (Inc.) of Leigh-on-Sea, United Kingdom.

32 Courtesy of the National Portrait Gallery, London.

44 Courtesy of the National Portrait Gallery, London.

52 Courtesy of the National Portrait Gallery, London.

60 Courtesy of the Brontë Society.

72 Courtesy of the Brontë Society.

77 Courtesy of the Brontë Society.

78 Courtesy of the Brontë Society.

81 Courtesy of the Brontë Society.

89 Courtesy of the National Portrait Gallery, London.

100 Courtesy of the Amherst College Archives and Special Collections.

109 From Freda Pratt and Carol Cooper, *A Friend in Deed* (Cornwall: R. Booth Bookbinders, Ltd, 1993.)

111 By permission of the Houghton Library, Harvard University bMS Am 1118.99b (28) © The President and Fellows of Harvard College.

113 By permission of the Houghton Library, Harvard University MS Am 1118.99b (29.1) © The President and Fellows of Harvard College.

122 By permission of the Houghton Library, Harvard University bMS Am 1118.99b (6) © The President and Fellows of Harvard College.

125 From Nancy Elkholm Burket and Jane Langton, *Acts of Light: Emily Dickinson* (Boston: New York Graphic Society, 1980). Courtesy of the artist.

129 By permission of the Houghton Library, Harvard University bMS Am 1118.99b (45) © The President and Fellows of Harvard College.

144 Courtesy of the Yale Collection of American Literature, Beinecke Rare

Book and Manuscript Library. Reprinted by permission of The Edith
Wharton Estate and the Watkins/Loomis Agency.

157   Courtesy of the Yale Collection of American Literature, Beinecke Rare
Book and Manuscript Library. Reprinted by permission of The Edith
Wharton Estate and the Watkins/Loomis Agency.

160   Courtesy of the Yale Collection of American Literature, Beinecke Rare
Book and Manuscript Library. Reprinted by permission of The Edith
Wharton Estate and the Watkins/Loomis Agency.

173   Courtesy of the Yale Collection of American Literature, Beinecke Rare
Book and Manuscript Library.

183   Courtesy of the Yale Collection of American Literature, Beinecke Rare
Book and Manuscript Library. Reprinted by permission of The Edith
Wharton Estate and the Watkins/Loomis Agency.

185   Courtesy of the Lilly Library, Indiana University. Reprinted by permission of The Edith Wharton Estate and the Watkins/Loomis Agency.

189   Courtesy of the Yale Collection of American Literature, Beinecke Rare
Book and Manuscript Library. Reprinted by permission of The Edith
Wharton Estate and the Watkins/Loomis Agency.

192   Courtesy of the Lilly Library, Indiana University. Reprinted by permission of The Edith Wharton Estate and the Watkins/Loomis Agency.

198   Courtesy of the National Portrait Gallery, London.

201   Courtesy of the Mortimer Rare Book Room, Smith College.

208   Courtesy of the Tate, London, 2007.

221   Courtesy of the Virginia and Leonard Woolf Collection, Gift of Frederick R. Koch, the Harvard Theater Collection, Houghton Library.

227   Courtesy of the Virginia and Leonard Woolf Collection, Gift of Frederick R. Koch, the Harvard Theater Collection, Houghton Library.

229   Courtesy of the Virginia and Leonard Woolf Collection, Gift of Frederick R. Koch, the Harvard Theater Collection, Houghton Library.

231   Courtesy of the Virginia and Leonard Woolf Collection, Gift of Frederick R. Koch, the Harvard Theater Collection, Houghton Library.

239   Copyright 1933 by Harcourt, Inc., and renewed in 1961 by Leonard
Woolf, reprinted by permission of Harcourt, Inc.

TEXT CREDITS

Grateful acknowledgment is made to the following for permission to reprint
both previously published and unpublished material:

The Belknap Press of Harvard University Press: Excerpts from forty-eight letters from *The Letters of Emily Dickinson*, edited by Thomas H. Johnson, copyright © 1958, 1986 by The President and Fellows of Harvard College, 1914,
1924, 1932, 1942 by Martha Dickinson Bianchi, 1952 by Alfred Leete Hamp-

Index

Page numbers in *italics* refer to illustrations.

ABOUT THE AUTHOR

MAUREEN ADAMS is a licensed clinical psychologist. Before teaching psychology at the University of San Francisco, she taught English at the University of Missouri. She and her husband live in Sonoma, California. This is her first book.